Rewriting the Victorians

Rewriting the Victorians

Theory, history, and the politics of gender

Edited by Linda M. Shires

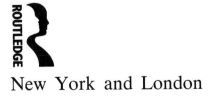

New York and London

First published 1992
by Routledge
a division of Routledge, Chapman and Hall, Inc.
29 West 35th Street, New York, NY 10001

Simultaneously published in Great Britain
by Routledge
11 New Fetter Lane, London EC4P 4EE

Typeset in 10 on 12 point Times by
Intype, London

Printed in Great Britain by
T J Press (Padstow) Ltd, Padstow, Cornwall

Library of Congress Cataloging in Publication Data
Rewriting the Victorians: theory, history, and the politics of gender
    / edited by Linda M. Shires.
        p.   cm.
    Includes bibliographical references and index.
    1. English literature—19th century—History and criticism—
Theory, etc.   2. Feminism and literature—Great Britain—
History—19th century.   3. Politics and literature—Great Britain—
History—19th century.   4. Women and literature—Great Britain—
History—19th century.   5. Great Britain—Civilization—19th
century.   6. Social problems in literature.   7. Sex roles in
literature.   I. Shires, Linda M.
PR468.F46T4   1992
820.9'008—dc20   91–23416

British Library Cataloguing in Publication Data
Rewriting the Victorians.
    I. Shires, Linda M.
    820.9008

ISBN 0–415–05524–5   ISBN 0–415–05525–3 (pbk)

Contents

Contributors

Susan P. Casteras, Curator of Paintings at the Yale Center for British Art, has organized numerous exhibitions on Victorian art for this museum and many others. Her most recent books and exhibition catalogues include *Images of Victorian Womanhood in English Art, English Pre-Raphaelitism and its Reception in America in the Nineteenth Century*, and *Pocket Cathedrals: Pre-Raphaelite Book Illustrations*. She also teaches at Yale.

Christina Crosby is Associate Professor of English at Wesleyan University and also teaches in the Women's Studies program. She is the author of *The Ends History: Victorians and the Woman Question*. She is currently working on a study of credit and representation.

Ina Ferris, Professor of English, University of Ottawa, is the author of *The Achievement of Literary Authority: Gender, History, and the Waverley Novels* (1991) and of many articles on Victorian fiction. She is presently researching the discourse of the book in the early nineteenth century.

Christine Krueger, Assistant Professor of English at Marquette University, is the author of *The Reader's Repentance: Women Preachers, Women Writers and Nineteenth-Century Social Reform* (1992) and co-editor, with Susan Sage Heinzelman and Zipporah Wiseman, of a collection of essays on feminism, literature, and law, forthcoming from Duke. Her current research involves feminism and the law in the nineteenth century.

Jules Law, Assistant Professor of English at Northwestern University, has written a number of articles on Joyce, Wittgenstein, and Derrida. He is also the author of *The Rhetoric of Empiricism from Locke to Ruskin* (1992).

Judith Newton is the Director of Women's Studies at University of

California, Davis. She is the author of *Women, Power, and Subversion: Social Strategies in British Fiction*; co-editor, with Judith Walkowitz and Mary Ryan, of *Sex and Class in Women's History*; and co-editor, with Deborah Rosenfelt, of *Feminist Criticism and Social Change: Sex, Class and Race in Literature and Culture*. She has published several essays on "new historicism" and on the intersection of feminist literary and historical work. She is currently preparing a collection of essays on feminism, literary criticism, and history, and, with Judith Stacey, a project on the politics of contemporary cultural criticism by men.

Jeff Nunokawa is Assistant Professor of English at Princeton University. He has published articles on Dickens, Tennyson, and mourning in the age of Aids. His current research projects include completion of a book about sexuality and economics in Victorian narrative and a study of male homosexuality in nineteenth-century English literature, tentatively entitled *The Disappearance of the Homosexual*.

Marion Shaw, Senior Lecturer in the English Department at the University of Hull, has published three books on Tennyson. She has co-authored a new book on Agatha Christie's *Miss Marple* (1991) and is currently engaged on a biography of the Yorkshire novelist and reformer, Winifred Holtby.

Linda M. Shires, Associate Professor of English at Syracuse University, has published numerous articles on Victorian poetry and fiction. Her most recent book, co-authored with Steven Cohan, is *Telling Stories: A Theoretical Analysis of Narrative Fiction*. Her current projects include a book on authorship and masculinity in Tennyson and Hardy, and a longer project on the French Revolution and Victorian movements of dissent.

Sally Shuttleworth is Lecturer in the School of English, University of Leeds. She is the author of *George Eliot and Nineteenth-Century Science: The Make-Believe of a Beginning*; co-editor with John Christie, of *Nature Transfigured Essays on Science and Literature, 1700–1900*; and co-editor with Mary Jacobus and Evelyn Fox Keller, of *Body/Politic: Women and the Discourses of Science*. Currently she is working on a study of Charlotte Brontë's fiction in the light of nineteenth-century medical and psychological discourse.

Preface

The essays in this collection intervene in traditional histories of the
Victorian period not only through the topics taken up by individual
contributors, but also through a common political edge. Our criticism
self-consciously grows out of our particular historical moment in post-
industrial capitalism, the 1990s, when disciplines continue altering their
shapes through an increasing cross-fertilization of methods and ideas.
Influenced by Marxism, feminism, sociology, anthropology, and post-
structuralist theories of language and subjectivity, this volume presents
itself as an example of the new cultural studies. The major intersections
which the book attempts to negotiate are those of history, theory, and
gender.

We make several major assumptions in this book. Cultural processes,
whether they serve conservative, progressive, or radical ends, we believe,
are effects of individual and institutional social relations. These relations
are based on standardized, if changing and cross-culturally varied, social
markers by which individuals award meaning to their culture and to
their own lives. The essays before you attend closely to the intertwined
categories of class, sex, nation, and gender, but age and race are equally
important denominators both to the Victorians and to us as critics. As
the title of the book indicates, we view gender as one of the primary
categories by which Victorians ordered their lives. As a theoretical concept, however, gender is never singular, but is always inflected by other
social categories. In addition, as Joan Scott (1989) and others have
demonstrated, categories such as class and gender reciprocally construct
each other, so that a particular class, for example, may be considered
"feminine" or "masculine." Further, Allon White and Peter Stallybrass
have argued persuasively that the body can be culturally "placed" on a
mental hierarchical grid which involves the relative values of gender,
race, class, nation, and topography of the city (Stallybrass and White
1986). Particular instances in the social formation and particular representations figure this type of cross-over differently, but certain trends can
also be detected at a particular historical moment. In the mid-Victorian

period, for instance, lower-class women are regularly thought of as connected to blacks, to certain nationalities figured as "licentious," such as the French, and even to urban geographical locations, such as gutter and whorehouse. Middle-class professional men, on the other hand, are usually connected (and connect themselves) to white Englishness and its dominant social spaces and institutions, while upper-class men are often feminized as they lose dominance over land and fortune to wealthy middle-class businessmen.

Our project here is specifically feminist and historical in that we are concerned with analyzing power relations between men and women in the Victorian period. Power is never inherently divisive, yet the conflicts we trace can be described correctly as power struggles: in particular, we analyze struggles for legitimacy and recognition, whether a conflict over turf, audience, and prestige in the mid-century press, or over control of the female body in the Victorian medical establishment, or over the ideological representations of the gendered subject in texts. We also take to heart what Anthony Giddens refers to as the "dialectic of control" (Giddens 1984: 283–4) whereby resources for control are always available to those with less power, though how and to what degree such resources are used can vary from one social context to another. History, and especially the history of gender relations, as we view it, is a process that may not always be divisive, but it is one that is always political and, to some degree, negotiable.

Although most of the contributors to the volume are white, middle-class women, I have attempted to provide a variety of topics and approaches by drawing together authors from different geographical, political, institutional, and personal locations. This book does not claim to invent a "new" Victorian period or to inaugurate a "new" Victorian studies or even to represent the multiple ways we read the Victorians today. Indeed, while this book was shaped with a bias and an agenda, it was not designed, for a number of reasons, to "cover" what is considered most important in the academy today. On the other hand, I do not imagine I can ignore my own historical positioning. I had hoped to include an essay on nation and race. The importance of such study is amply clear from the dominant Victorian tendency to engage in self-constructions defining Englishness against racial and national Otherness. These self-constructions have very much shaped the way we protectively still think about ourselves. In the global arena where the 1990s positions us, detailed study of race and nation is essential. The need for more study of the workings of imperialism and of the colonial subject is paramount in Victorian studies, and I wish I had been able to include some of the fine work being undertaken now in this area by many graduate students and by such diverse critics as Catherine Hall, Deirdre David, Cora Kaplan, and Patrick Brantlinger, but we will have to be content to read it and hear it elsewhere.

This collection maintains that we need to examine Victorian culture through analysis of institutions and through close attention to symbolic forms and representations. (I take up the related issue of the individual in an Afterword.) The public reception and manipulation of symbols, most of us would agree, is as important to social relations as the formulation of public policy. We analyze both struggles for power in institutions and in representations to investigate how ideologies of gender are concurrently maintained and subverted and to observe how new combinations and new ideologies may, using Raymond Williams's term, "emerge" at the same time (Williams 1986).

Students of theory and of the nineteenth century, in particular, will find much to ponder in the analysis of hegemonic institutions in the exceptionally fine essays on the press by Judith Newton and Ina Ferris and in Sally Shuttleworth's overwhelmingly convincing examination of the ideologies of motherhood (a topic of increasing importance to Victorianists and eighteenth-century scholars). The collection breaks new ground in the study of literary representations and their relationships to the politics of gender in the period. Several chapters closely examine individual texts such as Jules Law's elegant study of water rights and gender in *The Mill on the Floss*, Jeff Nunokawa's important contribution on historicizing the male gaze in *Tess of the d'Urbervilles*, and Marion Shaw's fascinating explanation of gender and confession in *The Strange Case of Dr Jekyll and Mr Hyde* and *The Island of Doctor Moreau*. Christina Crosby ambitiously identifies how a group, the Gothic revivalists, imagine history as both commodity and as fetish, while Susan Casteras isolates a particularly insidious gender narrative in mid-century painting – the cult of male child genius. Both consider the effect of such representations on women. Finally, two essays overtly concern powerful women, the French Revolution, and Victorians: my own cross-cultural study of the symbolic pairing of mother/maenad in both the French Revolution and again in England at mid-century and Christine Krueger's analysis of Gaskell's ideological construction of the female paternalist in her historical fiction about the French Revolution, *My Lady Ludlow*. These chapters argue for the strength of the female, while allowing for the cultural constraints placed on her.

All of the essays offered here were specially commissioned for the collection. They reveal that junctures of history and theory within Victorian Studies are both varied and vitally important to a rewriting of the period. They also reveal that there is no "right way" to view Victorian Studies in the twenty-first century. Indeed, the collection demonstrates, instead, the very accommodation of multiple points of view and contrary states that is itself a hallmark of the Victorian period and its literature.

WORKS CITED

Giddens, Anthony (1984) *The Constitution of Society*, Berkeley: University of California Press.

Scott, Joan (1989) *Gender and the Politics of History*, New York: Columbia University Press.

Stallybrass, Peter and White, Allon (1986) *The Politics and Poetics of Transgression*, Ithaca, NY: Cornell University Press.

Williams, Raymond (1986) "Forms of English Fiction in 1848," in Frances Barker, Peter Hulme, Margaret Iversen, and Diana Loxley (eds) *Literature, Politics, and Theory. Papers from the Essex Conference, 1976–84*, 1–16, New York: Methuen.

Acknowledgments

I take great pleasure in thanking the people and institutions whose assistance has made this book possible. First, of course, I thank all of the contributors collectively and individually for their hard work and their patience with me and with each other. My appreciation is also due to John P. Crowley, Chair of the Department of English at Syracuse University, and to Deans Samuel P. Gorovitz and Michael Flusché, who granted me an administrative leave for spring 1990, which aided my continuing this and other work. I am especially grateful to Elaine Showalter, Chair of the Department of English at Princeton University, who obtained further leaves for me to teach there during 1990–2, where this book was completed. I warmly thank them all for their kindnesses, past and present.

Graduate students and colleagues in English 576 at Princeton showed me that a group of scholars in a feminist classroom can consciously and conflictually face differences of age, race, ethnicity, gender, sexual preference, class, religion, disciplinary training, and theoretical approach and end up with vastly more than when they started. For this very special and inspiring series of debates, I thank Laurel Bollinger, Sylvia Brown, Mark Braley, Grant Farred, Franziska Gygax, Brian Hanson, Ann Jurecic, Takayuki Murakami, Amelia Sandy, Jeffrey Spear, Lee Talley, David Thomson, and Laura Yavitz.

I am much indebted to the friends and colleagues who supported me in this work, especially Steven Cohan who, in its initial stages, offered me good advice and a room of my own in London. Richard Kroll, characteristically generous with time and intellectual rigor, talked through ideas about historical process and the social formation. Janice Price at Routledge encouraged me in my editorial tasks with tact and her always infectious, subtle humor. Marc Conner worked long hours to help prepare the index. Finally, Chris Stansell brought good cheer at an important juncture.

My husband Uli's enduring engagement with the Victorians has fructified my own work in numerous ways, yet his ability to balance scholarship and teaching with our family life and with friendship has been just as valuable. This book is dedicated with love to my son Alexander Knoepflmacher and to my stepson Daniel Knoepflmacher who, born eighteen years apart, will read the Victorians differently than we do here, and differently from each other.

Chapter 1

Engendering history for the middle class
Sex and political economy in the *Edinburgh Review*

Judith Newton

Judith Newton, relying on Marxist categories of analysis to read across a variety of cultural texts and discourses, establishes the way men and women struggled to engender history for the middle class. While many analyses of middle-class culture still focus on class and on a male-centered society, Newton points to the intersection of class and gender and includes the labor and values of women. With examples from the *Edinburgh Review*, she argues that middle-class women of letters entered into the male struggle for cultural authority and formed their own "counter publics" (Fraser 1980). Demonstrating how women essayists' versions of the seemingly fixed laws of historical development promoted their own values as "value," Newton argues that "moral" or "cultural" revolution, like the creation of the modern state, involved the negotiation of gender as well as class. At the same time, the male legitimation of political economy as a new form of expertise, a new basis for cultural authority, and a master narrative of history involved the construction of a new discourse of masculinity as well, which may be read as responding to women's increasing power in the domestic sphere.

* * *

The 1830s in Great Britain were marked by struggles to increase the political and social power of middle-class men, by pressures from radicals and feminists to extend political and social authority more widely, by the social dislocations and increasing militancy of the working class, and by the gradual refashioning of "society" to include, under conditions of carefully negotiated control, male laborers and the poor. Not surprisingly, this decade is often characterized as a time of transition, deeply informed by a sense of "history," a heightened consciousness that the past was distinctly different from the present and that the future was liable to be marked by greater difference yet.[1] Public written histories, structured as narratives of the past or as accounts of the principles of historical development, offered a sense of control over time and change while extending to those who could interpret the flux a superior cultural authority.[2] Writing "history," indeed, in which self-interested norms and values implicitly governed "disinterested" accounts of the "laws" by which society as a whole progressed, was an important means by which struggles for cultural authority took place.

It was through struggles for cultural authority, in part, that "some values, norms, and qualities (appropriate to the life situation of some social groups) were elevated to become value, normality, quality of life itself" and that "a revolution in government" took place (Corrigan and Sayer 1985: 123).[3] Although this "revolution" signaled no simple triumph of the "middle class," essentially bourgeois and capitalist groups of men were incorporated into the English ruling class, forming an alliance with older aristocracy. At the same time, there was "a concerted attempt to disentangle 'the state' from interests, from clientage, from its previously more overt class and patriarchal register" so that the state came to represent "a neutral, natural, obvious set of institutionalized routine practices," which successfully laid "claim to the legitimate monopoly of national means of administration" (Corrigan and Sayer 1985: 123).[4]

Much has been made in accounts of British "state" or "cultural revolution" of the role played by professional middle-class men. Half in the market and half out of it, ambiguously related to the status of gentleman as well, their indeterminate social identity made them well placed to promote values and forms of social authority seemingly unbound to rank or wealth – the value of expertise, for example, and most particularly the value of 'disinterested' social knowledge. On the one hand, of course, professional ideals intersected with the entrepreneurial. The emphasis placed upon expertise, for example, overlapped with entrepreneurial celebrations of competition based on talent so that, in the process of offering their own values as the quality of life itself, male professionals may have shored up entrepreneurial values by displacing them onto higher ground.[5] But on the other hand, by emphasizing the disinterested nature of their expertise and by proposing that expertise as a basis for their own social authority and as a basis for state operations as well, professionals helped construct the state as a neutral set of routine practices seemingly divorced from the interests of class (Corrigan and Sayer 1985: 123; Perkin 1969: 429, 261; Wiener 1981: 8–30).

As with many accounts of the "middle class," in which "middle class" is largely masculine, "cultural" or "state" revolution is often conceived of as a "struggle over signs" conducted for the most part by sets of men.[6] And yet middle-class women, particularly women of letters, entered into these struggles too, forming their own "counter publics" (Fraser 1990). Women of letters articulated their own versions of the laws of historical development, offered their own values as "value" and the "quality of life itself," and in this way struggled for cultural space and social authority. Their more marginal position in relation to the market and the professional public world made them even better placed than professional men to enact the role of social "crank,"[7] to offer social analyses and critiques of the very market or social relations on which their class position to some degree hinged. And, like their male peers, women of letters promoted values seemingly unlinked to rank or wealth – the value of moral rather than intellectual expertise, the value of cooperation in opposition to the value of competition, whether of money or of merit. As with men, women's alternative values also intersected with entrepreneurial (and professional) ideals.

"Moral" or "cultural" revolution, therefore, like the creation of the modern state, involved discursive interchange between women and men, involved the negotiation of gender as well as class relations. And gender, in this context, must also be applied to relationships among men. For the creation of the modern state involved the renegotiation of male hierarchies which were based as much on conflicting masculinities as on conflicting class ideals.[8] Establishing distance from and authority in relation to the discourses of middle-class women, for example, played a crucial role in the legitimizing processes by which men of letters, in particular, established new forms of authority in relation to other males. This chapter examines the role of masculine identity in a struggle for social authority that was carried on by men who moved in what would appear to have been the most masculine of discursive worlds, that of the principal writers for the *Edinburgh Review*.

The *Edinburgh Review* was the first of the great political quarterlies and the most successful. In the 1830s, for example, it had a circulation of 12–14,000 (in contrast to the *Quarterly*'s 10,000, *Blackwood*'s 8,000, and the *Westminster Review*'s 2–3,000.) And in addition it may have had four or five readers for every copy (Heyck 1982: 33). The *Review* was founded in 1802 by a group of young intellectuals whose backgrounds were mainly urban professional middle class and whose ostensible purpose in creating a journal was "personal amusement" and "the gratification of some personal and national vanity."[9] In the latter regard the *Review* was certainly functional. Politically marginalized and professionally impeded by the fact of their entertaining Whiggish politics in Tory-dominated Edinburgh, the founders of the *Review* created an ideal vehicle for establishing social authority on other grounds.

First of all, the *Review* reviewed and therefore claimed authority in relation to texts on a wide range of topics, from political economy to women's novels, to scientific treatises, to debates in Parliament, to various kinds of reform, and collections of Greek poetry. The *Review*'s goal, according to Jeffrey, was "to go deeply into *the Principles*" on which the judgment of a work rested and "to take large and Original views of all the important questions to which these works might relate" (Jeffrey 1966: 1, 416). Even the length of the essays – individual issues averaged 10–12 pieces and 250 (roughly equivalent to 500 manuscript) pages – laid claim to interpretive authority as did the unusual vigor with which reviewers characteristically expressed their ideas, while the anonymity of the contributors helped to establish the illusion of a unified, institutional, and more than merely human voice. Readers of the *Review*, moreover, crossed class lines. Despite the fact that the *Review* is often characterized as a key institution of middle-class life, its implied audience was, to a significant degree, Whig aristocracy, including many figures among the governing elite (Fontana 1985: 7–8). The breadth of their audience, the range of classed individuals which they addressed, made the reviewers' claims to social authority particularly far reaching.

The most central and overt basis for the *Review*'s claims to interpretive authority lay in the expertise of its writers in political economy. The latter itself was an aggregate of converging views rather than a single specific doctrine, but its characteristics might be described as follows: a reading of historical progress which sees the development of civilization as "characterized by the successive emergence of different modes of production"; an assumption that "despite the greater degree of inequality of resources which it exemplified, modern commercial society is more compatible with the material welfare of the great majority and with political liberty than any other earlier form of social organization"; an assertion of the belief that market society was ruled by rational laws and was thus a possible object of scientific understanding and that "any transformation of society for the better could only rest upon the knowledge of such laws and on the observation of the constraints which they indicated" (Fontana 1985: 8). The *Review* was to become the major vehicle for this "scientific reading" of the laws of historical development in the early nineteenth century.

Many of the *Review*'s claims on behalf of political economy were set forth by John Ramsay McCulloch, the *Review*'s principal writer on political economy during the 1830s. McCulloch, who entered the Civil Service in 1838, was also to write several books on statistics and to champion statistical knowledge as a basis for social policy (O'Brien 1970). He was doubly positioned, therefore, as a man of letters and as a governmental agent, to promote the "science" of political economy (based on statistical "facts") as a master theory of history, as a standard against which all other readings of history could be assessed, and as a basis for state operations conceived of as natural, neutral, and divorced from class interests.[10]

The meta-theoretical claims which the *Review* made on behalf of political economy, however, were launched in a context of cultural ambivalence toward expert knowledge in general and "scientific" knowledge in particular. The growth of a mass market for information, to take one example, and the multiplication of popular and elementary texts conveying knowledge in simple and accessible forms prompted intellectuals like John Stuart Mill to characterize the 1830s as an era marked by the dogma of common sense and indifference to theory and expertise (Yeo 1984: 7). The distinction between common sense and informed judgment, moreover, was particularly difficult to make in the moral and social sciences. Indeed, writers on political economy often refer to themselves as chemists or physicians in an attempt to claim the greater authority of natural science. Political economy, finally, was a relatively recent contender for the status of science and, as I will suggest, a fairly embattled one as well.

The relation of reviewers to their male audience (essays on political economy routinely position their readers as male) was further complicated by the fact that their political and personal agendas involved them in conflicting or at least complex representations of their "science." As liberals, for example, reviewers sought to establish the authority of political economy on the basis of its being a democratic, commonsensical knowledge, available to all (and therefore deserving of cultural dominance in a properly "open" society). At the same time, they made equally determined attempts to establish political economy as a "recondite" knowledge, which only experts like themselves could master. Political economy was at once a knowledge "useful at all times, eminently useful among the people in times of distress and emergency" (Coulson 1831: 338–9) and a form of scientific theory so difficult and "abstruse" that only "those who have minds best prepared and most leisure to learn" could really understand it (Jeffrey 1825: 6).

Another source of difficulty in staking claim to social authority on the basis of this "scientific" reading of the world was that political economy was under attack in the 1830s, in both working-class and Tory journals, as an articulation of class and sectional interests. As marginalized middle-class men seeking professional advance, the chief reviewers were naturally prone to believe in a "science" which demonstrated the universal benefits of a society open to the pursuit of self-interest. But political economists like McCulloch were also regularly accused of being "in the pay of capitalists" as well and so of not being objective or scientific at all (Thompson 1984: 22). Partly, though not solely, in response to these attacks, reviewers maintained an ambivalent relation to entrepreneurs and therefore to an important section of their reading audience. On the one hand, for example, the reviewers' insistence that commercial progress based on self-interest is a key to moral progress as well as to material well-being seems a strategy for joining forces with entrepreneurs by displacing entrepreneurial values onto higher ground. But on the other hand, this insistence also works to establish the reviewers' transcendent relation to material production and entrepreneurs. *Review* essays are marked both by persistent celebrations of material production and by persistent efforts to transcend the concerns of wealth and industry which are continually linked to the body and to "sensuality" and therefore to what is less "exalted" than the "intellectual" (Jeffrey 1825: 5).

The *Review*'s essays on women appear to have functioned as sites on which some of these discursive tensions might be offset or resolved. The *Review*, to be sure, maintained a strict division between essays on "historically significant" topics like political economy and the essays on women writers. Women, indeed, even working-class women for the most part, do not even appear in essays on the former and are not officially addressed as readers. But if the reading audience for essays on political economy is implicitly male, the audience for essays on women is implicitly dual. While the female writer, and through her, genteel women in general, are corrected, warned, exhorted, categorized, selectively praised, defined as different from and more embodied than male writers, male readers are implicitly positioned as persons identifying with the reviewer. Since the thrust of *Review* essays on women was to place limits on women's access to the public sphere, they offered a "knowledge" about women that most male readers could be assumed to see as objective, disinterested, and "true." Since these same readers, we assume, were willing (only too willing) to see gender "knowledge" of this sort authoritatively reaffirmed, essays on women situated reviewers in a position of far less negotiation about their authority than did essays on political economy. Essays on women helped establish the *Review*'s expertise and interpretive authority for male readers in other, more problematic spheres.

To some extent, of course, the *Review*'s essays on ostensibly neutral subjects such as Greek poetry and scientific inventions, performed a similar function. But the *Review*'s essays on women also provided sites on which to establish the masculine credentials of the *Review* and of its chief reviewers, first by constructing the *Review* generally as a powerful institution for maintaining women's subordination through interpreting and delimiting the significance of their entry into public discursive spheres, and second by distinguishing women's limited authority as interpreters of history from the reviewer's own meta-theoretical expertise and authority (crucial in the case of women writing on natural science and on political economy).

Verification of masculinity as a form of distance from, superiority to, and control over women was of particular importance to liberal reviewers in the 1830s. Reviewers, for one thing, claimed social authority on the basis of mental abilities which were potentially more accessible to women than the rank or money on which more entrenched forms of masculine social authority were based. (And of what value is a form of masculine authority which women can share, particularly if that authority must contend with more established and less accessible forms of masculine power?) Liberal constructions of the public sphere, moreover (including those of political economy as defined by the *Review*) opened up the public sphere to feminine appropriation as the overtly hierarchical and paternalistic ideologies of landed men did not.

Seventeenth-century liberalism, for example, while officially restricting women to the domestic sphere and implicitly omitting them from the category of "rational individual" and citizen, did not directly deny the rationality of women. Indeed it offered terms for self-understanding ("rational individual," for example,) which feminists like Mary Wollstonecraft and Harriet Martineau effectively appropriated on women's behalf.[11] By the 1830s the rationality of genteel women and the necessity of extending and improving their education was a well established liberal position, although the goal of women's education was restricted in much male liberal discourse to improving their performance as wives and mothers.[12] Such discourse on the education of women, moreover, became particularly significant in the context of debate over parliamentary reform, a debate in which the *Review* played a leading role and a debate which raised many questions about the education and enfranchisement both of women and of working-class men (Fontana 1985: 147–80).

Review essays on women's writing, which increase in numbers during the 1830s, became sites on which the democratic tendencies of the reviewer's own liberal philosophies could be delicately encountered and on which the reviewers' status as "rational individuals" in an open society, a status increasingly appropriated in the discourse of middle-class women, could be upgraded or displaced by a more exclusive cultural authority – that pertaining to "men of science." This authority, to some degree, was already being constructed through scientific societies. Like other professional bodies, which proliferated in the 1830s and 1840s in Great Britain, scientific organizations such as the Royal Society, the Statistical Society, and the Political Economy Club, to which reviewers variously belonged, helped establish the social value of a specific expertise. Unlike comparable organizations in other fields, scientific brotherhoods were not tied to a particular profession, but they were restricted to those dedicated to the pursuit of, and presumably capable of, "scientific" knowledge, whether of the "facts" expressed by numbers, the laws governing wealth, or the physical world. Like other professional organizations, therefore, they helped establish the authority of a particular expertise while also conferring the identity of experts, "men of science," upon their members.[13]

By grouping their cross-class membership under the aegis "men of science," scientific brotherhoods and clubs eroded vertical class distinctions between middle-class professionals and members of more established class position. They were particularly important, therefore, in constructing the social authority of professional men while also forging new cross-class alliances or brotherhoods. Working-class men were omitted from such brotherhoods but were frequently a target audience for the spread of scientific knowledge through Mechanics Institutes. Those who most distinctly defined the outside to these insiders' clubs were women.[14]

As with other professional organizations, scientific societies helped demarcate a newly burgeoning field as the sphere of gentlemen. They reinforced in this way the overt emphasis on gender exclusion, expressed, for example, in the language of the Reform Bill and the Municipal Corporations Act, which accompanied the partial erosion of exclusions based on class in the 1830s. In contrast to the fields of medicine or law, however, the more amorphous field of scientific theory was not secured from women by training or official career structures. Scientific brotherhoods, for all their exclusivity, did not prevent women like Mary Somerville, Mrs Marcet, and Harriet Martineau from publishing on natural and political science in the 1830s and entering thereby into a scientific public sphere, nor did they prevent them from enjoying immense popularity as well. So the *Review*, like other male-run journals, played an important gatekeeping role.

Liberal reviewers excluded women from these inner circles on different grounds from those invoked, say, by Tory reviewers writing on the same women writers for the *Quarterly Review*. The latter were given to emphasizing natural mental divisions between women and men and were fond of exercising a species of discursive violence against women, by reminding readers, for example, of how eminent women of science had (unhappily) been burned and butchered or otherwise excluded from the public sphere by men (Whelwell 1834; Scrope 1833). Liberal reviewers were too immersed in discourse about the necessity for women's education, too wed to notions about the role of free choice and effort as keys to success in the public sphere for that.

Instead they based women's exclusion from authentic scientific expertise on a division of labor, freely chosen by women in part, but also based on women's bodies and finally on women's greater embodiment than men. Women might aspire to practical and useful scientific knowledge but not, in their greater embodiment, to the theoretical (Brewster 1834; Empson 1833). In the *Review*'s essay on Harriet Martineau, female political economists are represented as active and practical, as "missionaries" and "disciples" of male experts. Significantly, female political economists are also pictured as active in the "outer court" while the real experts on political economy are represented as having "retired for awhile into the inner sanctuary" (Empson 1833: 8). The active, physical life outdoors is associated with the feminine and embodied while the indoor, stationary, and disembodied life of contemplation is reproduced as male.

The emphasis on women's embodiment here positions male readers

and reviewers in still another cross-class brotherhood or club and repli-
cates the gender boundaries of scientific societies. But the same emphasis
on disembodiment also reinforces a hierarchy which reviewers explicitly
establish (in essays on political economy) between themselves and entrepreneurs. Indeed, in the pages of the *Review*, the active, producing
entrepreneur, whose masculine credentials were better established and
less accessible to women as well, is frequently linked with the body,
embodiment, and practical life, and therefore with increasingly feminized
sites. It is the theorists of material production, with their sedentary at-
home labor – more sedentary than middle-class women's by a long shot
– who are defined as truly masculine and free of crude self-interest in
these new and disembodied terms.

In establishing the distance of reviewers from the feminine and
embodied, *Review* essays on women may have strengthened the masculine authority of the *Review* and may have helped forge cross-class
alliances between reviewers and male readers, while also weakening the
association of chief reviewers with trade and with entrepreneurial and
other forms of class interest. *Review* essays on women may have lent
credence to the reviewers' insistence on the objective, disinterested,
scientific nature of political economy, the knowledge for which the
Review in many ways "stood." To stop here in an analysis, however,
would be to see gender as in the service of social relations in the public
sphere. It would be to ignore the fact that men lived in and were
ambivalently invested in domestic relations too, and it would obscure
the ways in which domestic relations, the anxieties and the investments
which they involved, impacted on the so-called public world.

The familiarity of "separate spheres" ideology should not obscure for
us the tensions which those ways of representing the world produced.
The *Review*'s allocation of middle-class women to the home, with its
compensating assertion of women's domestic power – women "are the
proper legislators for, as well as ministers of, the interior" – is seldom
made without discomfort.[15] Home, indeed, as constructed in the pages
of the *Review*, is not a place about which many reviewers feel at ease.
It is another sphere in which boundaries must be drawn, fortified, and
policed. For despite wish-fulfilling claims that women are "less
ambitious" than men, women's ambition would appear to be lurking
everywhere, not excluding what has been defined as the domestic sphere.

The novel, for example, is sometimes tentatively defined in the pages
of the *Review* as a predominantly domestic and feminine genre, as a way
of being in the home while in the public sphere: "there are some things
women do better than men; of these, perhaps, novel-writing is one"
(Lister 1830: 446). But female writers have 'stuffed the pages of an
ordinary love tale with grave and weighty disquisitions," thereby "allur-
ing" the masculine reader "to the well-cushioned sofa of the novel

reader" but leaving him "seated in the uneasy chair of the scholastic disputant" (ibid.: 444). Women's ambition is also expressed through the "education they give their children and in advice they bestow on their husbands," resulting in that "senseless heartless system of ostentation which pervades society" (Bulwer-Lytton 1831: 379). Even motherly ambition on behalf of children, Lister maintains, may become the secret cause of "the tarnished character and venal vote of the husband" (1830: 444).

As those contained, moreover, women are nonetheless identified with what contains them, that is with the home. Thus, in a review of Anna Jameson's work on Shakespeare's heroines Jameson is praised for choosing "the department" in which her powers may be "most efficiently and conspicuously exercised," "the female characters of Shakespeare":

> study and observation may afford a sufficient glimmer of light to illuminate the common apartments and familiar passages, as it were, in the labyrinth of the female heart, but they desert us entirely, or only lead us astray, when we endeavour, by their fitful ray, to thread our way through the more mysterious recesses of the edifice; – its sacred retirements, its "chambers of imagery", its wells of feeling, its vault of secrecy, suffering or crime. The torch that would guide us surely through these must be held by a female hand.
>
> (Anon. 1834: 181, 183–4)

The home and, by extension, women, as the place from which men freely come and go, the place in which they read novels on a "well cushioned sofa," becomes the labyrinth in which unfortunate men become entrapped and die. The sexual anxiety suggested by the traditional figure of labyrinthine women seems obvious, and it is worth noting that the labyrinthine nature of women's sexual and reproductive organs was already being illuminated and mapped by male medical experts, making a female guide unnecessary. But, on another and related level, the figure of the labyrinthine woman also suggests the fear of being contained or held by those who share the mother's embodiment or sex.

Leonore Davidoff and Catherine Hall, in their study of nineteenth-century middle-class life, remind us that middle-class sons "had the task of breaking away from intense but *dependent* relationship with their mother (or substitute female caretaker)" (1987: 356). The intensity and dependency of mother/child relations, moreover, and the power of mothers in middle-class homes may have been intensified in the 1830s and 1840s by some of the strategies that functioned to contain women's participation in the newly fluid public realm. The actual physical separation of the home from the workplace, for example, which isolated women in the family, may have intensified the relation between mother and children, mother and sons (ibid.). The ideology of separate spheres, in granting women a compensatory power as "ministers of the interior," may have imaginatively underscored an actual increase in the mother's domestic influence. It might be argued, indeed, that one effect of ideologies which emphasized genteel women's containment in the home was, ironically, to augment male anxiety about the domestic woman and the mother's power.

Anxieties about mothers and domestic women, moreover, do not surface in essays on women alone. Indeed, if *Review* essays on women offset some of the discursive tensions produced in essays on political economy, essays on political economy might be seen as a species of dream work useful in working through anxieties generated by relations in the middle-class home. Although women themselves, for example, do not appear in essays on political economy, embodiment and the intimate relationships over which women presided in the middle-class home are not simply excluded, in some tidy dualism, from "real" history in the *Review* – real history being scientific accounts of the public world as inhabited by men. Instead, relationships, roles, and functions associated with middle-class women are regularly employed in essays on political economy to structure, soften, and enliven the reviewer's "scientific" reading of men's relations to men and the nature of industrial progress.

McCulloch's "Philosophy of Manufacturers," for example, published in 1835, conceives of "history" in a way which appears to leave women out. For history is commercial progress conceived of as a giant "race" while the public world, where history takes place, consists of implicitly male individuals pursuing their own self-interest (McCulloch 1835: 455). But the public world is divided in this essay into a domestic and a nondomestic front, one competitive and the other communal. Thus the race for commercial progress is offered not as a struggle between English men in the domestic market but as a patriotic and unified struggle between England and other industrial capitalist nations in "the race of improvement," a struggle in which English men are domestically united "at home" (ibid.).

Shared and familiar understandings about the gendered division of the social world and about the relative harmony of domestic relations soften the essays' representation of men's class relations. McCulloch, however, does not imagine this community in familial terms, as the full logic of separate spheres would dictate. Rather, male domestic relations are implicitly compared to the workings of a factory which in itself is compared (in a quotation from Ure) to the operation of a giant machine. Each individual that is, an individual stripped of any embodied or material identity, asserts "his energies in his own way" and in concert "produced results that must appear all but incredible to persons placed under less exciting circumstances" (McCulloch 1835: 461). Domestic society, like factories, appears to be ' "a vast automaton, composed of various mechanical and intellectual organs, acting in uninterrupted concert for the production of a common object, all of them being subordinated to a self-regulated moving force" ' (ibid.: 434). So, domestic relations are appropriated but also reimagined in disembodied, masculinized, and carefully atomized form.

Although women are overtly excluded from the essay's narrative of industrial progress, qualities dominantly associated with women in nineteenth-century representation, such as nature, embodiment, and birth, are also employed at times to familiarize, naturalize, and assign life-giving functions to material and largely machine-based production. Early in his essay, for example, McCulloch's "scientific" reading of history as competitive material progress is overlaid with traditional and quasi-religious discourse in which "nature," through the provision of natural physical and moral resources, is discovered to be the cause of industrial development.

Yet this effort to create a unifying and legitimizing myth is in tension with the desire to present entrepreneurs and then political economists as the motor of history. Male human agency begins to erode the agency of nature early in the essay, when manmade machines first rival natural resources in importance and then displace them. Later in the essay machines completely outstrip nature in importance as they begin to intervene in history, calling "into employment multitudes of miners, engineers, and ship-builders, and sailors," "causing" the construction of canals and railways, and otherwise taking on the role of the entrepreneur (McCulloch 1835: 458).

Implicit in this shift from natural resources to machines is an ambivalent set of attitudes toward nature and by extension, I would suggest, to mortality and embodiment. From the beginning of the essay, nature is most often seen as raw material, as that which may be used and therefore controlled by men for material advance. That steam engines supplant waterfalls suggests the alignment of entrepreneurial men with what can be controlled, for "steam may be supplied with greater regularity, and being more under command than water . . . is therefore a more desirable agent" (McCulloch 1835: 457). Horses, unlike machines, are alive and therefore mortal: "What a multitude of valuable horses would have been worn out in doing the service of these machines and what a vast quantity of grain would they have consumed!" (ibid.: 458).

This alignment with what can be controlled, however, with what is not mortal, represents an alignment with what is not alive. But this is not an alignment which the essay will finally embrace. In a replay of Frankenstein myth what is dead must be made to live. As machines begin to act human and to intervene in history much like entrepreneurs, entrepreneurs are praised for producing machines in an "all but miraculous creation" (ibid.: 472). Thus, through a series of displacements, entrepreneurs appear to give birth, by immaculate conception, to themselves and machine-based industrial production is enlivened through a discursive appropriation of women's life-creating functions. This appropriation, of course, expresses both identification with and escape from embodiment.[16]

The reference to "all but miraculous creation" also positions entrepreneurs as more godlike than God, in their invention of machines that do more than nature to further material progress. Since the invention/ creation of key machines was the work of "a few obscure mechanics," it appears at first that this central role is relatively open to men from below. But artisans, as well as entrepreneurs, prove less significant in this history than would at first appear. In the hands of the lower class inventor, the spinning frame "how ingenious soever, was of no use, and all traces of it seem to have been lost" (ibid.: 471). The real credit belongs to Arkwright, who invented it "a second time" by showing "how it might be rendered the most prolific source of individual and public wealth" (ibid.). It is the unembodied interpretation of material invention/ life creation which makes it useful to the social world just as it is the objective, disembodied political economist who "in carefully investigating" the causes of progress ensures the continuation of that commercial race set in motion by more materially bound entrepreneurs.

In the pages of the *Review*, the legitimation of political economy as a new form of expertise, as a new basis for social authority, and a master narrative of history involved the construction of a new discourse on masculinity as well. The "rational individual," compromised by its appropriation in feminist discourse, was reconstructed as a Cartesian mind while the more emotional and embodied qualities present in earlier forms of masculinity were displaced onto women and onto competing subgroups of men (Davidoff 1990). The construction of this discourse, however, should be read in relation to multiple interests and investments, not all of which have solely to do with power and status in the public sphere.

The construction of disembodied masculinity might be read as an attempt to establish the masculine credentials of chief reviewers by distinguishing reviewers from female competitors in the field and by implicitly laying claim to a superior form of masculinity with respect to entrepreneurs. It might be read as an attempt to suggest the reviewers' distance from class and personal interests and as an attempt to legitimize the objective, scientific nature of political economy. This same emphasis on disembodiment might be read as an attempt to perpetuate women's confinement to the domestic sphere and it might be read, finally, as an attempt to deal with newly augmented anxieties in relation to women's power in the home, anxieties continually evoked by some of the reviewers' own discursive strategies. Anxiety over the middle-class mothers' and women's powerful embodiedness may centrally explain that "dread of unruly forces" and of the "biological and economic processes on which life exists" which other writers have marked in the new class of professional intellectuals.[17] That same anxiety perhaps lay at the heart of Foucault's technologies of power and at the heart of his own equation of this degendered knowledge with the "truth" of the modern age.[18]

NOTES

1 Such characterizations, of course, began with the Victorians themselves. See, for example, Mill "The Spirit of the Age": "The idea of comparing one's own age with former ages, or with our notion of those which are yet to come, had occurred to philosophers; but it never before was itself the dominant idea of any age," (1965: 28). See also Houghton (1957: 1–23, 34–5); Knights (1978: 10–12); Heyck (1982: 122–3); Dale (1977: 1–4).

2 Knights (1978: 22). See also Heyck (1982: 28), and Klancher (1987: 5), on the "complex contention" over texts which marked the early nineteenth century.

3 See also Brantlinger (1977: 11–34). On the "crisis of hegemony" in the 1830s see Richards (1988: 75).

4 See Perkin (1969: 267) on the process by which social justification through service, expertise, selection by merit, efficiency, and progress became identified with the aims of government.

5 On the roles of professional middle-class men and especially men of letters in the construction of Victorian ideologies see Heyck (1982: 24–46); Perkin (1969: 252–70, 428–37); and Cooter (1984: 70).

6 See, for example, Perkin (1969) and, despite their consciousness of the exclusion, Klancher (1987) and Corrigan and Sayer (1985). For an account of middle-class formation in which gender and women are central see Davidoff and Hall (1987).

7 Perkin applies this term to professional men on the grounds that their indeterminate class position enabled them to choose sides, often to come to the side of a class not their own (1969: 257).

8 These categories overlap in ways that are highly problematic. I am using the term masculine identity to refer mainly to strategies for maintaining difference from women and strategies for maintaining women's subordination to men. I am not proposing that this is all there is to masculine identity. For an account of the relation between masculine identity and the state see Connell (1987: 155–7).

9 Francis Jeffrey to Francis Horner, 11 May 1803 cited in Fontana (1985: 3). For an account of the reviewers see also Stewart (1985: 19–27).

10 McCulloch initially placed theory-making in a hierarchical relation to statistical fact-gathering. See Goldman (1983: 611). On the identification of science as a tool for constructing an ordered society see Berman (1978: 109).

11 See Eisenstein (1981: 44–7) and Elshtain (1981: 121–7). For accounts of feminist appropriations of liberalism see Eisenstein (1981: 89–113) and Rendall (1985).

12 See Rendall (1985) Chapter 4, "Educating Hearts and Minds," for an analysis of the way that arguments for women's education moved beyond arguments for improving women as mothers and wives.

13 On the political economists as a scientific community, see O'Brien (1975: 11–16). On the way in which marginal men gained and propounded social

identity through the institutions and groups of science culture see Inkster (1983: 39–42). See also Cooter (1984: 70–1) and Reader (1966).

14 See Davidoff and Hall (1987: 274, 310, 312, 425) on the exclusion of women from scientific culture.

15 For a discussion of gender as "a primary field within which or by which power is articulated" see Scott (1988: 44–5).

16 For similar analyses of seventeenth-century science see Merchant (1980: 193) and Keller (1979).

17 Knights (1978: 17).

18 For further analysis of this idea see Balbus (1986: 110–27).

WORKS CITED

Anon. (1834) "Mrs. Jameson's *Characteristics and Sketches*," *Edinburgh Review* 60: 180–201.

Balbus, Isaac (1986) "Disciplining Women: Michel Foucault and the Power of Feminist Discourse," in Seyla Benhabib and Drucilla Cornell (eds) *Feminism as Critique: The Politics of Gender*, Minneapolis: University of Minnesota Press.

Berman, Morris (1978) *Social Change and Scientific Organization: The Royal Institution 1799–1844*, Ithaca, NY: Cornell University Press.

Brantlinger, Patrick (1977) *The Spirit of Reform: British Literature and Politics, 1832–1867*, Cambridge, Mass.: Harvard University Press.

Brewster, David (1834) "Mrs. Somerville on the Physical Sciences," *Edinburgh Review* 59: 154–77.

Bulwer-Lytton, E. G. E. (1831) "Spirit of Society in England and France," *Edinburgh Review* 52: 375–87.

Connell, R. W. (1987) *Gender and Power: Society, the Person and Sexual Politics*, Stanford, Cal.: Stanford University Press.

Cooter, Roger (1984) *The Cultural Meaning of Popular Science: Phrenology and the Organization of Consent in Nineteenth Century Britain*, Cambridge: Cambridge University Press.

Corrigan, Philip and Sayer, Derek (1985) *The Great Arch: English State Formation as Cultural Revolution*, Oxford: Basil Blackwell.

Coulson, Walter (1831) "McCulloch's Principles of Political Economy," *Edinburgh Review* 52: 338–9.

Dale, Peter Allan (1977) *The Victorian Critic and the Idea of History: Carlyle, Arnold, Pater*, Cambridge, Mass.: Harvard University Press.

Davidoff, Leonore (1990) " 'Adam Spoke First and Named the Orders of the World': Masculine and Feminine Domains in History and Sociology," in H. Corr and L. Mamieson (eds) *The Politics of Every Day: Continuity and Change in Work, Labour and the Family*, London: Macmillan.

Davidoff, Leonore and Hall, Catherine (1987) *Family Fortunes: Men and Women of the English Middle Class 1780–1850*, London: Hutchinson.

Eisenstein, Zillah R. (1981) *The Radical Future of Liberal Feminism*, Boston: Northeastern University Press.

Elshtain, Jean Bethke (1981) *Public Man, Private Woman: Women in Social and Political Thought*, Princeton, NJ: Princeton University Press.

Empson, William (1833) "Mrs. Marcet – Miss Martineau," *Edinburgh Review* 57: 3–39.

Fontana, Biancamaria (1985) *Rethinking the Politics of Commercial Society: the 'Edinburgh Review' 1802–1732*, Cambridge: Cambridge University Press.

Fraser, Nancy (1990) "Rethinking the Public Sphere: Toward a Socialist Feminist theory of Democracy," talk delivered at a conference on "Negotiations, Strategies, Tactics: Discourse and Praxis in the Humanities and Social Sciences," University of California, Davis.

Goldman, Lawrence (1983) "The Origins of British 'Social Science': Political Economy, Natural Science, and Statistics, 1830–35," *The Historical Journal* 26 (3): 587–616.

Heyck, T. W. (1982) *The Transformation of Intellectual Life in Victorian England*, London: Croom Helm.

Houghton, Walter E. (1957) *The Victorian Frame of Mind 1830–1870*, New Haven, Conn.: Yale University Press.

Inkster, Ian (1983) "Introduction: Aspects of the History of Science and Science Culture in Britain, 1780–1850 and Beyond," in Ian Inkster and Jack Morrell (eds) *Metropolis and Province: Science in British Culture, 1780–1850*, London: Hutchinson.

Jeffrey, Francis (1966) *Contributions* I, xi cited in "The Edinburgh Review, 1802–1900," in Walter Houghton (ed.) *Wellesley Index to Victorian Periodicals*, vol. 1, Toronto.

—— (1825) "Political Economy," *Edinburgh Review* 43: 1–23.

Keller, Evelyn Fox (1979) *Reflections on Gender and Science*, New Haven, Conn.: Yale University Press.

Klancher, Jon (1987) *The Making of English Reading Audiences 1790–1832*, Madison: University of Wisconsin Press.

Knights, Ben (1978) *The Idea of the Clerisy in the Nineteenth Century*, Cambridge: Cambridge University Press.

Lister, T. H. (1830) "Mrs. Gore's *Women as They Are; or, the Manners of the Day*," *Edinburgh Review* 51: 444–62.

McCulloch, J. R. (1835) "Philosophy of Manufacturers," *Edinburgh Review* 61: 453–72.

Merchant, Carolyn (1980) *The Death of Nature: Women, Ecology and the Scientific Revolution*, New York: Harper & Row.

Mill, J. S. (1965) "The Spirit of the Age," in J. B. Schneewind (ed.) *Mill's Essays on Literature and Society*, New York: Collier Books. First published in 1831.

O Brien, D. P. (1970) *J. R. McCulloch: A Study in Classical Economics*, New York: Barnes & Noble.

—— (1975) *The Classical Economists*, Oxford: Clarendon Press.

Perkin, Harold (1969) *The Origins of Modern English Society 1780–1880*, London: Routledge & Kegan Paul.

Reader, W. J. (1966) *Professional Men: The Rise of the Professional Classes in Nineteenth Century England*, New York: Basic Books.

Rendall, Jane (1985) *The Origins of Modern Feminism: Women in Britain, France and the U.S. 1780–1960*, New York: Schocken.

Richards, Paul (1988) "State Formation and Class Struggle, 1832–48" in Phillip Corrigan (ed.) *Capitalism, State Formation and Marxist Theory*, London: Quartet Books.

Scott, Joan Wallach (1988) "Gender: As a Category of Historical Analysis," in *Gender and the Politics of History*, New York: Columbia University Press.

Scrope, G. Poulett (1833) "Miss Martineau's *Monthly Novels*," *Quarterly Review* 49: 136–52.

Stewart, Robert (1985) *Henry Brougham 1778–1868: His Public Career*, London: The Bodley Head.

Thompson, Noel W. (1984) *The People's Science: The Popular Political Economy of Exploitation and Crisis 1816–34*, Cambridge: Cambridge University Press.

Whelwell, William (1834) "On the Connexion of the Physical Sciences," *Quarterly Review* 51: 54–68.

Wiener, Martin J. (1981) *English Culture and the Decline of the Industrial Spirit 1850–1980,* Cambridge: Cambridge University Press.

Yeo, Richard (1984) "Science and Intellectual Authority in Mid-Nineteenth Century Britain: Robert Chambers and *Vestiges of the Natural History of Creation,*" *Victorian Studies* 28: 5–31.

Chapter 2

From trope to code
The novel and the rhetoric of gender in nineteenth-century critical discourse

Ina Ferris

Following recent sociologists of literature such as Pierre Bourdieu and Alain Viala, Ina Ferris holds that the internal relations of the literary field (rules, codes, genres, etc.) are as important as external relations (for example marketing or format) for the distribution of cultural power. She analyzes the rhetoric of gender at two important moments in the relationship between critical discourse and the novel: the early decades when the novel began to be allowed into the literary sphere, and the mid-century, by which time it had become a major literary genre. Taking as its object of study neither individual works nor authors nor readers, this chapter examines discursive structures that enable particular responses and, thus, regulate the literary field. Orienting herself in rhetoric and history, Ferris establishes a sociopoetic base for a feminist literary pragmatics.

* * *

In its review of Hannah More's *Coelebs in Search of a Wife*, the *Monthly Review* praised the work as an attempt to correct the "false taste" and "pernicious principles" of the ordinary novel. Deploying a stock metaphor of the period, the review imaged More's text as a vaccine that sought "to counteract the poison of novels by something which assumes the form of a novel . . ." (1809: 128). The "poison" that More sought to counteract, as the review did not need explicitly to spell out, was the syndrome of female reading. Characterized as addictive, sensational, and irresponsible, female reading was a trope well entrenched in both fictional and critical discourse by the turn of the century, and it was activated by women writers like Mary Wollstonecraft and Jane Austen, as well as by male critics and novelists (Uphaus 1987). The trope typically featured a passive, languorous body displaying itself on a sofa and neglecting domestic duties as it "devoured" the texts that fed its romantic and sexual fantasies. The text of a proper novelist like Hannah More, on the other hand, encouraged an upright reading that maintained the decorum of gender, and the *Monthly Review* goes on to define *Coelebs in Search of a Wife* as "a lecture to the fair sex on 'their being, end, and aim'," a lecture that aimed at repelling "the tyranny of fashion" and demonstrating to women "what they ought to pursue, in order to qualify themselves for wives; and to inculcate those religious and moral principles by which they ought to be governed" (1809: 128). Conspicuously absent from this description of intent and effect is any sense of fiction, fantasy, or, more generally, of literariness. More's narrative and her language are identified as a form of social discipline, her targeted readers as subjects to be reformed.

The *Monthly*'s review of Hannah More represents a standard moment in a standard middle-class periodical of the day, and it serves to underline the way in which the novel was admitted into mainstream nineteenth-century critical discourse as part of a project (largely initiated by the authoritative *Edinburgh Review*)[1] to shape and control reading practices. The point is worth insisting on, for the focus of early nineteenth-century critical discourse on the reading, rather than the writing, of the genre meant that the novel entered the critical sphere as social and ethical (rather than literary) discourse. More precisely, it was harnessed by the middle-class reviews as part of a cultural pragmatics that sought to forge a diverse and unstable group of the newly literate into the civic coherence of a "reading public."

Whatever the actual increase in literacy at the turn of the century, the advent of "multitudes" of new readers functioned prominently in the elite reviews as a discursive motif, especially when novels were at issue.[2] As the genre most closely identified with new classes of readers outside the genteel and gentlemanly space of the republic of letters, the novel stood as a sign of a new cultural force that the reviews had to begin to take into serious account if they were to extend and consolidate their own cultural power (Baym 1984).[3] The orthodox *British Critic* was not alone in regarding novels as "works which have so powerful, though imperceptible, an influence on the public mind," an "influence" that demanded "strict examination" by critical reviewers (*British Critic* 1814: 160). For its part, the leading Tory journal, the *Quarterly Review*, was led to observe, as it set out to review Edgeworth's *Tales of Fashionable Life*: "If the importance of a literary work is to be estimated by the number of readers which it attracts, and the effect which it produces upon character and moral taste, a novel or a tale cannot justly be deemed a trifling production" (Stephen and Gifford 1809: 146). The statement is symptomatic. At once admitting and denying the importance of the novel, the rhetoric of the *Quarterly Review* draws on a familiar double logic whereby the novel is granted cultural power but denied literary value. Herein, rather than in the gender binary itself, lies the well-known "double standard" of criticism identified by Elaine Showalter (1977).

The passage in the *Quarterly Review* works with two notions of literary importance: one derives from the reception of a work and foregrounds the problem of taste; the other, implicit in the passage, looks to the axis of production and raises the question of truth. For the reviewer these are not simply different mediations of a work; they stand in opposition. To be popular, the review suggests, is in some sense to be untruthful; at the same time, it is also in some sense to be meaningful. Meaning in such a context is interactive and extraformal, a matter of performance and response, and it is noteworthy that when novels are reviewed in these early years of the century (whether generically or as individual works), they are usually reviewed as if they were acts, not texts. So critics speculate on what fiction does to readers and to the social formation; they worry over questions of regulation (who should read what?); and so forth. Even a cursory glance at the periodicals yields a whole set of articles bearing titles like "On Novels and Romances," "On the Ill Effects of Novel Reading," "On Novel-Reading, and the Mischief Which Arises from its Indiscriminate Practice." By contrast, one finds few articles entitled "On the Depravity of Poetry Reading."

Critical identification of the significance of novels with the social context of reception meant that gender assumed a special valence in the discourse about fiction that it would maintain for the rest of the century. In the first place, the generic novel-reader (the "fair one on the sofa") was typically characterized as young and female; and in her inexperience and presumed impressionability, she came to function metonymically for all the new readers whose entry into the culture of literacy the reviews were monitoring, much as the genre itself signaled the pressure of that new literacy on the literary republic. The *Quarterly*'s review of Edgeworth cited above goes on to justify critical attention to novels on the basis not only of the number but also of the vulnerability of novel-readers, arguing that the genre attracts "readers of a more ductile cast whose feelings are more easily interested, and with whom every impression is deeper, because more new" (Stephen and Gifford 1809: 146). Such readers, the reviewer maintains, are "so easily imposed upon" that public duty demands the subjection of the circulating library to "the inspection of a strict literary police . . ." (ibid.). Incorporated into a discourse of civic discipline, approved fiction like that of Hannah More or Maria Edgeworth was represented as maintaining the proprieties not only of gender but also of class, and the *Edinburgh Review* noted with approval that Edgeworth's *Popular Tales* taught the "homely virtues" of prudence and economy to "that great multitude who are neither high-born nor high-bred," thereby countering the "pernicious absurdities" of a Thomas Paine or a William Wordsworth (1804: 329–30). Francis Jeffrey's early and highly influential reviews of Edgeworth in the same journal, notably those in the decade between 1804 and 1814, were equally concerned with questions of audience and effect, as when he commended her *Popular Tales* for having rendered "an invaluable service to the middling and lower orders of the people," and applauded her *Tales of*

Fashionable Life for attempting "to promote the happiness and respect-ability of the higher classes" (Jeffrey 1809: 376).

The *Edinburgh Review* noticed less than a dozen novels in its first ten years of publication (1802–12), the years of its own greatest influence, and half of these notices were devoted to Maria Edgeworth, whom Jeffrey congratulates in 1809 for "having done more good than any other writer, male or female, of her generation" (1809: 376). It is no accident that the novelists and novels regularly reviewed in the early years of the century were (like Edgeworth) those placed in the category of utility. The writing of didactic and domestic novelists not only preached but itself enacted the virtues of restraint and deferment proper to civil society. Thus Jeffrey noted with approval the "self-denial" that led Edge-worth to resist the temptation to produce "brilliant and fashionable" writing in order to produce that which was "useful and instructive" (Jeffrey 1812: 103). If Edgeworth's "sober" virtues came in time to seem constricted and constricting, especially after the entrance of Scott's Waverley novels, her writing possessed a special exemplariness at a crucial moment in the history of the novel and the literary republic. It rescued fiction as meaningful form (rather than irresponsible escape and self-indulgence), and it did so because of its generic exercise of gender, exchanging in its "self-denial" the personal satisfactions of brilliance for the social good of\ usefulness and instruction.[4]

Not only as reading but also as writing, then, the novel was inextricably entangled in gender codes; more specifically, the utility that justified the form was very much a matter of femininity. This is not to dismiss the role of other critical articulations of the novelistic field – there was a lively interest, for instance, in working out taxonomies of fictional genres and historical lines of development – but the critical project in which the novel was most prominently featured was that of the problem of reading, and in this project gender was central.[5] It was central precisely as a trope, and I have in mind here the old, rhetorical sense of the term as figurative language rather than the more usual current sense of any discursive construct, especially one that represents a belief or set of values from which we wish to distance ourselves. Certainly, non-figurative generalizations about "womanhood" and "truly feminine power" appear over and over again in the early nineteenth-century reviews, and the routine slide into figurative language itself testifies to a profound internal-ization of gender-constructs. It is not that reviews of the period operated subversively – far from it – but that their figurative turn marked a potential gap and so gave to the reproduction of gender a (limited) mobility that was soon to disappear. In this discourse, particularly as practiced by the monthlies and magazines, gender emerges as less a systematic code or a scientific "fact" than a loose and highly concrete set of analogies, associations, and metaphors.

The figurative ground for gender chosen by the discourse is typically the social body, for in order to enact the kind of reform and discipline sought by reviewers (and proper novelists), the novel could not be abstracted from the temporal and mundane realm of social and historical process. Standing as it did under the sign of utility, the novel was defined as less a literary than a social act, both as a form of writing and as a form of reading; and the critical idiom through which novels were mediated kept constantly in the foreground the link between writing and world on which their value in the discourse depended. Thus the vocabulary used for proper novels (and for "feminine" writing in general) is marked by the referential doubleness whereby its characteristic terms ("delicate," "amiable," "gentle," and so on) apply equally to persons and to texts, so that texts in this discourse begin to assume a worldly and bodily configuration. They often do so explicitly, as when reviewers transform texts into exemplary female bodies, either positive or negative. For the *Monthly Review*, reviewing Sydney Owenson's *The Lay of an Irish Harp*, for example, Owenson's text is a neurasthenic body, "a being that is all nerve and agitation" (*Monthly Review* 1808: 375). And John Wilson Croker, reviewing Fanny Burney's *The Wanderer* in the *Quarterly*, conflates author, text, and heroine as he transforms Burney's text into "an old coquette who endeavours, by the wild tawdriness and laborious gaiety of her attire, to compensate for the loss of the natural charms of freshness, novelty, and youth" (1814: 126). When approved fictions are under review, the fictional text most frequently assumes the eroticized shape of the graceful lady, and the *Edinburgh Review* is simply more direct than most in asserting at the end of its review of Amelia Opie's *Simple Tales* that her writings "would do very well to form a woman that a gentleman should fall in love with" (*Edinburgh Review* 1806: 471). Indeed, the whole context of courtship informs much of the critical rhetoric in this period when there were very few woman reviewers and many prominent women novelists, and male reviewers tended to approach women writers and readers with the gallantry and archness they deemed proper to encounters with "the fair sex."

In all this we can recognize a familiar tactic: the dissolving of female mind into body that has historically allowed for the erasure of women's writing. There is no writing in Croker's image, for example, only a woman. But at the same time, Croker's own writing is very much there; it neither seeks nor pretends to transparency. Moreover, the female body that is evoked in such moments (even in Croker) is less a natural than a socialized body. One cannot look past it to some essential or "natural" truth, so that the critical move of embodiment when women's language is at stake works, oddly, to underline the constructedness of gender.

The scene of the text in this discourse is worldly and even playful, as critical discourse casts readers, writers, and reviewers in parodic dramas of domesticity and romance. A review of Amelia Opie's *Tales of the Heart* in (Gold's) *London Magazine* (1820) affords a striking example. Itself a heavily jocular and clumsy review, the article is useful precisely because its very awkwardness makes more readily apparent than do more skillful reviews the methods and motifs of embodiment. The reviewer sets the tone in his opening lines: "Novels, those dear delightful, condemned, yet irresistibly fascinating productions, boast no class of readers so numerous, no admirers so enthusiastic, as those still more fascinating beings, the young ladies of this fair island" (*London Magazine* 1820: 178). Activating here the doubled reference characteristic of this discourse, the reviewer defines novels from the outset in terms applicable to the "dear delightful" and "irresistibly fascinating" young ladies who consume them. With genre and gender so doubling one another, he goes on to place himself outside their interplay by casting himself as an old-fashioned paterfamilias "blessed with blooming and enticing daughters" who pressure their fondly exasperated parent for fiction. What can one do? he asks:

> we can't keep the girls always at school nor always at work, nor always at play; their minds and their imaginations crave for some sort of sustenance, some degree of exertion, that shall amuse without fatiguing them – Novels are the very thing, and novels they must and will have.
>
> (ibid.)

As a sign of the desire that eludes the supervision of school, work, and play, novels are regarded with suspicion by "miserable prejudiced dotards" like the reviewer. But to his relief there exist novelists like Amelia Opie, novelists whose fiction works to "confine the imagination within due bounds." So long as they continue to write, he declares, the young women under his control will not be "debarred" from reading novels. Opie herself meanwhile emerges in his review as "a priestess" who wields a "potent" and "fascinating" influence over the imagination and the affections.

By staging the whole problem of the novel through a concrete figuration of comic fathers, spoiled daughters, and enchanting priestesses in a tale of displaced eroticism, the review of Opie points to the way in which this critical discourse takes on a distinctly sensuous accentuation when it comes to novels, but a sensuousness that is always (officially) in the service of social decorum. It is ladies and gentlemen (or their negative counterparts) who figure in these scenes of the text, as the reviews seek to channel the asocial energies conventionally associated with novel-reading in the interests of modern and civil society. Women's writing was generally held to have a special relationship to both modernity and civility, and a long two-part article "On the Female Literature of the Present Age" in the *New Monthly Magazine* voiced a common view when it opened with the declaration: "There is no more delightful peculiarity in the literature of the present age than the worth and the brilliancy of its female genius. The full developement [*sic*] of the intellect and imagination of women is the triumph of modern times" (1820: 271). Female genius turns out to be remarkably like the ideal lady, being marked by "sweet fancies," "delicious conceits," and "gentle influences." Creating "nooks of graceful loveliness," it is said to shed a "delicate and tender bloom." The language here, with its appeal to the senses (particularly those of taste and touch), is symptomatic of the way in which the article as a whole materializes as it idealizes what it calls "the female mind." On the one hand, such a move reifies; on the other, it blocks precisely the abstraction that allows for reification.

The article in the *New Monthly*, like the general discourse in which it participates, works to both ends. Its survey of over two dozen women writers depends on and produces a composite female figure whose traits are slotted in as the individual women pass in review. Despite significant variations in the individual portraits and despite their accommodation of such unfeminine qualifiers as "bold" and "original," certain stock traits are reiterated, and they coalesce into the ideal lady whose outline governed the article from the beginning. Thus Felicia Hemans is marked by "grace and beauty," Mary Brunton by "harmony and proportion," and Jane Austen by "simple elegance" and a "harmonious mind." Austen in fact is characterized entirely in terms of the perfect lady, and the reviewer regrets that she died just when she was able to feel "that the mild influences of her powers were extensively diffused to purify and to soften" (*New Monthly Magazine* 1820: 637). Suggestively, he places Austen right after Sydney Owenson (Lady Morgan) from whose "dazzling brilliancy" he turns with some relief in order to "repose on the soft green of Miss Austen's sweet and unambitious creations" (ibid.). The banality of the language obscures the oddness of this moment. The writer deploys a rapid series of metaphoric shifts to raise the possibility of reposing on Austen's text-turned-bosom before displacing the body of the mother-lover that he has summoned into the idyllic pastoral and national space of the "soft green" English landscape. The figural slide here from text to body to landscape depends on the operation of tropes that have been well assimilated by the culture but nevertheless remain clearly tropes. The sequence depends (modestly) on the mobility of signifiers that allows them to be embedded in different codes and to form different metaphoric combinations. Throughout the article scenarios shift, metaphors change, and there is a sense of (restrained) pleasure in the play of signification. Although the figuration that marks early nineteenth-century critical prose routinely naturalizes gender by conflating women's writing and women's bodies, it also maintains the sense of a gap in the openness of its metaphoric transformations. There is little sense of a transparent, stable, or "scientific" language for gender; instead, gender typically activates and is itself defined through the imprecision of the figurative power of words.

By mid-century, however, the informality and salutary incoherence of gender in the early decades had largely given way to formalization and codification. Despite the slippage inevitable in any discursive construct, by the 1850s the whole issue of gender was more fully rationalized. Richard Holt Hutton's representative piece on male and female writing for the *North British Review* in 1858, "Novels by the Authoress of 'John Halifax'," is a case in point, and it will serve as my exemplary mid-century text. Hutton, co-founder of the *National Review* and future literary editor of the *Spectator*, here takes the occasion of a review of Dinah Mulock to define how "feminine fictions, as distinguished from those of men, are strong or defective" (1858: 468). The division of the fictional field that Hutton goes on to elaborate yields a familiar shape: men are linked to intellect, imagination, and breadth; women to emotion, fancy, and close observation. Reviewers earlier in the century had deployed the same binary, as when the article on female literature discussed earlier declared that the anonymous *Glenarvon* (by Caroline Lamb) had to be by "a female pen" because qualities like its "quick sensibility" and "nice apprehension and intuitive discernment" revealed a "manifestly feminine" cast (*New Monthly Magazine* 1820: 633). But if the two reviews reproduce the same binary, they embed it in different rhetorical structures. Where the 1820 article adopted the form of a loosely organized survey and marked out a series of traits, Hutton works analytically from a model of gender whose implications for narrative he systematically draws out. He proceeds, not from traits that imply gender (as did the *New Monthly Magazine*), but from concepts of gender that determine its traits. Hutton's approach, that is, depends on the formulation "woman = delicate" rather than on the reverse formulation ("delicate = woman") that structures the piece in the *New Monthly*. Both formulations are tautological and both work to exclude those who do not possess a particular trait from the general category, but "woman = delicate" makes delicacy a condition of womanliness in a way that "delicate = woman" does not. It may be possible to be a woman and yet not be delicate, as it may also be possible for delicacy to signify something other than womanliness. To move from trait to category is to leave open possibilities that reversing the direction of implication closes off, and in Hutton gender operates very much as a closed system.

What this reflects in part is that for critics like Hutton the novel was a more serious and "literary" (if still somewhat suspect) genre than it had been for early nineteenth-century reviewers. One mark of its new status was a shift of interest to the writing rather than the reading of novels, and here a closed paradigm of gender was invoked to govern entry into the field. This does not mean that the direct sociocultural interest in reception which marked the early decades evaporated. We have only to recall the often lampooned concern for "the Young Person" in Victorian criticism, while the reading of women, as critics like Kate Flint (1986) have been reminding us, continued to be a persistent and explicit concern throughout the century. But after the decisive intervention of Walter Scott's Waverley novels, the novel was granted a measure of literary authority and occupied a different cultural space; more particularly, his historical novel, together with its critical reception, effected a re-gendering of the genre, making possible a "manly" kind of fiction that intensified the gendered division of novel-writing (Ferris 1989). Hutton's article insists on a sharper separation of male and female modes of fiction than do the earlier reviews, so testifying to the heightened contest over generic territory between the genders that helped to shift attention away from reading to writing in the course of the century.

At mid-century the critical reviews were generally more secure in their own readership (the "reading public" forged by reviews like the *Edinburgh* was now firmly in place), and critical discourse itself was becoming increasingly stratified into specialized discourses. In its literary stratification in particular, critical discourse was shedding the link with the mundane that had motivated its earlier practice. Questions of taste and reading (while still posed) more and more gave way to questions of truth and form, and the scene of the text in this discourse began to lose its concreteness and sociability – even as the domestic circle of actual novel-reading outside the discourse intensified those very traits. In Hutton's text there are no bodies, and the physical and social world of readers, texts, writers, and reviewers constructed by earlier critical discourse drops out of sight to be replaced by abstract "capacities" and "powers" whose metaphoric ground is the cosmic ground of space and time. Hutton valorizes "the imagination alone, grasping its own thought" as it meditates in the unworldly space of "a sphere beyond the range of ordinary observation" (1858: 476). Controlled by an insistent binary of height/ depth, his discourse locates truth and literary value somewhere "beyond" the ordinary world. The realm of the ordinary (identified with women) serves only as a "surface" or "visible expression of deeper wisdom" that stimulates the true (male) imagination to "decypher and interpret" it (ibid.: 467). No longer attached even to the rarefied bodies of ladies and gentlemen, gender floats free, more difficult to locate and more coercive.

At the same time, it is more visible – and hence open to contestation. That is, it no longer goes almost without saying, as it had tended to do earlier in the century. Indeed, in Hutton gender becomes a master-sign, absorbing everything it encounters and processing it as part of itself. His model of gender organizes a whole series of literary terms – plot, narration, character, and so on – into male and female modes, so that by the end of the article nothing is left out, and the whole fictional field is laid out in two parallel lines. And he could easily continue, for the model is potentially capable of accounting for an infinite number of forms of writing and forms of experience. There is little room here for metaphoric slides or an excess of signification, as Hutton seeks to bring language into order and to transform world into idea. His model of gender in fact derives precisely from his valorization of such a transformation of world into idea, for its distinction between the genders rests on a distinction in imagination in which the imagination is defined in terms of impersonality and abstraction. Hutton argues that "proper *imaginative* power" lies in a capacity for detachment that women do not, as a class, possess: unlike men, he claims, they are typically absorbed in and by the visible, the circumstantial, and the personal.[6]

Women are thus identified with the temporal, characterized as operating in a concrete and saturated time; their entire existence, Hutton reiterates, is taken up with the "daily," the "circumstantial," and the "*visible*" (ibid.). Being so caught up in "the human *dress and circumstance* of life," women are unable to remove themselves from "mere external *symptoms*" in order to "meditate deeply on the living realities which lie beneath" (ibid.: 477). By contrast, men in Hutton's scheme are linked to the freedom of space, able to leave the temporal world at will in order "to go apart" and to discern underlying laws and systems "as if no outer world for the time existed at all" (ibid.). Imaginative power lies in this ability "to go apart," a phrase that becomes a leitmotif in the essay.[7] "Women's fancy," Hutton writes, "deals directly with *expression* . . . and seems unequal to go apart, as it were, with their conception, and work it out firmly in fields of experience somewhat different from those from which they have directly gathered it" (ibid.: 474). Because of their entanglement in time and their consequent inability "to go apart," women are excluded from the properly literary, whose sign for Hutton is poetry. Women have not produced first-rate poetry, he argues, because the poet "must penetrate and battle for a time, nay even *live*, far beneath the surface of life, in order to create fine poetry"; but women's imagination is "not *separable*, as it were, in anything like the same degree [as that of men], from the visible surface and form of human existence" (ibid.: 467).

Instead, women have a special connection to narrative, the genre of those interested in "visible surface" and in temporal notions like "event" and "growth." Because women are interested in "the full dress of circumstance," for example, women novelists are better able than their male counterparts to construct "that flow of event which is one of the greatest necessities of the writer of fiction" (ibid.). But skill in constructing the "flow of event" is a trivial matter, a sign of the female limitation to the temporal sphere which stood in conventional opposition to the literary, distracting one with its circumstances and visibility from the truth that lay "far beneath." Thus confined to the temporal, women are inevitably – and inherently – simply superficial. On this point Hutton is tactful but insistent, and his insistence underlines the way in which the cultural discourse that detemporalized women as angels of the hearth contained within it a contrary discourse that insisted on their inescapable temporality. In both discourses, of course, women were inherently domestic, but the angel of the hearth was granted access to the atemporal binary of height/depth from which the woman as writer was definitively excluded. So Hutton admits that Charlotte Brontë delved into "depths" and "secret roots," but those depths and secrets, he hastens to add, were all located in her own psyche.

To become a properly literary form in Victorian culture, then, the novel had to "go apart," as Hutton puts it. This meant not only that it had to shed its worldliness but that it needed to purge itself of the very narrativity that marked its generic identity. The novel, in other words, had to be split apart as a genre and emptied out if it was to achieve status as a serious form. Women functioned in an analogous way in the discourse of gender, and they were equally linked to temporality and equally dependent for their cultural seriousness on the severance of that link. In appropriating the novel, critical discourse could thus draw on the code of gender to naturalize a critical regime whereby denarrativized fictions (those shaped by what Hutton calls an "intellectual frame") were allowed into the literary sphere while the narrative power of the genre itself remained outside. The scheme of exclusion is familiar, as is its post-structuralist accentuation whereby that which is inside (literariness, masculinity) turns out to depend on that which is outside (narrativity, femininity). But familiarity should not obscure the strangeness of such generic and cultural definition nor the working of cultural power which the model inscribes. Operating by negation, splitting, and inversion, Victorian critical discourse entangled women, novels, and criticism itself in a project of legitimation that required a denial of the very categories of narrative and history on which all three at the same time depended.

NOTES

1 On the significance of the *Edinburgh Review* for middle-class culture, see Klancher (1987) and Shattock (1989).
2 Richard Altick's classic study (1957) of the reading public remains the best introduction to the history of reading in the nineteenth century, though it is focused on a lower stratum of the public than that targeted by the elite reviews with which I am concerned. For a more theoretical approach that relies on Habermas's notion of the public sphere, see Peter Hohendahl (1982). Hohendahl argues that the pressure of a marked increase in literacy helped to fragment the classical public sphere at the end of the eighteenth century and hence to

shape the new critical formations of the nineteenth century. On criticism and the public sphere, see also Eagleton (1984).

3 Baym's study focuses on the nineteenth-century United States, but critical discourse about the novel was informed by similar assumptions on both sides of the Atlantic. Baym's fine study is one of the few to offer a historical analysis of the discursive context of reception.

4 The reception of Edgeworth also underlines the important distinction in the period between the indirect "influence" proper to women and the direct "power" proper to men. On this distinction, see Newton (1985).

5 For the purposes of this chapter, my discussion of gender leaves aside the problem of masculinity and the novel during this period, but the two genders always imply one another. See Ferris (1989, 1991).

6 Although Hutton refers constantly to "men" and "women," his categories of masculinity and femininity are partly abstracted from biological gender. Dickens, for example, is judged to be "in some remarkable points feminine . . ." (Hutton 1858: 477). When men novelists are at issue, gender will often stand in for class, as was the case with Dickens (widely regarded in the reviews as vulgar interloper in the literary republic) and in the much earlier debate between the "feminine" Richardson and the "masculine" Fielding.

7 Hutton thus offers a striking illustration of Pierre Bourdieu's (1979) well-known point that the key to "aesthetic," as opposed to "popular," taste is the valorization of distance.

WORKS CITED

Altick, Richard (1957) *The English Common Reader*, Chicago: University of Chicago Press.

Baym, Nina (1984) *Novels, Readers and Reviewers: Responses to Fiction in Antebellum America*, Ithaca, NY: Cornell University Press.

Bourdieu, Pierre (1979) *Distinction: A Social Critique of the Judgement of Taste*, trans, Richard Nice, London: Routledge.

British Critic (1814) Review of Maria Edgeworth's *Patronage*, NS 1: 159–73.

[Croker, John Wilson] (1814) Review of Mme D'Arblay's (Fanny Burney) *The Wanderer, Quarterly Review* 11: 123–30.

Eagleton, Terry (1984) *The Function of Criticism: From "The Spectator" to Post-Structuralism*, London: Verso.

Edinburgh Review (1804) Review of Maria Edgeworth's *Popular Tales*, 4: 329–37.

—— (1806) Review of Amelia Opie's *Simple Tales*, 8: 465–71.

Ferris, Ina (1989) "Re-Positioning the Novel: *Waverley* and the Gender of Fiction," *Studies in Romanticism* 28: 291–301.

—— (1991) *The Achievement of Literary Authority: Gender; History, and the Waverley Novels*, Ithaca, NY: Cornell University Press.

Flint, Kate (1986) "The Woman Reader and the Opiate of Fiction: 1855–1870," in Jeremy Hawthorn (ed.) *The Nineteenth-Century British Novel*, London: Edward Arnold. Stratford-upon-Avon Studies, 2nd series.

Hohendahl, Peter Uwe (1982) *The Institution of Criticism*, Ithaca, NY: Cornell University Press.

[Hutton, Richard Holt] (1858) "Novels by the Authoress of 'John Halifax'," *North British Review* 29: 466–81.

[Jeffrey, Francis] (1809) Review of Maria Edgeworth's *Tales of Fashionable Life*, *Edinburgh Review* 14: 375–88.

—— (1812) Review of Maria Edgeworth's *Tales of Fashionable Life, Edinburgh Review* 20: 100–26.

Klancher, Jon (1987) *The Making of the English Reading Audiences, 1790–1832*, Madison: University of Wisconsin Press.

[Gold's] *London Magazine* (1820) Review of Amelia Opie's *Tales of the Heart*, 2: 178–80.

Monthly Review (1808) Review of Sydney Owenson's *The Lay of the Irish Harp*, NS 57: 374–8.

—— (1809) Review of Hannah More's *Coelebs in Search of a Wife*, NS 58: 128–36.

New Monthly Magazine (1820) "On the Female Literature of the Present Age," 13: 271–5; 633–8.

Newton, Judith Lowder (1985) *Women, Power, and Subversion: Social Strategies in British Fiction, 1778–1860*, London: Methuen. First published in 1981.

Shattock, Joanne (1989) *Politics and Reviewers: The Edinburgh and the Quarterly in the Early Victorian Age*, London: Leicester University Press.

Showalter, Elaine (1977) *A Literature of Their Own*, Princeton, NJ: Princeton University Press.

[Stephen, H. J. and Gifford, W.] (1809) Review of Maria Edgeworth's *Tales of Fashionable Life, Quarterly Review* 2: 146–54.

Tuchman, Gaye, with Nina E. Fortin (1989) *Edging Women Out; Victorian Novelists, Publishers, and Social Change*, New Haven, CT: Yale University Press.

Uphaus, Robert (1987) "Jane Austen and Female Reading," *Studies in the Novel* 19: 334–45.

Chapter 3

Demonic mothers
Ideologies of bourgeois motherhood in the mid-Victorian era

Sally Shuttleworth

Sally Shuttleworth draws on Marxist categories to investigate the operations of ideological contradiction and displacement with respect to Victorian constructions of motherhood. The dual labor these constructions had to perform for the bourgeois class, enhancing its claims to moral and hence social supremacy and ensuring its healthy reproduction, led to irreconcilable ideological contradictions. Enlarging Michel Foucault's work on the disciplining of the bourgeois body, Shuttleworth argues that the functions of maternity, even more than sexuality itself, were fiercely regulated and controlled. Unlike Foucault, however, she highlights the operations of ideological contradiction and the ways in which class and gender ideologies clashed, destabilizing each other. Class issues are displaced into sexual terms, and sexual are displaced into class terms: demonic figures of maternal excess, for example, are aligned both with the degenerate aristocratic classes, and with the working classes and the fallen sisterhood.

*　*　*

Motherhood was set at the ideological centre of the Victorian bourgeois ideal. Virtually any reference to motherhood in the social texts of the era seemed to call forth, as if by necessity, yet one more recitation of the maternal creed. We hear endlessly of the mother's sacred mission to rear children, and of her spiritual grace which, filling the domestic sphere, uplifts her weary husband on his return from the corrupting world of Mammon. Few ideological constructs seem to arouse such uniform responses in the era; men and women, conservatives and reformers alike, seem to endorse this identikit picture. Even with the beginnings of the women's movement in the 1860s, female reformers were reluctant to voice a challenge to the sacred ideals of motherhood. Yet the very ideological centrality of these ideals ensured that motherhood was not the still point around which other ideological contradictions might turn, but rather a field of potent conflict in itself. Far from guaranteeing, by its seemingly unchallengeable status, areas of overt ideological conflict, it acted as a focal point for many of the most problematic areas of Victorian ideology.

Ideals of motherhood had to perform important ideological labor: they helped constitute and maintain the gendered social hierarchy and its division of labor, they vindicated the middle class's claims to social leadership through moral superiority, and sanctioned, by their maintenance of a strict division between the realms of home and work, whatever questionable practices the bourgeois male might have to pursue in business. But motherhood was not solely a spiritual mission, as so many descriptions seemed to suggest. It was also an intensely physical process, and a mode of social productivity vital to the middle class's maintenance of power. From the beginnings of the foundation of the bourgeois ideal in the mid-eighteenth century, we start to hear dire warnings, which reach a crescendo in the Victorian era, that middle-class women are failing to fulfil their reproductive duties, producing sickly, puny children, while the threatening mass of the working classes are producing bouncing, healthy babes.

As Foucault (1984) has argued, the nineteenth century was an age dedicated to the regulation of the middle-class body, and perhaps even more than sexuality, the functions of maternity were the object of fierce scrutiny and control. Indeed maternity encompassed the domain of female sexuality, for all the workings of female sexual desire were traced directly to the operation of the reproductive system. Woman, the medical textbooks insisted, was ruled by her "uterine economy" from the first onset of puberty to the cessation of her reproductive life with the "climacteric," or menopause.[1] The maternal function dominated womanhood not only with the actual bearing of children, or the wild outbreaks of an "ovarian perversion of appetite" or puerperal insanity that childbirth might occasion, but in all the daily operations of the mind and body throughout a woman's reproductive life. Female emotion, whether hysterical and out of control, or spiritually elevated and refined, sprang from the seat of maternity; sexuality and tenderness were deemed equally the products of the uterine economy. The two seemingly opposed models of womanhood constructed in nineteenth-century bourgeois ideology – refined angel, or helpless prey to the workings of the body – come together in discourses on maternity, for woman's mission is both to ensure, physically, the healthy reproduction of the race, as well as the spiritual superiority of the middle class.

Contradictions within constructions of the maternal role were not confined to the split between materiality and spirituality, but were indeed legion. For example, conflicts between the projections of motherhood and wifehood abound. Emphasis on female domestic supremacy seemed to offer potentially dangerous images of female empowerment, while the intense ideological focus on woman's reproductive role threatened to marginalize male creativity. On a practical level, theorists were exercised by the problem of whether a woman's first concern should lie with the comfort of her husband or the upbringing of her children. Sarah Ellis solved the dilemma by producing two separate texts, *The Wives of England* (1843b) and *The Mothers of England* (1843a), both of which speak, to the virtual exclusion of the other sphere, of the all-encompassing centrality of their chosen theme. When conflict is unavoidable, Ellis pays lip service to the primary importance of the male, despite frequent projections of him as a spoilt and petulant child. The thinking underlying this priority is explicitly voiced in another contemporary text: Mrs Warren's semi-fictionalized account, *How I Managed My Children from Infancy to Marriage*:

> During all these years, though I became so devoted to my children, I never allowed them to interfere with my time when my husband came home. . . . I would suggest to every woman never to allow her children to usurp the time and loving attention due to the husband. If she does, home will be no home to him; he will become irritable and seek comfort elsewhere.
>
> (Warren 1865: 41–2)

Although a woman's central concern is with her children, self-interest dictates an outward subservience to the controller of the purse-strings.

The mother was not an unproblematic figure in Victorian discourse. The angel was shadowed by potent images of disruptive physicality, while wifehood and motherhood seemed to impose conflicting demands. This ideological confusion is perhaps best summarized in the details of a psychological case that seemed to haunt the male imagination of the era, being repeated frequently in medical texts of the time. It concerns a woman who, through an extreme "ovarian perversion of the appetite," developed "such a cannibalish longing for the flesh of her husband, that she killed him, ate as much of him as she could while fresh, and pickled the remainder" (Anon. 1851: 31).[2] In this monstrous concatenation of different ideological images, uncontrollable maternal urges unite with commendable attributes of housewifely zeal and economy literally to eat into and destroy male dominance. So absorbed is the woman with the needs of her reproducing body, and the fulfilment of her housewifely role, that her husband is efficiently and neatly subsumed, negated by the conjoined powers of maternity and domestic management. While such demonic images are no doubt extreme, they are not unusual and highlight the ideological anxieties underlying the projections of female angelic subservience. Like the working classes, women represented to the bourgeois male imagination an ever-present threat to their dominance, a threat, moreover, that was enshrined within the sanctuary of their own home. In the following analysis I will look in more detail at some of the fears accruing around the middle-class female body, and attempts to regulate her maternal functions. The discourse of maternity was

promulgated through a wide range of texts. This discussion will focus
initially on the popular advice texts, and more specialized medical works
which together laid the ideologically-riven ground of Victorian projections of motherhood, while the final section will consider the more complex textual terrain of fictional constructions.

HEALTHY REPRODUCTION

In his *Advice to Mothers* (1803), a text that laid the framework for later
discussions in the Victorian era, William Buchan warned that "It is little
short of intentional murder on the part of a weak, languid, nervous, or
deformed woman to approach the marriage-bed" (Buchan 1809: 9). Not
only would such a woman fail in her social duty of producing healthy
offspring to perpetuate the nation's prosperity, she would also be burdened with ineradicable guilt for her heinous crime against the social
good. This ideological construction of a languid, nervous woman who
fails in her bounden duty to her country seems to shadow the bourgeois
rise to social power. From the earliest stages, fears are voiced that
"degeneracy" within these classes will impede industrial progress. Thus
Thomas Trotter warns at the beginning of the nineteenth century that
England's commercial ascendancy is under threat from "the increasing
prevalence of nervous disorders; which, if not restrained soon, must
inevitably sap our physical strength of constitution; make us an easy
conquest to our invaders; and ultimately convert us into a nation of
slaves and idiots" (Trotter 1812: x). As the century progressed, middle-
class women, with their languid airs and nervous ailments, were increasingly singled out as the prime culprits of this feared decline (fears that
were not in any way allayed by England's growing commercial success).
The bourgeois woman was caught in an unyielding ideological double-
bind: separated, increasingly, from the polluting domain of work, she
was nevertheless then fiercely criticized for her debilitating idleness.

   The era's advice books on womanhood and motherhood were virtually
all directed to this social class of woman, and all carried the same
message: idle, artificial habits, copied from a degenerate aristocracy,
endangered the health and wealth of the nation. Sarah Ellis was uncom-
promisingly specific about the designated audience for *The Women of
England*. Other advice books, she observed, had been written for ladies,
"while that estimable class of females who might be more specifically
denominated *women*, and who yet enjoy the privilege of liberal education, with exemption from the pecuniary necessities of labour, are
almost wholly overlooked" (Ellis 1838: preface). The category of true
"womanhood" takes on an extraordinarily privileged status in her text:
the true woman would be neither an aristocratic lady (a term that takes
on increasingly pejorative connotations), nor subject to the degrading

demands of pecuniary labour which helped to unsex the vulgar lower orders, but rather an educated member of the middle classes.

Like all her contemporaries, Ellis is not sparing of her strictures on "the sickly sensibilities, the feeble frames, and the useless habits of the rising generation" (1838: 11) which are threatening the "nation's moral wealth" (ibid.: 13). In a sweeping statement she asserts that:

> By far the greater portion of the young ladies (for they are no longer *women*) of the present day, are distinguished by a morbid listlessness of mind and body, except when under the influence of stimulus, a constant pining for excitement, and an eagerness to escape from every thing like practical and individual duty.
>
> (ibid.: 11–12)

Whereas an earlier generation were lambasted for not being true "ladies," the Victorian females were excoriated for not being true "women" – a category that encompassed both healthy reproduction and domestic usefulness. From a biological definition, "womanhood" has been transformed into a class-based moral assessment, but one that was nonetheless founded on the quality of biological performance with regard to reproduction.

The language of biological imperatives was pressed into service to underscore the middle-class concern with reproduction as a vehicle for the perpetuation of social dominance. According to J. M. Allan, "Woman craves to be a mother, knowing that she is an imperfect undeveloped being, until she has borne a child" (1869: 35). True selfhood, and indeed biological completion, only comes with successful maternity. But the latter was deemed to be threatened by the competing demands of wifehood. Thus Pye Henry Chavasse in his *Advice to a Wife on the Management of her own Health* endorsed the current ideological claim that a wife's highest duty was to bring healthy children into the world, but warned that if she pursued the customary round of marriage visits, she would irredeemably damage her own health and chances of reproductive success. A woman's conduct at this stage will determine "whether she shall be the mother of fine, healthy children – or – if, indeed, she be a mother at all – of sickly, undersized offspring" (Chavasse 1864: 1–2). As in all these works, "advice" seems to come in the guise of alarmist warnings. From the first hours of marriage, the young bride is faced with an impossible choice: if she fulfils her social duties as a wife, she will ensure her total failure as a mother.

Bourgeois motherhood was enshrined in sanctity but framed by prohibitions. The class basis of the criticism directed at the middle-class woman was quite specific: by aping the manners and vices of the upper classes she had weakened her constitution to such a degree that the debilitated middle classes were under threat from the rising vitality of the working classes. Women who miscarried, had puny infants, or failed to supply sufficient milk were directed to look at the working-class women who labored in the fields and yet still produced healthy offspring. While frequently vilified, in their roles as servants or wet-nurses, as vulgar corrupters of infant purity, working women were nonetheless held up to their middle-class counterparts as models of industry and reproductive success.

Behind all this concern with the middle-class mother's reproductive powers lay the beginnings of the eugenics debate. Long before Darwin's *Descent of Man* (1871), the idea of marital selection on the grounds of improving class and species health had been part of public discussion. Buchan, at the beginning of the nineteenth century, had observed that social degeneracy would be arrested if country squires could "be induced to pay half as much attention to the breed of men as to that of dogs, horses, and cattle" (1809: 107). By the mid-century, breeding anxiety was focused directly on the middle classes. T. J. Graham, in his treatise on the management of infancy, speaks confidently of the "laws of selection," and warns that the middle classes must be careful to avoid the mistakes which had precipitated the aristocracy into degeneracy: "It is only by attending to the law of selection, that the organization and qualities of offspring can be improved: and, on the other hand, that the disastrous consequences of improper intermarriages can be avoided" (Graham 1853: 28). Advice books abound with warnings about avoiding early marriages (which will entirely debilitate the women and produce puny children), marriages too close in blood, or ones where there is known to be a weak constitution, hereditary insanity, or morbid disposition in the family (Combe 1854: 18). John Reid, writing in 1821, had spoken of the "criminal indiscretion" of those who marry although "radically morbid in intellect," comparing the act unfavorably to that of shooting someone, which destroys only one life:

> But he who inflicts upon a single individual, the worse than deadly wound of insanity, knows not the numbers to which its venom may be communicated; he poisons a public stream out of which multitudes may drink; he is the enemy, not of one man, but of mankind.
>
> (Reid 1821: 285–6)

By the mid-century this secret poisoner and enemy of the public weal was more narrowly defined. Although some texts looked at the problems of weak mental or bodily constitutions in both sexes, the emphasis had shifted predominantly onto female weakness. Symbolic associations of women with disease were strengthened by the received wisdom that not only were women more prone to insanity than men, they were also more responsible for hereditary transmission: "insanity descends more often from the mother than the father, and from the mother to the daughters more often than to the sons" (Maudsley 1867: 216). Women, it seems, were the main pollutants, the primary poisoners of the public stream.

Sacred though the social role of motherhood might have been, the female body was seen as a fertile source of anarchic disruption. Bucknill and Tuke, in their influential *Manual of Psychological Medicine*, noted their surprise that even more women did not become insane under the pressures of pregnancy (Bucknill and Tuke 1874: 348). All stages of a woman's reproductive life were marked by potential violence: the cannibalish longings of pregnancy might be succeeded by the onset of puerperal insanity when murderous acts were frequently committed, usually against husbands and children. Bucknill and Tuke cite the case of a woman, thirteen days after her confinement, who "cut off the head of her child with a razor" (ibid.: 273). Even the operations of a woman's menstrual cycle could evoke equivalent violence – whether the blood flowed, or failed to appear. Maudsley cites the case of a woman who, afflicted with a desire to kill her children, was cured by the return of her menses, while another killed her three children when her menstrual blood started to flow (Maudsley 1867: 308–9). Motherhood, and all processes leading up to it, were firmly associated in Victorian eyes with murderous lust.

As physical body, vehicle of reproduction of the nation's wealth, the middle-class woman was subjected to extreme regulation. Failure to adhere to the strict regimes laid down by the medical establishment would lead to ideological reclassification: angel no longer, but a source of corruption and poison. In an era of appalling childbirth fatality, the medical establishment took no part of the blame, shifting the burden of guilt entirely onto the shoulders of the woman.[3] The mild Mrs Warren informs the reader how her ignorance and self-indulgence during her first pregnancy nearly killed both herself and her child. Should the expectant mother avoid exercise and resort to stimulants then "the child-spirit sent from the hand of God appears on the earth in human flesh, corrupt with the vices and taint of the mother" (Warren 1865: 8). A mother's guilt is such that it cannot be hidden. Both the temperament and physical constitution of a child, Andrew Combe declares, are "a legible transcript of the mother's condition and feelings during pregnancy" (Combe 1854: 26). Not only was it incumbent upon an expectant woman to control all physical aspects of her life, such as diet, social habits, and exercise, she also had to police her feelings, for these too would be inscribed upon the child, turning it into an informant, or public statement of her guilt.

All at costs, a pregnant woman was advised to avoid strong emotions and thoughts. Buchan, in his usual alarmist fashion, cited the case of a woman who, in a paroxysm of rage, "brought forth a child, with all its bowels hanging out of its little body" (1809: 12). Victorian texts warned of the dangers of anxiety, passion, and morbid thoughts during pregnancy, all of which could bring on miscarriage or mark the child for life. Pregnant women who were prey to anxiety, Combe observes, would give "birth to children who continued through life a prey to nervous, convulsive, or epileptic disease, or displayed a morbid timidity of character which no subsequent care could counteract" (1854: 24). Miscarriages could similarly be provoked by the slightest infringement of the rules for diet, social behavior, and exercise. As Thomas Bull warned in his *Hints to Mothers for the Management of Health*, an expectant mother should follow every rule and injunction laid down by her medical adviser, no matter how strict, for "by *one* act of disobedience she may blast every hope of success" (Bull 1837: 138). So perverted was the female body, one miscarriage was deemed to be sufficient to establish a "habit" which the woman could not break. Male discipline and female obedience was the name of the game, yet the woman was hedged around with so many restrictions that obedience itself seemed almost designed as a deliberate impossibility: a pregnant woman should take exercise but not too much, rest but not be idle, take cold baths but refrain from catching cold. All the rules seemed calculated to drive her into that very state of anxiety which she was warned was fatal, and a clear result of her own weakness and disobedience.

BREAST-FEEDING

The disciplining of the bourgeois mother's body did not cease with successful childbirth, but if anything increased in intensity. The image of the mother giving suck to her innocent babe was a potent one in Victorian ideology, but one that was riddled with class anxieties and demonic undertones. From the end of the eighteenth century, breast-feeding had been ideologically designated as a middle-class duty. Neither animals nor savages, Buchan had observed, were so monstrous as to withhold "the nutritive fluid" from their young (1809: 30). The Victorians similarly employed the discourse of the "natural" to enforce the bourgeois mother's obedience. Inability to breast-feed, like miscarriages, was again taken as a sign of her lack of discipline, her failure to forgo luxurious practices and the artificial round of social life (Combe 1854: 67). Mere feeding was insufficient, however; the *quality* of production also had to be strictly controlled. Cloaked beneath the rhetoric of the natural lie the assumptions and discourse of contemporary capitalist economics. Isabella Beeton advised the readers of her *Book of Household Management* that,

> As Nature has placed in the bosom of the mother the natural food of her offspring, it must be self-evident to every reflecting woman, that it becomes her duty to study, as far as lies in her power, to keep that reservoir of nourishment in as pure and invigorating condition as

possible; for she must remember that the *quantity* is no proof of the *quality* of this aliment.

(Beeton 1861: 1034)

This insidious distinction between quantity and quality performs a crucial role in class control: supplying milk of the correct class quality becomes a matter of conscious *study*, requiring the policing both of bodily habits and thought. Milk becomes a metonymic projection of womanhood; so seemingly pure and innocent, it can yet be a vehicle of class corruption. Unregulated emotion, mothers were warned, could turn their milk into a literal poison. Anger or a fretful temper would give the milk an "irritating quality" (Carpenter 1846 quoted in Graham 1853: 163). Nor does the emotion have to be extreme before such deleterious effects take place. Beeton's *Housewife's Treasury* paints a scenario of a mother confined upstairs with her new babe, listening to domestic turmoil below (the result, of course, of her previous faulty management): she "frets and fumes, and at last poor baby, the one least able to bear it, has to stand the consequences. Its food is upset and deranged, and turned into draughts of poison almost" (Beeton 1880?: 419). While extreme worry will most likely *kill* the child, readers are warned, even mild worry will have very harmful effects. Just as the physical state and temperament of the child when born is a "legible transcript" of a mother's self-regulation during pregnancy, the child's response to a mother's milk becomes one more moral indicator of a woman's self-control, or lack thereof. To this end, the milk is endowed with near magical powers of directly transcribing maternal emotional states into physical effects. Indeed it becomes the medium for the transmission of moral qualities, for the child was said to inherit the temperament of the mother or wet-nurse (Chavasse 1864: 169).

Although the texts extolled the delights of suckling one's own child, they also warned that it would be necessary to engage a wet-nurse if a mother came from a family with a "hereditary taint," whether a disposition to consumption or insanity, for "the milk of such mothers may be changed into a noxious agent, – even a deadly poison" (Conquest 1848 quoted in Graham 1853: 194). They should also instantly desist if their menses returned, for their milk would then be inevitably "depraved," a term which draws on the moral language of vice, taint, and corruption that pervades this discourse. On this occasion, the "depravity" seems to lie in the linking of the ideas of sexual activity and nursing, since menstruation was still regarded by some doctors as the time when women were sexually "on heat."[4] Discussion of the employment of wet-nurses is also sexually charged and produces an extreme ideological mystification of the milk, as all the fears of working-class pollution are condensed into this image of fluids circulating from the lower orders to the higher.

Graham warns against the selection of a nurse with a less than perfect moral character:

> Her very blood, and therefore her milk, is commonly tainted by her bad disposition and evil tempers; and she never fails by her voice, manner, looks, etc., to stir up, more or less, the evil passions of the child, and thus to injure it physically, intellectually, and morally.
>
> (Graham 1853: 169)

Through the agency of the wet-nurse, the vulgarities and perversions of the working class are given physical imprint on the cherished minds and bodies of their masters.

The sexual undertones of this fear of working-class invasion are given overt articulation in the case Graham quotes from a Swedish physician: "in a respectable family in Stockholm the father, the mother, three children, the maid servant, and two clerks, were infected with the venereal disease by a nurse who was admitted into the family, without previous inquiry into her character" (1853: 191). As in the contemporary Aids scare, fear of pollution is enough to activate class, gender, and sexual prejudices to such a degree that all reasonable notions of cause and effect with regard to transmission are overturned: the very presence of a morally dubious working-class woman in a middle-class household, offering that highly sexualized organ, the breast, to one of its members, is enough to poison the blood of all who reside in it.

In making a connection between the transmission of "tainted milk" and that of venereal disease, Graham is drawing to the surface the class and sexual undertones which pervaded critiques of the bourgeois mother. In failing to fulfil her reproductive duty, in placing pleasure before the demands of motherhood and thus transmitting her own taints and vices to her children, she was in many ways falling out of her own class and thus joining the fallen sisterhood. The discourse which surrounded prostitution in the mid-Victorian era follows, significantly, exactly the bifurcation which characterized bourgeois ideologies of motherhood. In W. R. Greg's famous article in the 1850 *Westminster Review*, prostitutes are characterized initially as too womanly for their own good: perfect angels, they fall, not from evil desires, but from "pure unknowingness," and an exaggeration of woman's best qualities, a "strange and sublime unselfishness" (Greg 1850: 459). Their angelic nature is revealed even when fallen in the fact that they make excellent, affectionate mothers and nurses. With the mention of venereal disease, however, the whole tone of the article changes, and prostitutes become "the hundreds of female devils who prowl about day and night seeking for their prey" (ibid.: 478). The dramatic shift in representation, from tender angel to contaminating demon, follows exactly the same trajectory pursued by the ideological discourse on bourgeois motherhood. The same emotive images to be found in motherhood texts of poison being introduced into the very bosom of the family, and innocent babes being tainted from birth, are recycled in articles on venereal disease, which becomes one more version of the notion of women polluting the "public stream," only this time the source is the working-class female. This ready translatability of an existing discourse into different class terms, with the middle-class woman switching role from polluter to innocent victim, draws attention to the class and sexual concerns underpinning the discourses on bourgeois motherhood. Like the working class, the middle-class woman represented a disruptive and corrupting threat to class stability, a threat rendered all the more dangerous by her key position within that class formation. She stood accused, like the working class, of following her own desires, consulting her own pleasure rather than her duty to the nation.

SEXUALITY AND MATERNITY

The question of female pleasure, and of the relationship between sexuality and maternity, formed one more problematic area within Victorian ideologies of motherhood. Breast-feeding, although ideologically prescribed, was still an arena suffused with sexuality and worrying images of self-pleasuring. Medical texts and advice books spoke of the "positive pleasure derived from the act itself" (Graham 1853: 161) and suggested that "the pleasure of the young mother in her babe is said to be more exquisite than any other earthly bliss" (Chavasse 1864: 168, quoting *Good Words*, October 1861). Such exquisite pleasure was also dangerous, however, suggesting an unwelcome autonomy, an exclusion of the male from sexual gratification, and hence an activity crying out for external regulation.

As in all ages, breast-feeding highlighted the implicit conflict between a woman's marital and maternal roles, a conflict particularly pronounced in the Victorian era when the ideal of female beauty, with the exaggerated attention paid to the bust and hips, focused on woman's reproductive powers. According to one scientific commentator of the era, woman was most pleasing to man during "the period of activity of the reproductive organs," and her "greatest beauty of form" was to be found in "those parts peculiar to her organization": the bust and pelvis. The description of the bosom, "on which the organs for nutrition of the tender offspring are developed" spirals off into ecstatic, sexual contemplation:

It is to her bosom that woman instinctively clasps all that she rightly loves – her bosom, remarkable for the unsurpassable beauty of its voluptuous contours and graceful inflexions, the white transparent surface of which is set off with an azure network, or tinged with the warm glow of the emotions and passions that make it heave in graceful undulations.

(Anon. 1851: 19–20)

The woman's use of this bosom, so central to the Victorian male's sexual imagination, had to be severely regulated and controlled. Both the frequency and duration of breast-feeding were subject to rigid discipline. A mother should feed only at set, regulated times, and never on demand, like an animal. Some of the severest strictures are reserved for mothers who always have the child at their breast: overfeeding, all commentators agreed, could not only sow the seeds of later disease, but also kill outright (Graham 1853: 103). Breast-feeding should continue for nine months, but should quickly cease thereafter if the mother was not to become "nervous, emaciated, and hysterical" or the child to die of "water-on-the-brain, or, of consumption" (Chavasse 1864: 186).

One of the most significant prohibitions was against falling asleep while feeding, or allowing the infant to sleep in the maternal bed. Mrs Beeton speaks of

> that most injurious practice of letting the child *suck* after the mother has *fallen asleep*, a custom . . . which . . . is injurious to both mother and child. It is injurious to the infant by allowing it, without control, to imbibe to distension a fluid sluggishly secreted and deficient in those vital principles which the want of mental energy, and of the sympathetic appeals of the child on the mother, so powerfully produce on the secreted nutriment, while the mother wakes in a state of clammy exhaustion, with giddiness, dimness of sight, nausea, loss of appetite, and a dull aching pain through the back and between the shoulders. In fact, she wakes languid and unrefreshed from her sleep, with febrile symptoms and hectic flushes, caused by her baby vampire, who, while dragging from her her health and strength, has excited in itself a set of symptoms directly opposite, but fraught with the most injurious consequences – "functional derangement."

(Beeton 1861: 1034)

In this extraordinary passage, the seemingly innocent picture of a mother asleep with her babe in her arms becomes a scene of uncontrolled debauchery. The baby becomes a sexualized demon, a vampire sucking at her breast, while her symptoms mirror those ascribed to women who indulged in "lesbian pleasures." Indeed, masturbation itself was similarly referred to in contemporary discourse as a vampire sucking away vital strength.[5] The milk itself is said to suffer, no longer expressing a mother's mental energy, or *conscious* sympathetic response to her child. The supreme sin actually lies in this state of unconsciousness: maternity is no longer being policed and externally controlled. From being a conscious, and hence socialized, mental response to the demands of her role, breast-feeding has become an instinctive, physical function, outside the sphere of social regulation. Hence the demonic sexual overtones. Breast-feeding remained unthreatening only to the degree that it functioned as a conscious social duty, prescribed and regulated from without, and not a pleasurably physical, solipsistic bonding of mother and child.

MATERNAL EXCESS

The final problematic area of maternal ideology I would like to consider is that of the mother who allows her feelings for her offspring to run to excess. Emotional immoderation in the mother, Buchan had warned, could produce an insidious "relaxing effeminacy" in her offspring which clearly threatened to undermine the moral fibre of the nation (Buchan 1809: 77–81). Sarah Ellis similarly speaks witheringly of mothers with "ungoverned springs of tenderness and love, which burst forth and exhaust themselves, without calculation or restraint" (Ellis 1843a: 106). Even maternal love should be subjected to an economic calculus. Ellis's imagery also suggests that maternal emotion partakes of the same volatile, disruptive nature, as female sexual passion, or insanity, which, women were warned, was liable to burst forth suddenly if not kept under constant watchful guard.

While fears of unregulated emotion, and especially female emotion, were rampant in the Victorian era, Ellis pins this particular form directly onto a conflict between the roles of mother and wife. "We must not forget," she warns with reference to maternal love, "that while wholly given up to this feeling, so sacred in itself, there is such a thing as neglecting, for the sake of the luxury it affords, the duty of a wife" (ibid.: 252). In a significant transposition, "luxury" ceases to denote an artificial social state, but designates instead a form of female emotional autonomy. The threat posed to a husband by a wife luxuriating in maternal feeling is overtly sexualized:

> wherever a mother thus doats upon her children, she is guilty of an act of unfaithfulness to her husband, at the same time that she places herself in a perilous position, from whence the first shock of disease, or the first symptom of ingratitude, may cast her down into utter wretchedness.
>
> (Ellis 1843a: 253)

Although the passage is enigmatic, it is perhaps not over-reading to suggest that this act of maternal "unfaithfulness" is rewarded by the husband "seeking comfort elsewhere," and the transmission of venereal disease. The undisciplined bourgeois mother is once more aligned with the fallen sisterhood. The affections, Ellis warns, must not "be concentrated into one focus, so as to burn with dangerous and destructive intensity" (ibid.). The image crystallizes many of the contradictions in Victorian projections of motherhood: the sacred passion can itself be demonized, turned into an avenging force which destroys both the angelic mother herself and the concord of the domestic hearth, revealing all too clearly the precarious balance of the patriarchal bourgeois order.

FICTIONAL REPRESENTATIONS

Mothers in Victorian fiction are distinguished by their absence. On the one hand this is a literal absence – heroes and heroines are notoriously motherless – and can be accounted for both in terms of hard historical fact, the high mortality rate associated with maternity, and in terms of generic fictional conventions: the romance structure dictated that the narrative end with marriage. Maternal absence also conferred, however, a form of shadowy power, allowing such figures to exert far more influence than that customarily given to the mothers permitted a more overt presence in the Victorian fictional text. Motherhood is simultaneously marginalized and given ideological centrality. This uneasy configuration is given literal embodiment in a series of novels which feature a mother who is yearned for in her absence, but who is actually present: Mrs Pryor in Charlotte Brontë's *Shirley* (1849) for example, or Lady Dedlock in Dickens's *Bleak House* (1853), or the Princess in Eliot's *Daniel Deronda* (1876). Perhaps the most extreme form of the absent/present mother is to be found in Mrs Henry Wood's *East Lynne* (1861), which features a mother who, presumed dead by her family, returns to look after her children in the guise of governess. *East Lynne* also differs from the other texts in this mode in that it focuses not on the offspring's emotional needs for a mother, but rather on the feelings of the mother herself.

The dramatic shift of narratorial focus revealed in *East Lynne* is typical of the genre of sensation fiction which emerged in the 1860s. While earlier fiction had not generally endorsed angelic notions of motherhood, neither had it foregrounded maternal emotion or explored the reverse, underside of bourgeois maternal ideology. Many of the sensation novels confronted these aspects of contemporary ideology head on, continuing into the vicissitudes of married life and producing representations of violent, undisciplined, or monstrous mothers which took to an extreme the negative formulations of the advice literature and medical texts. Perhaps the most famous example is Mary Braddon's *Lady Audley's Secret* (1862), where the heroine, whose only inheritance from her mother, she claims, is insanity, violates all the principles of motherhood in abandoning her child in order to pursue, under cover of her angelic appearance, a "demonic" career of self-interest. Wilkie Collins, in contrast, focuses in *Jezebel's Daughter* (1880) on an evil woman whose only redeeming quality is love for her daughter, while in the "thesis" novel, *The Legacy of Cain* (1888), he deliberately foregrounds the nature-nurture debate, directly paralleling the development of two girls, one the daughter of a convicted murderess, the other of a respectable, but selfish and unprincipled, woman.

In all these texts, contemporary medical debates on hereditary insanity, and the impact of maternity on the female mind and body, are explicitly highlighted. There is, however, a significant shift in the discourse. While the medical texts and advice books overtly promulgated contemporary ideology, sometimes seeking to reconcile contradictions, but more often letting conflicting constructions of womanhood stand side by side, the fictional texts actively explore and expose those contradictions. Structurally, they are also more complex than the other texts: overt agreement with dominant ideological projections, expressed directly by the narrator, or in the conformist endings adopted, is often undercut by the sympathies generated, or implicit critiques offered, in the course of the narrative. The two texts I would like to consider briefly, in conclusion, Mrs Henry Wood's *St Martin's Eve* (1866) and *East Lynne* (1861), both follow this pattern.

St Martin's Eve has all the ingredients of contemporary ideological debate: a "demonic" mother, in the figure of the primary heroine, Charlotte St John, and an insistent preoccupation with the "unwholesome" transmission of hereditary taints. In the opening section of the novel Charlotte's mother surprisingly opposes, for reasons she will not disclose, her daughter's marriage to the local lord, stating that, "I would almost rather see you die, than married to George St John" (Wood 1905: 27). The reason for such extraordinary vehemence soon becomes clear to the alert reader. Charlotte's father, we learn, died very suddenly in mysterious circumstances. Charlotte herself, however, appears oblivious of any causes for concern and, ignoring her mother's warnings, goes ahead with the marriage. Suspicions of hereditary insanity are confirmed when the birth of Charlotte's son calls forth a wild, jealous love. Charlotte is not the kind of demonic mother who rejects her child, but one who loves to excess. She will not leave her child to accompany her husband, a member of parliament, to London for,

> The frail little infant of a few days had become to her the greatest treasure earth ever gave; her love for him was of that wild, impassioned, all-absorbing nature, known, it is hoped, but to few, for it never visits a well-regulated heart.
>
> (ibid.: 39–40)

Both the tone and substance of the comments echo contemporary advice books: Charlotte violates both her wifely duty and the requisite maternal self-regulation.

Charlotte's condition is exacerbated, and transformed into apparent madness by a crucial economic fact: her son is not the heir to the property, for there exists a previous heir, born to St John in his first marriage. Maternal passion leads to a jealous hatred of the heir, and to sudden outbursts of angry violence against him when Charlotte appears as one "mad," totally devoid of self-control. When the heir apparently burns himself to death we have our suspicions, shared by the surgeon and confirmed at the conclusion of the book, that Charlotte has been instrumental in his death. Her sins are not rewarded, for her own son dies shortly thereafter, not, interestingly, from the seeds of her own insanity, but from the hereditary taint of consumption which had destroyed his father. With such a fatal cocktail of inheritance, it is not surprising that the doctor remarks, in seemingly unfeeling vein, that it is best that the child die.

Throughout there is a reiterated suggestion that it is better to die than to transmit an unhealthy constitution, and thus poison the "public stream." In the secondary plot, which counterpoints that of Charlotte, the aristocratic and angelic Adeline dies of consumption (a disease associated with aristocratic overbreeding) and a broken heart. While Charlotte's unregulated energies find aggressive outward expression, Adeline's feelings implode. At her funeral, her lover Frederick, who was partly responsible for her death, thinks, in spite of his regrets, "that all things might still be for the best. Had she lived to bear him children – and to entail upon them her fragility of constitution – " (ibid.: 374). Contemporary ideological concerns with sexual selection, and the health of the ruling-class body, seem to ride rough-shod over dramatic sympathy. Frederick's subsequent opposition to the idea that Charlotte might marry his uncle (and thus disinherit him) is framed in similar terms. Any other woman, he tells himself, he would welcome, "But to marry *her* – with that possibility of taint in her blood . . ." (ibid.: 382). Both women, angel and demon alike, are to him potent sources of class pollution. Under his relentless pursuit and eagle eye, Charlotte's self-control cracks, signs of insanity emerge, and she is locked up in an asylum for good. The surgeon, Mr Pym, who has been a shadowy, all-knowing figure throughout, confirms the facts of her case. It was from her father, not her mother, that Charlotte inherited insanity, but his wild outburst four days before Charlotte was born clearly affected the mother and hence the baby in the womb.

On the surface, *St Martin's Eve* appears a textbook account of the dangers of maternal excess, and of transmitting hereditary "taints" to one's offspring. Wood follows with scrupulous care the precise details and language of contemporary medical accounts. Yet the sympathies generated in the novel run counter to this message: Charlotte's outbursts are all connected with the very obvious injustices of a patriarchal legal and economic system which insistently disinherits women, a fact which suggests justifiable rage rather than madness as the cause of her behavior. In addition, despite extensive narrational laudation, the hero Frederick, who gains all the wealth in the end, does not appear in a particularly appealing light. Although his uncontrolled outbreak of anger is partly responsible for Adeline's death, within a very short time he is pledging his love to a less aristocratic and hence healthier, more dynastically suitable bride. Prudence and common sense might dictate that we approve and applaud his actions, in line with Victorian concerns with the "law of selection," but the romantic sympathy generated by the novel lies firmly with the two heroines, for whose respective incarceration and death he is in part responsible. Female madness or consumption, outward demonic excess, or angelic repression are, the book suggests, but two sides of the same coin: the only responses permitted to women under patriarchal oppression. And both are equally fatal.

While contemporary ideologies of motherhood formed one of the central concerns of the sensation novel, they never receive straightforward endorsement. Mrs Henry Wood's *East Lynne*, which has driven successive generations of readers and theatre-goers to their handkerchiefs, brought such narrative ambiguity to a fine art. The novel highlights the class-based assumptions of contemporary advice texts: bourgeois prudence and self-control is set against aristocratic excess, but, as in *St Martin's Eve*, the overt message of the novel seems to run counter to its sympathies. Isabel, the delicate, aristocratic heroine, represents, on the surface, the worst excesses of a degenerate upper-class lineage, revealing a uterine economy entirely out of control. The forces of sexual desire (painted initially in very graphic terms, but subsequently masked under the morally more acceptable explanation of marital jealousy) cause her to violate the sacred code of motherhood and abandon her bourgeois home, husband, and children for the aristocratic rake, Francis Levison. Another form of excess, however, this time of maternal feeling, drives her back (having luckily suffered severe disfigurement in the mean time so as to render her virtually unrecognizable) to take up the post of governess to her own children, and to watch her ex-husband bestowing the same endearments as in her own marriage on his new, bourgeois bride. In behavioral terms, Isabel thus conforms to the most extreme aspects of aristocratic indiscipline held up to middle-class women as a terrifying model of immoral, socially degenerative conduct. Although the narrator is careful to stress Isabel's mistakes, her suffering, as the Victorian critics were quick to point out, seems nonetheless to elevate her spiritually. The more she sins, the more angelic she becomes.

The descriptions of Isabel's insensate maternal longings parallel those of Charlotte St John, but the weakness is viewed in a more sympathetic light. Once installed as governess, Isabel's passion for her children, which she is never able to suppress or restrain, is contrasted sharply with the bourgeois, wifely restraint of Barbara. While the aristocratic Isabel is depicted primarily as a sexual being and a mother, the middle-class Barbara is primarily a wife. The conflict between maternal and wifely roles in Victorian ideology is here refracted across class lines, revealing, in the process, the direct connections between bourgeois economic and domestic ideology. The economic values of regulation, order, and restraint are associated with the middle class and with wifely subservience, while the messier, physical aspects of maternity and sexual desire are connected with upper-class indiscipline. Yet the novel is by no means clear cut in its ideological allegiances. Its troubled responses to the question of good motherhood are revealed most clearly in a long lecture that Barbara gives to Isabel on the correct way for a mother to bring up her children.

According to Barbara, mothers should not keep their children constantly about them, or as some mistaken mothers do, "wash them, dress them, feed them; rendering themselves slaves, and the nurse's office a sinecure" (Wood 1984: 341). Indeed the physical, troublesome daily care of children should be devolved onto the nurse so as not to weary the mother, who will then be more fitted for her daily duty of gathering the children round for "higher purposes," to instil in them a sense of Christian and moral duty. If the mother is too much with the children, her moral authority is weakened and indiscipline arises: "The children run wild; the husband is sick of it, and seeks peace and solace elsewhere" (ibid.). Barbara's highly regulated and hierarchical version of wifehood takes the separation of moral and physical upbringing to an extreme, while placing the comfort of the husband to the fore. Perhaps surprisingly, Isabel concurs, her agreement standing as a tacit acknowledgment of her own mistakes: "Lady Isabel silently assented. Mrs Carlyle's views were correct" (ibid.).

Such agreement, however, is conspicuously withheld when Barbara enters onto the subject of breast-feeding, which is linked, significantly, with the question of maternal versus wifely priorities. Breast-feeding, she insists, must give way before the claims of her husband: "If I and Mr Carlyle have to be out in the evening baby gives way. I should never give up my husband for my baby; never, dearly as I love him" (ibid.: 343). Isabel's ominous silence confirms the view that the text is not willing to endorse this assertion of wifely duty over the physical claims of maternity. Indeed, despite Isabel's own earlier agreement to Barbara's maternal system, when set against Isabel's passionate excess it appears cold and unfeeling, too calculating. As we view with Isabel's eyes, so we participate in all her exquisite maternal torture. Regulation itself comes to appear almost unseemly. Although Isabel comes from a line of consumptive, spendthrift aristocrats, she has all the sympathy of romance lacking in the healthy, self-controlled bourgeois class (whose qualities are aped by the lower-class Afy – a debased Aphrodite – who also lives with Francis Levison, but without shame, and out of sheer self-interested calculation). Like angelic mothers, restrained bourgeois wives do not generate much narrative excitement or interest.

Similarly, Archibald Carlyle, the hero of the tale, has, like his counterpart in *St Martin's Eve*, an unappealing side. Not only does he take advantage of the Earl of Mount Severn's debts and illness to buy himself an aristocratic estate on the cheap, he also puts the demands of his business before thoughts of Isabel. There is clearly a fine line to be drawn between self-interested calculation and responsible management. Despite narratorial insistence to the contrary, bourgeois prudence is not the stuff from which romantic heroes are made.

The romantic structure of the tale vindicates the values of passion, both sexual and maternal, over the controlled calculation which defines the bourgeois world: "Let people talk as they will, it is impossible to drive out human passions from the human heart. You may suppress them, deaden them, keep them in subjection, but you cannot root them out" (ibid.: 496). While Wood speaks of the need for constant self-watchfulness to keep the passions in check, the novel actually stresses the uncontrollability of passion. Against contemporary ideological projections, Wood insists that true passion *cannot* be controlled; Isabel preserves, and indeed increases, her angelic status precisely because she is powerless to control the workings of both sexual and maternal desire. Her powerlessness thus aligns her with the "angelic" fallen sisterhood who were too womanly for their own good. Barbara, although initially given to sexual excess, learns to regulate her feelings and is rewarded with wifedom and the subsequent extinction of all independence or narrative interest in her personality.

The writings of the sensation novels offer a fascinating insight into the workings of Victorian maternal ideology. We find here, writ large, all the demonic figures and anxious preoccupations with heredity which filled contemporary medical texts and advice literature. Notions of hereditary taints abound, and of woman as outwardly fair and controlled, but inwardly the hidden source of corruption of both her class and race. Yet the very excess with which some of these traits are painted draws attention to their unstable foundations. The sensation novel took the demonic underside of the Victorian bourgeois male's imagination and turned it back upon itself. The pages are full of unregulated motherhood: women who abandon their children or destroy them through love, who lash out in excesses of both sexual and maternal emotion, overturning all domestic peace around them. Yet the true villains of the piece, despite the "safe" moral commentary offered by the narrators, tend to be the calculating and colorless males who pursue these women to their doom, a pursuit frequently tied to their own economic or social advantage. The novels expose the degree to which the demonization of the maternal body is linked to the regulatory, economic ideologies of the era, and the maintenance of bourgeois male dominance.

NOTES

1 For further details see, for example, Jalland and Hooper (1986), Showalter (1985), and Shuttleworth (1990).
2 The case is also cited, for example, sixteen years later by Henry Maudsley (1867: 303).
3 Andrew Combe opens his treatise with the alarming facts of infant mortality based on statistical data culled from the *Annual Reports of Births, Deaths and Marriages* in England in 1842–3: "of all the children born alive in England, 14 per cent die within the first year, and 20 per cent within the first two years" (Combe 1854: 2). In this work Combe does not express any interest in the rate of maternal deaths in childbirth.
4 For further details on this point, and a more general discussion of Victorian responses to menstruation, see Shuttleworth (1990).
5 Although Victorian fears of masturbation were focused primarily on the male, frequent concern was also expressed about female "self-pollution." For a popular treatment, and description of symptoms, see Goss (1829: 59–66). A description of onanism as "a vampire feeding on the life-blood of its victims" is to be found in another very popular "quack" text (Perry 1854: 54).

WORKS CITED

Allan, J. M. (1869) "On the Differences in the Minds of Men and Women," *Journal of the Anthropological Society of London* 7, cited in P. Jalland and J. Hooper, *Women from Birth to Death. The Female Life Cycle in Britain 1830–1914*, Brighton: Harvester, 1986.
Anon. (1851) "Woman in her Psychological Relations," *Journal of Psychological Medicine and Mental Pathology* 4: 18–50.
Beeton, I. (1861) *The Book of Household Management* London: S. O. Beeton.
—— (1880?) *Beeton's Housewife's Treasury of Domestic Information* London: Ward, Lock & Co.
Buchan, W. (1809) *Advice to Mothers, on the Subject of their own Health; and the Means of Promoting the Health, Strength, and Beauty of their Offspring*, Boston: J. Bumstead. First published 1803.
Bucknill, J. C. and Tuke, D. H. (1874) *A Manual of Psychological Medicine* 3rd edn, London: J. & A. Churchill.
Bull, T. (1837) *Hints to Mothers for the Management of Health*, cited in P. Jalland and J. Hooper, *Women from Birth to Death. The Female Life Cycle in Britain 1830–1914*, Brighton: Harvester, 1986.
Carpenter, W. B. (1846) *A Manual of Physiology*, London: J. & A. Churchill.
Chavasse, P. H. (1864) *Advice to a Wife on the Management of her own Health; and on the Treatment of some of the Complaints Incidental to Pregnancy, Labour and Suckling*, London: J. Churchill. First published 1839.

Combe, A. (1854) *A Treatise on the Physiological and Moral Management of Infancy, being a Practical Exposition of the Principles of Infant Training for the Uses of Parents*, Edinburgh: Machlachlan & Stewart. First published 1840.

Conquest, J. T. (1848) *Letters to a Mother*, London: Longman & Co.

Ellis, S. Stickney (1838) *The Women of England, their Social Duties, and Domestic Habits*, London: Fisher, Son, & Co.

—— (1843a) *The Mothers of England, their Influence and Responsibility*, London: Fisher, Son, & Co.

—— (1843b) *The Wives of England, their Relative Duties, Domestic Influence, and Social Obligations*, London: Fisher, Son & Co.

Foucault, M. (1984) *The History of Sexuality, Vol. 1*, trans. R. Hurley, Harmondsworth: Penguin.

Goss & Co. (1829) *Hygeniana: a Non-Medical Analysis of the Complaints Incidental to Females, in which are Offered Important Admonitions on the Peculiar Debilities Attending their Circumstances, Sympathies and Formation*, London: Sherwood & Co.

Graham, T. J. (1853) *On the Management and Disorders of Infancy and Childhood*, London: Simpkin, Marshall & Co.

Greg, W. R. (1850) "Prostitution" (Review Article), *Westminster Review* 53: 448–506.

Jalland, P. and Hooper, J. (1986) *Women from Birth to Death. The Female Life Cycle in Britain 1830–1914*, Brighton: Harvester.

Maudsley, H. (1867) *The Physiology and Pathology of the Mind*, London: Macmillan.

Perry, R. and L. & Co (1854) *The Silent Friend: a Practical Work, Treating on the Anatomy and Physiology of the Organs of Generation, and their Diseases, with Observations on Onanism and its Baneful Results*, London.

Reid, J. (1821) *Essays on Hypochondriasis and other Nervous Afflictions*, 2nd edn, London: Longman, Brown, Green & Longman.

Showalter, E. (1985) *The Female Malady: Women, Madness, and English Culture, 1830–1980*, New York: Pantheon.

Shuttleworth, S. (1990) "Female Circulation: Medical Discourse and Popular Advertising in the Mid-Victorian Era." in M. Jacobus, E. Fox Keller, and S. Shuttleworth (eds) *Body/Politics: Women and the Discourses of Science*, London: Routledge.

Trotter, T. (1812) *A View of the Nervous Temperament; being a Practical Enquiry into the Increasing Prevalence, Prevention, and Treatment of those Diseases*, 3rd edn, London: Longman, Brown, Green & Longman.

Warren, Mrs (1865) *How I Managed my Children from Infancy to Marriage*, London: Houlston & Wright.

Wood, Mrs H. [Ellen] (1905) *St Martin's Eve*, London: Macmillan. First published 1866.

—— (1984) *East Lynne*, New Brunswick, Rutgers University Press. First published 1861.

Chapter 4

Water rights and the "crossing o' breeds"

Chiastic exchange in *The Mill on the Floss*

Jules Law

With his study of the river in George Eliot's *The Mill on the Floss*, Jules Law elaborates a theory of the text as a formal expression of social tensions which are, though material, themselves mediated and symptoms of deep-rooted historical contradictions. In following the lead of Fredric Jameson and other Marxist and post-Marxist theorists of culture, Law offers a genuinely fresh interpretation of George Eliot's novel by calling into question those readings which thematize the river without also taking account of historical and material references related to it, such as steam power, agricultural technology, and water rights. Law makes sense of the role played by the river – translating the river's material influence into its social and symbolic significance – by drawing on both rhetorical and materialist criticism. In offering the syntactic figure of chiasmus (symmetrical crossing) as the figurative clue informing the representation of the river and of the social logic of the text, Law relates exchange explicitly to gender and power. He argues that the river must be grasped as a symbolic form in the widest sense possible: that which has its own material significance in the text, that which recapitulates the novel's philosophical themes, and that which reproduces gender-specific structures of social action and interaction.

* * *

There is even in the material facts a half-hidden symbolism indicating the idea of the story . . . [T]he mere material facts of the river playing such a great part in Maggie's life give one the feeling that she is swept along by a current of circumstances she can neither resist nor control.
(unsigned review, *Spectator* 1860: 113)

The flooded river has no symbolic or metaphorical value.
(Leavis 1960)

For at least one hundred years after its publication, critical disagreement over the merits of *The Mill on the Floss* has centered on the status of the novel's dominant "material facts" of river and flood, and on the relationship of those elements to the novel's abrupt, improbable, and

catastrophic ending. Critics have either lamented Eliot's inability to relate
the motifs of river and flood plausibly to the novel's psychological and
social tragedies or have praised the river as a profound instance of the
implacable forces encountered by the heroine. Yet even those readings
which have granted critical importance to the influence of the river on
the characters' lives have remained curiously general, equating the river
either with historical forces broadly conceived or abstracting from the
river motif an allegory of inexorability which is then used to characterize
everything from economics and technology to the psychological constitution of the central characters. Such thematization of a text's "material
facts" is an inevitable and productive moment in critical reading; and in
the case of *The Mill on the Floss* such thematization has produced
a number of significant insights concerning the novel's sexual politics.
Nonetheless, there are good reasons to suspect that both from an historicist and a formalist point of view we have not yet adequately characterized the complex dynamic which links the river to the lives – and the
catastrophic fates – of the novel's characters. The sense we make of the
role played by the river in the novel needs to proceed simultaneously
from two very different critical impulses: first, to determine more particularly the rhetorical features which link the representation of the river to
other formal structures in the novel, and second, to understand as
specifically as possible the relationship of the novel's historical and
material references – e.g., steam power, agricultural technology, water
rights – to the novel's plot. The thematization of historical references
will always play a key role in any negotiation between these two critical
impulses, but we must be prepared for thematization to lead us back to
narrowly historical questions as well as away from them.

Criticism of *The Mill on the Floss* over the past quarter-century – since
Leavis's stringent remark – has continued to concern itself with the
problems surrounding the novel's closure, while moving slowly away
from questions concerning the function and status of the river. In contrast
to criticisms raised by Leavis and by Barbara Hardy concerning the
obtrusiveness and irrelevance of the novel's river and flood imagery, U.
C. Knoepflmacher, Sandra Gilbert, and Susan Gubar have argued for
the importance of the river as an expressive symbol in the novel,[1] and
Nancy Miller has joined Gilbert and Gubar in reading the novel's
"implausible" conclusion as an acute instance of the historically persistent
and critical relationship between women's writing and the politics of
closure.[2]

The critically and politically important re-evaluations of the novel's
closure inaugurated by Gilbert, Gubar, and Miller have found their most
significant extensions in the work of Mary Jacobus and Margaret
Homans, both of whom, in different ways, have redirected discussions
of the problem of closure away from the figure of water and toward the

novel's thematically resonant scenes of reading and writing. According to Homans, Maggie Tulliver is a figure for the dangers of literal reading, and "The huge fragments of machinery that overtake Maggie and Tom in the flood are literalization itself" (Homans 1986: 130). For Jacobus, Maggie is associated with metaphor – its ambiguity, its impropriety, its unsettling of the "language or maxims of the dominant culture" (1981: 213–18) – and the flood at the end of the novel merges the novel's literal and figural elements in a utopian-feminist gesture "beyond analytic and realistic modes" (ibid.: 221–2).

Homans's and Jacobus's readings seem crucial to me because in moving beyond the specific metaphorics of water they are able to uncover more general rhetorical structures governing representation and interpretation in the novel, structures which link the novel's gender politics, its topographical setting, and the issues surrounding its extravagant closure. Clearly, however, such analyses also bypass the perhaps naïve literalism that once looked to the dominant "material fact" of the river to explain Maggie's fate. It is to this material fact that I would like to return, keeping in mind that Homans's and Jacobus's careful readings of the complex relationship between rhetoric and literality preclude any simple distinction between the novel's material and symbolic elements.

The river in *The Mill on the Floss* must be grasped as a symbolic form in the widest sense possible: a form that recapitulates the novel's philosophical themes, its gender-specific structures of social interaction, and the psychology of individual characters, but which nonetheless has its own irreducible significance as a material determinant in the plot.[3] Here is where an analysis of the novel's rhetorical strategies and of its "allegory of reading" are of critical importance. For in order for the river to be grasped as a comprehensive symbolic and material fact in this way – in order for it to be thematizable – it must be seen to possess distinct and recursive formal features. References to the river, to its effects, and to its thematic resonance must be *recognized* as they recur in new and changed contexts, and often we are aided in making this formal identification by way of rhetorical figures suggested to us elsewhere in the text.

What I am suggesting is that the river in *The Mill on the Floss* is depicted as having a material effect upon the characters which is direct and causal, but that it functions simultaneously as a symbolic expression of social and psychological patterns that are only contingently linked to it. These latter patterns can neither be reduced to the material facts of the river nor distinguished from them entirely. A larger rhetorical pattern, isomorphic with the river's distinctive formal characteristics (as they are rhetorically presented), governs the relationship between river and individual characters, between river and social structure, and between individuals and social structure. But this pattern *is* ultimately only rhetorical; it is the structure of social experience and social relations as the characters themselves see and represent it. And these rhetorical characterizations – revealed most clearly as such at the points where they break down – may turn out to have motives worthy of investigation.

To that end I would like to propose a particular syntactic figure as the figurative clue which informs the representation of the river and of a certain social logic in *The Mill on the Floss*. That trope is *chiasmus*, the figure of syntactic reversal or symmetrical crossing. Though the figure is most prominent in those scenes where characters or narrator note the ostensible "crossing o' breeds" that has produced a "feminine" boy, a "masculine" girl, a Tulliver-like Dodson or simply an un-Wakemlike Wakem (e.g. Eliot 1961: 12, 13, 30, 54–5, 158), the temporal logic of crossings, reversals, and exchanges runs much deeper in the novel. The Tulliver mill changes hands and then reverts to its original owners; Maggie floats with the tide and then reverses her direction to return home; and the novel's central chapter on rhetoric underscores its radical critique of literality, metaphor, pedagogy, and misogyny precisely by way of the syntactic figure of chiasmus. Before we investigate these movements in detail, however, we must examine the process in the novel that motivates chiastic reversal and which furthermore gives definition to objects and people in such a way as to make them appear proper objects of symmetrical exchange. That process is the "checking" of spontaneous impulses.

The Mill on the Floss begins with an action which is immediately "checked." The first sentence reads: "A wide plain, where the broadening Floss hurries on between its green banks to the sea, and the loving tide, rushing to meet it, checks its passage with an impetuous embrace" (Eliot 1961: 7). In the next few lines, however, the direction pursued by the Floss is reversed, apparently anticipating the ultimate fate of both Maggie's and her father's impulsiveness. From out of the amorous embrace of river and sea, black ships laden with "seed" and "the dark glitter of coal" proceed upriver to St Ogg's, emblems of sexual, commercial, and technological penetration which will alter forever the lives of many of the novel's central characters. This proleptic overlapping of the novel's sexual, social, and economic narratives of destruction is accomplished through the dominant, ubiquitous symbol of water. And criticism of the novel has been sensitive to both the sexual-psychological and the economic-historical dimensions of the water symbolism.[4] Yet if the novel's most potent images are indeed those of water out of control – of irresistible, overwhelming forms of energy – this potency tends to obscure the narrative's deep ambivalence about how to *characterize* material, historical, and psychological energies. Is there a discernible "flow" to feelings and events?

Two questions are raised by the novel's opening paragraph. First, what precisely are the "checking" forces which oppose the seaward flow of the river and the apparently impulsive temperaments of the main characters? And second, is the reversal of direction and of impulses figured in this passage a symmetrical, containable reversal, or does it suggest a more radical disruption of equilibriums which cannot be given any simple, symmetrical characterization? We may approach these questions by looking both at the pattern of psychological "checks" in the novel and at the struggle for legal and technological control over the narrative's principal material symbol: the river.

The "check" of the river Floss by the ocean tide is echoed endlessly in the novel's psychological rhetoric. Maggie, in particular, is consistently "checked" both by domestic authority and by her own sense of priorities and obligations:

> She rebelled against her lot, she fainted under its loneliness, and fits even of anger and hatred towards her father and mother, who were so unlike what she would have them to be – towards Tom, who *checked her*, and met her thought or feeling always by some *thwarting difference* – would flow out over her affections and conscience like a lava stream, and frighten her.
>
> (Eliot 1961: 252, my emphasis)

In this passage, Maggie is identified with the river Floss, and Tom with the "checking" or constraining tide. There is some ambiguity here, however, since the very checking of Maggie's impulses produces a new flow – in this case the lava flow of resentment – which Maggie herself evidently wishes to check. The latter dynamic is even more readily apparent in an earlier passage, when the thought of prolonged absence from her prostrate father "checks" a "violent" outpouring of grief: "With these last words, Maggie's sobs burst forth with the more violence for the previous struggles against them. . . . But Maggie soon checked herself abruptly: a single thought had acted on her like a startling sound" (ibid.: 169–70).

The rhetoric of "checking" also occurs in a less apocalyptic and more ironic register throughout the novel, as more or less prudential considerations motivate various characters to desist or pause in the pursuit of a particular course of action, or as various characters chastise and correct one another's petty foibles and behavioral tics.

One source of "checking," then, is *conscience*, and we would be mistaken in distinguishing categorically between authentic and inauthentic forms of social conscience in the novel (for example, Maggie's vs. Aunt Glegg's), since Eliot takes great pains to emphasize that the distinction between idealism and pragmatism in the analysis of individual motives is a highly problematic one, and that the relative proportion of the two in any one action is difficult to determine. We might also be tempted to think of "checking" as a process which arises out of a consideration of the consequences of one's actions; but Eliot denies this too. The process of checking arises from the recognition of analogies (in her later novels this phenomenon will be known distinctively as "sympathy") rather than from any apprehension of causes and effects, even if the characters themselves do not see it quite this way. Mr Tulliver, for instance, regresses from his determination to enforce the repayment of an onerous debt owed him by his sister, and this out of a sympathetic identification with Maggie:

> It had come across his mind that if he were hard upon his sister, it might somehow tend to make Tom hard upon Maggie at some distant day, when her father was no longer there to take her part; for simple people, like our friend Mr Tulliver, are apt to clothe unimpeachable feelings in erroneous ideas, and this was his confused way of explaining to himself that his love and anxiety for "the little wench" had given him a new sensibility towards his sister.
>
> (ibid.: 76)

Eliot's point is that Mr Tulliver misreads his own change: he has constructed a scheme of symmetrical relations in which his own sympathetic actions – his moral self-checking – can be figured as the negation of a future dynamic. The moral action of forbearing on the loan is in fact hardly a negation or reversal of any future system of relations or sequence of causes and effects, but it gives him satisfaction to imagine it in these terms. Such a conception fits perfectly with the generally chiastic logic of crossings and reversals by which he constructs his own domestic identity.

It is an essential postulate of Mr Tulliver's family mythology that character traits "crossed" the lines of gender when his children were born:

> "Tom hasn't got the right sort o' brains for a smart fellow. I doubt he's a bit slowish. He takes after your family, Bessy. . . . It seems a bit of a pity, though, . . . as the lad should take after the mother's side i'stead o' the little wench. That's the worst on't wi' the crossing o' breeds: you can never justly calkilate what'll come on't. The little un takes after my side, now: she's twice as 'cute as Tom."
>
> (ibid.: 11–12)

Not only is the self-serving distribution of character traits here pure postulation; the apparently scandalous chiasmus depends even further on an assumption that character is normally inherited along lines of gender, and that the inheritance of a mother's traits by her son and of a father's by his daughter is an *inversion* – a precise crossing over of characteristics.

Notwithstanding the narrator's warning that "Nature" might be "secretly preparing a refutation" of Maggie's and Tom's apparent temperaments (ibid.: 30) – a warning which ironizes the putative scandal of gender asymmetry by hinting at the possibility of a *double*-cross – Tulliver, along with most of the other characters in the novel, persists in an antithetical view of the world that makes of every anomaly (every irritating "check" produced by the contemplation of untoward or unanticipated consequences) a veritable reversal or crossing of terms.

Flow, check, and reversal: this simple and reciprocal dynamic appears to govern not only the individual motives and actions of characters at distinct points in the narrative, but the larger pattern of the narrative as well. This would seem to point to the river, or to something that the river stands for, as the source of the novel's tragedy. And yet the catastrophe of the novel in the largest sense – the destruction of the Tulliver family – is not precipitated by a literal flood, a flood of events, or a flood of feelings, but by an upstream farmer's deployment of irrigation dykes, a development which may (or *may not*) jeopardize the water power for the Tulliver Mill, and which drives Tulliver to seek legal redress. Here is where the material reality of the river as a source of labor (and the struggle for legal and technological control over its energies) intersects with, and is refracted throughout, the novel's social and sexual structures.

We might note that the novel's rhetoric encourages us to believe that the driving forces behind Tulliver's litigious impulses are psychological, domestic, and sexual, and that they are fully comprehended by the metaphor of water. Tulliver, it is acknowledged by virtually everyone in the novel, is "given to lawing" (ibid.: 86). This seems to be a "given" of his personality, as obscure and inexorable as the floods of desire which supposedly drive Maggie, yet clearly related in some way to the question of his domestic authority. Throughout the novel, Tulliver's energies and ambitions are described as deeply rutted (ibid.: 70, 75), "channel[led]" (ibid.: 172) and "vent[ed]" (ibid.: 172, 175). Yet what if Mr Tulliver's litigious impulses regarding his water rights are not, in the first instance, temperamental?

Water and mill are the two central symbols in the novel, yet both are on the verge of historical transformation. Between 1825 and 1845, steam engines were beginning to compete with natural hydraulics as a power source for mills. Mr Deane, for instance, believes that Dorlcote Mill might be improved as an investment if its output were increased by the addition of steam power (ibid.: 215, 347). At the same time, the development of methods for mass-producing iron piping (for irrigation) and clay tiles (for drainage), and the dissemination of agronomic knowledge through newly created colleges and publications of agricultural science, resulted in an expanded, more productive phase of farming (Chambers and Mingay 1966; Jones 1985: 14ff., 52ff.; Mechi 1855: 366–8). All of this took place roughly in the same time period covered by the novel (1829–44).

This explains why, in the four generations during which the Tulliver family had owned Dorlcote Mill, there had been no previous crisis of this nature or these proportions. Tulliver had indeed pursued litigation previously to defend his water rights; but his opponent in that case had been the builder of a *dam*, and the lawsuit was settled successfully through arbitration. The body of laws and precedents concerning water rights, known collectively as Riparian doctrine, was by the 1820s apparently adequate for adjudicating conflicts of interest created by the known quantities and effects of established technologies such as dams, watermills, and canals. But the new issues of water rights posed by technological advances in irrigation opened up an entirely new area of litigation – one in which the outcome of Tulliver's suit cannot have been foreseen with any clarity.[5] The suit over irrigation rights (set in 1829–30, in the novel), involving no precedents, cannot be settled through the relatively inexpensive para-legal process of arbitration, and this is something Tulliver had not anticipated.[6]

The point has to be emphasized: the catastrophe of Tulliver's ruinous lawsuit and his subsequent loss of mill and personal property cannot be reduced either to personal impulsiveness or to inexorable economic and technological transformation imposed from without.[7] The latter, materialist, interpretation might seem tempting given the way in which the river and mill motifs are assimilated throughout the novel into a rhetoric of "progress" and change. Both the narrator (in an ironic tone) and Mr Deane (in a self-satisfied way) refer to the ever-accelerating pace of modern life, in which the "slow" temperament of traditional St Ogg's is on the verge of invasion and transformation by "these days of rapid money getting" (Eliot 1961: 109) and "this steam . . . [that] drives on every wheel double pace, and the wheel of fortune along with 'em" (ibid.: 345). History, like Mr Tulliver, seems to be impulsive and irresistible, according to this interpretation. Nothing could appear more inevitable than that a new technology ("irrigation") overwhelm and displace an older mode of production ("milling").

Nonetheless a close inspection of the historical context reveals that the bearing of irrigation technology on water rights was, in 1829–30, an issue genuinely in suspense. Any survey of the historiographical literature on nineteenth-century British farming will reveal what common sense might have anticipated: that in a country with Britain's climate and topography, artificial irrigation was hardly in demand.[8] What the purpose or fate of Eliot's/Pivart's irrigation was we cannot know; but irrigation dykes remained an undeveloped technology, and irrigation rights an unexplored legal issue throughout the century in England. It was simply impossible for a miller to know with any certainty in 1829–30 whether or not his livelihood was threatened by the deployment of an irrigation system upstream – though the question could not have arisen even a few years earlier, and would have been anachronistic not many years later. Eliot has chosen the brief period during which industrial capabilities were advanced enough to produce a technology which actual agricultural practice would soon render irrelevant.

Tulliver cannot know what Pivart's "irrigation" portends; and what the novel does is to depict the psychological, social, and rhetorical effects of this uncertainty. It is inevitable that the novel – or at least a critical reading of the novel – thematize this historically, economically, and legally specific dimension of the plot. Thus in a sense we are simply replacing an older thematization (the river as emblem of irreversible historical forces) with a new thematization: the river and the struggle for control over it as expressive of a host of competing, contradictory, socially constructed and potentially reversible forces. Besides being more historically accurate, I would argue, this thematization yields a different reading of the novel's other basic structures, including the relationships of its central characters and its movement toward closure. For *The Mill on the Floss* does not represent the purely reactive and inevitable response of impulsive characters to a simple set of historical developments. Rather, it represents the displaced responses of characters and language to historical circumstances which are genuinely, objectively uncertain. We are witness to a situation in which net gains and losses of social power are not immediately encoded and distributed by the social structure, but are displaced into rhetorical excesses or silences, and into disproportionate reactions at the level of the family dynamic. That is why readings of the river as emblematic of irresistible, linear forces (whether internal or external) cannot adequately explain either the abruptness or the extravagance of the novel's conclusion.

I argued earlier that new readings of a text's explicitly historical references are directed as much by new readings of the text's formal patterns as by new information from without the text. Does the novel, then, have a symbol or an extended narrative figure which helps us read the complex displacement of larger historical disruptions into its domestic structure? Are there formal patterns which correspond to the way in which "historical" developments impinge on Maggie's fate? What we are looking for is not only a way of characterizing the story's legal and technological struggles on the one hand and its psychological and interpersonal struggles on the other; we are looking as well for the dynamic which links these two levels. For that connection need not be one of simple reduplication or echoing.

Here is where we might turn to the novel's central scene of reading and teaching, in which Tom is prepared (however badly) for a life in the world outside of books and Maggie consigned (in Tom's and Stelling's views) to the "superficial" parlor virtues of mere verbal agility. For it is here that the novel's most sustained commentary on the relationship between domestic life (figured as feminine) and the economic sphere (figured as masculine) intersects with the novel's most explicit meditation on the nature of formal and rhetorical structures. The scene is a good place to begin in looking for the distinctive way in which social and economic uncertainties are played out in Maggie's own life.

As befitting a chapter which opposes "rules" of "Syntax" to Maggie's purely creative and idiosyncratic translations of the Eton grammar book's "mysterious" exempla (ibid.: 131), this scene of pedagogy abounds in oppositions of syntax to rhetoric. The narrator's famous critique of metaphor – both a lament and an ironic affirmation – is underscored and undermined precisely by way of a syntactic figure, in this case a figure of reversal and exchange:

> O Aristotle! if you had had the advantage of being "the freshest modern" instead of the greatest ancient, would you not have mingled your praise of *metaphorical speech*, as a sign of high *intelligence*, with a lamentation that *intelligence* so rarely shows itself in *speech* without *metaphor*, – that we can so seldom declare what a thing is, except by saying it is something else?
>
> (ibid.: 124, my emphasis)

The chiasmus of this sentence virtually literalizes the ironic potential of metaphor by charting it as a *reversal* of form: metaphor – speech – intelligence; intelligence – speech – metaphor. While what the sentence states explicitly is that metaphor negates itself by saying "something else," the sentence's syntax dramatizes this negation as a reversal of word order. This echoes the chiasmus buried in the chapter's earlier and equally ironic description of Stelling's teaching methods,[9] and it prepares us for the syntactic rhythms that govern the chapter's crucial elaboration of gender in a passage only two paragraphs later. That passage concerns the "emasculat[ion]" of Tom by Stelling's "tonic" pedagogy:

> Yet, strange to say, under this vigorous treatment Tom became more like a *girl* than he had ever been in his life before. He had a large share of *pride*, which had hitherto found itself very comfortable in the world, despising old Goggles, and reposing in the sense of unquestioned rights; but now this same pride met with nothing but bruises and crushings. Tom was too clear-sighted not to be aware that Mr Stelling's standard of things was quite *different*, was certainly something higher in the eyes of the world than that of the people he had been living amongst, and that, brought in contact with it, he, Tom Tulliver, appeared uncouth and stupid: he was *by no means indifferent* to this,

and his *pride* got into an uneasy condition which quite *nullified his boyish* self-satisfaction, and gave him something of the *girl's* susceptibility.

(ibid.: 125, my emphasis)

The passage plots the decline of Tom's self-confidence in terms of an exchange of gender identities;[10] yet as we line up the corresponding terms of the chiasmus we notice that more than syntactic order has been reversed. There is a double reversal going on here, with several of the terms from the first half of the chiasmus reappearing in negative form. The term "different" in the first half of the passage is matched by the phrase "not indifferent" in the second half, and the "girl" of the first half corresponds to the "nullified boy" of the second. Difference and femininity, by this equation, are constituted as negatives, or at best, double negatives.

Eliot is performing two distinct critiques here with one and the same device. At one level this may be read as a critique of the patriarchal gender system in which femininity is understood negatively in reference to a normative and putatively universal masculinity. This critique requires first that we pay attention to syntactic form; it is by noticing the chiastic rhythm of the chapter and by being alert for the distinctive patterns of chiasmus that we recognize the curious reversal of terms which disturbs Tom's identity in this passage. Yet once we have noticed – and thus come to expect the completion of – this syntactic pattern, we are prepared to notice the contortions (in the form of the double negative) required to fulfil it. We recognize the invidious social construction of femininity precisely by noticing a chiasmus which goes awry, by noting the discrepancy between those "crossings" we expect and the relations we actually encounter. But this is a critique of reading as much as of social arrangements.

Interpreting creatively in order to maintain a chiasmus is an indispensable gesture in Eliot's general social critique – on a level with the necessary thematization of historical references – and yet it is also one of the most fundamental errors made by most of the characters in the novel. For almost everyone in *The Mill on the Floss* attempts to read perverse crossings, reversals, and deviations of form into the network of social relationships around them. We can see this, for instance, in the view, widely held in St Ogg's, that the "crossing o' breeds" has produced strange results in the novel's second generation: a passive Tom, a rebellious Maggie, a Lucy Deane more closely modelled on her aunt Bessy than on her own mother, and a noble Philip Wakem.[11] But it is equally clear that each of these readings is a self-serving and self-revealing postulation on the order of Mr Tulliver's lament over his wife's and son's putative mental sluggishness. The citizens of St Ogg's, no less than the critic, are eager to discern recursive formal features in the social text. Eliot's point is that this always involves a process of misreading; we make sense of social relations by giving them figurative characterizations which depend on highly ideological notions of continuity and discontinuity, identity and difference.

Interestingly enough, when Eliot chooses to problematize the tendency of her characters to see disturbing chiasmuses in the social fabric, she does this not by revealing the "true" figure of social relations, but by multiplying and ironizing chiastic structures (as in the passage on "Nature's" reversal of Tom's and Maggie's apparent temperaments (cited above, pp. 57–8), or even the passage in which Mr Tulliver strives pre-emptively to reverse Maggie's fate at the hands of her brother (above, p. 57)). We may speculate that there are various reasons for the privileging of this specific figure, a figure that is not prominent in Eliot's other novels. Those reasons range from the particularly rich ironic potential contained in a figure of *reversal* (though *The Mill on the Floss* is certainly no more ironic than, say, *Middlemarch*), through the obvious thematic affinity between chiasmus and the river/tide motif (the tide reverses the flow of the river during Maggie and Stephen's boat ride), to the intentional echoes of Darwinian biology throughout the novel. (*The Origin of the Species*, published in 1859, has as one of its dominant themes the "crossing" of species (Darwin 1968: 435–7).) In this novel the figure of chiasmus is clearly an important clue in the decoding as well as the encoding of domestic ideologies, but no single factor determines the selection of this figure; we must be prepared to see a range of proximate, though not directly determining, factors converging here. Rhetorical patterns are necessary guides to social critique, but they cannot themselves perform, let alone explain, the critique they enable.

Perhaps we are now in a position to ask whether the figure of chiasmus (or more properly, of the failed chiasmus), established in the domains of rhetoric and of gender, can be applied to the narratives of material and economic change which bring about the novel's closure. Looking at *The Mill on the Floss*, we can see that the apparently symmetrical and reciprocal economic plot – that is, the narrative of a family's loss of property, possessions, and good name, and of restitution of these through hard work – fails to constitute a full and satisfactory chiasmus, or even an elegantly flawed one. Mr Tulliver loses the mill in anger, and his enemy buys it out of revenge, but the reciprocity effected at the level of the second generation is hollow: Wakem Senior cares little, and his son not at all, about giving up the mill;[12] Tom Tulliver is not appeased by the prospect of regaining it. To make matters even more complicated, the legend of the river being angry when the mill changes hands (Eliot 1961: 221, 233) is fulfilled only when the mill *returns* to its original owner, not when it is lost. There appears to be no chiasmus here. Not only does the return of the mill fail to perform any compensatory function; it fails to reaffirm normative relations even by way of contrast.

As opposed to the domestic sphere, where characters insist on the presence of chiastic relationships even while lamenting them, the economic narrative is characterized precisely by Tom Tulliver's refusal to see a satisfactory chiastic exchange in the return of Dorlcote Mill to the Tulliver-Dodson family's sphere of influence. But why should the return of the mill fail so spectacularly to fulfil the rhetorical and domestic logic established elsewhere by the novel, and how can we relate the novel's ending to this failure? Eliot's departure, at the novel's end, from the norms of realism and verisimilitude has been much lamented, and critics have pointed out quite rightly that not every foreshadowed ending is an adequately motivated one (Hardy 1970, cited above, note 1). But is adequate motivation the point? Part of the novel's dynamic, as I have tried to show, depends on the radical uncertainty surrounding a new technology and its legal and social ramifications; there is a strong thematic connection between the catastrophe precipitated by "irrigation" and the formal scandal of the novel's abrupt ending.

In a sense it is precisely the unexpectedness of endings, and the unpredictability of consequences, that the novel prepares us for. Despite Mrs Tulliver's frequent lament that Maggie has – or will end up being – drowned, Maggie's fate is anticipated most precisely in a proleptic passage where she does not, in fact, drown: Philip Wakem's *interrupted* dream:

> he fell into a doze, in which he fancied Maggie was slipping down a glistening, slimy channel of a waterfall, and he was looking on helpless, till he was awakened by what seemed a sudden, awful crash.
>   It was the opening of the door. . . . It was his father who entered . . .

(Eliot 1961: 373–4)

The "crash" which so abruptly terminates Philip's dream clearly foreshadows the hurtling mass of machinery which destroys Maggie and Tom at the novel's end, even to the point of providing a gratuitously sudden and violent ending to a scene already haunted by the threat of drowning. Philip's dream also echoes several other key scenes of abrupt and dramatic awakening: the narrator's own arousal from a dream, which initiates the narrative proper at the close of the first chapter (ibid.: 8), and perhaps more importantly, the "bang" of the patriarchal "oak chest" which arouses Mr Tulliver from his first coma (ibid.: 195–6). This latter scene is particularly significant because it is the first of a series of deathbed, will-writing, and dying-curse scenes which punctuate the middle section of the novel (pp. 195–315), complicating and confusing the legacy Mr Tulliver leaves his children. These are the scenes which ensure that no simple chiasmus – no mere return of the mill – will satisfy the Tulliver men. For Mr Tulliver bequeaths a number of duties to Tom: not only to regain the mill and to hurt Wakem, but to "be good to" Maggie (ibid.: 314) as well. These last two requests turn out to be mutually exclusive, and thus the most chiastic possible fulfillment of Tulliver's wishes – in which Wakem not only returns the mill but is humiliated and hurt by the results – requires that Maggie be sacrificed; it requires, in fact, that reversals of fate extend far beyond the simple reciprocal exchange of positions envisioned by Tulliver. Mr Wakem can be hurt only if Maggie hurts Philip; Philip can be hurt only if Maggie is hurt. The cost of chiastic resolution at the level of the economic plot is enforced at the domestic and sexual level: specifically, in the relentless domination of Maggie by her father, brother, and lovers, in the destructiveness of those relationships; and ultimately, in the destruction of Maggie herself. That this structure of revenge and sacrifice, this articulation of the economic and domestic spheres, can itself be described as chiastic is hardly a consolation.

Maggie's "fate" is compared by the narrator to a "full and rapid" though "unmapped river" (ibid.: 351). And there is little doubt that the "material fact" of the river – to use the *Spectator*'s phrase – influences Maggie's fate in the most literal and direct ways even as it provides a symbol for forces beyond both Maggie and the Floss. But the task of translating the river's material influence into its social and symbolic significance remains a burden for both characters and readers. "It is astonishing what a different result one gets by changing the metaphor!" exclaims the narrator in a frequently cited passage (ibid.: 124). Yet the narrative remains as resistant to a change in its dominant metaphor as it is insistent that the metaphor's significance remains yet to be determined – yet to be *figured*. The narrator refuses to say just what it *means* for Maggie's fate to be like a river.

The narrator's warning concerning the unreliability of metaphor ("O Aristotle . . .") is, as we have seen, emphasized precisely through the contrasting syntactic figure of chiasmus. If chiasmus is the figure which helps us see just how figurative is the construction of identities and fates in the novel – if it is precisely the figure that highlights and exposes the metaphoricity of verbal texts and of social identities – then we might claim for chiasmus the role of privileged figure or clue. But if the point of chiasmus is to ironize the cognitive claims of rhetoric in the most general way possible, then chiasmus is clearly an object of its own critique. It is enough, in the final analysis, that chiasmus – like any rhetorical device, including metaphor – both underscore and undermine the significance of "material facts." For only by shuttling back and forth between deliberately naïve questions of historical factuality and an equally deliberate scepticism concerning the indeterminacy of rhetoric can we tease out the novel's most intricate and most disturbing structures.

NOTES

1 According to Hardy, prefigurations of the novel's ending in the pervasive references to drowning "remain figures in the frame, not in the picture," and the river "imagery" throughout "does not prepare us for the part played by the river in reaching the conclusion and solving the problem" (1970: 47). For Knoepflmacher the river is a successful "metaphor for the sweeping progress of history," and the flood expresses "those deterministic 'laws' within and without [Maggie's] psyche" (1968: 180, 220). Gilbert and Gubar agree that the river thematic is appropriately expressive of both psychological and historical forces: "Maggie is nature's child, for her rapt, dreamy feelings constantly carry her away in floods of feeling suggestive of the rhythms of the river that empowers the mill"; "When the mill is entangled in unintelligible but inexorable legal battles over water rights, it becomes clear that the forces of culture are inalterably opposed to those of nature" (1979: 492).

2 Gilbert and Gubar interpret the apocalyptic ending of the novel as Eliot's lesson in the dangers and utopian potentials of female "renunciation" (see particularly Gilbert and Gubar 1979: 491–4, 523–32). Miller sees the ending as a "demaximization" of literary closure, in at least two senses: as a strategic violation of the verisimilitude expected by conventional literary sensibilities (Eliot's "men of maxims"), and as a testimony to the artificially constrained range of possibilities for action encountered by women both in and out of fiction: "Mme de Lafayette quietly, George Eliot silently, both italicize by the demaximization of their heroines' texts the difficulty of curing plot of life, and life of certain plots." "The attack on female plots and plausibilities assumes that women writers cannot or will not obey the rules of fiction. It also assumes that the truth devolving from *veri*similitude is male. . . . It does not see that the maxims that pass for the truth of human experience, and the encoding of that experience in literature, are organizations, when they are not fantasies, of the dominant culture" (Miller 1981: 46).

3 This formulation does not correspond to any single theory of symbolic form, but it is intended to be roughly compatible with articulations of the "symbolic" as they are found in recent Marxist and post-Marxist work on literature and culture, most notably Fredric Jameson's *The Political Unconscious* (1981), Franco Moretti's *The Way of the World* (1987) and the work of Jean Baudrillard. Both Jameson's and Baudrillard's conceptions of the symbolic borrow heavily from anthropological theory: Jameson from Lévi-Strauss (Jameson 1981: 76–80) and Baudrillard from Lévi-Strauss and from Mauss's and Malinowski's work on "gifts" (Baudrillard 1981, intro. and chs 1–2; 1975, chs 1, 3; 1976: 202–15). The common element in these works is a willingness to see cultural artifacts as formal expressions of social tensions which are – even though "material" – themselves mediated and "symbolic" symptoms of deeper-rooted historical contradictions. Following Lacanian psychoanalysis, both Jameson and Baudrillard doubt whether this deepest level of the "real" is susceptible to analysis. But both are willing to treat social structures – even if always and already mediated – as the *material* and not only the symbolic ground of individual literary production. Without wishing to gloss over the complicated polemic internal to current left thought – in terms of which there are significant differences between Jameson, Baudrillard, and Moretti – I

believe we can deduce three levels of experience and expression from Jameson's formulation which may serve to outline the hybrid concept of the "symbolic" common to much of contemporary New Left thinking: the "Real," which may be affected through political praxis but cannot be analyzed or "known" as such, and is thus bracketed when we speak of literary texts; the "social" ground of literature, in which "material" elements are always already invested with "symbolic" significance; and "symbolic acts" which are constitutive of individual literary texts. The advantage of this formulation is that it allows historical and material considerations to enter into the interpretation of the individual text while retaining a respect for the heterogeneous, subjective, connotative, and affective qualities both of social experience and of formal symbolic expression. At the very least this allows us to describe the social ground of literary texts in terms of a wide variety of collectivities and intersubjective experiences beyond the strict confines of "class" and "production": e.g. sex, gender, race, religion.

4 See, for instance, Knoepflmacher (1968) and Gilbert and Gubar (1979).

5 Syson touches on the generally uneven impact of technological developments on water-mills and water power in the mid-nineteenth century (1965: 45ff).

6 After the suit has been lost, damages and costs exacted, his mortgage foreclosed and his family's personal possessions auctioned off, Tulliver laments: "I know, I know. I shouldn't ha' gone to law, they say. But who made it so as there was no arbitratin', and no justice to be got?" (Eliot 1961: 236).

7 Eagleton, in his otherwise excellent discussion of ideology in George Eliot's work, still implies that the loss of the mill is part of a larger pattern of "struggling tenant farmers becoming enmortgaged and forced to ruin by the pressures of urban banking and agricultural industry" (1976: 115), a connection which I believe is simply unwarranted. See a similar remark by Gilbert and Gubar concerning the external imposition of legal predicaments, above, note 1. For a more subtle description of the dialectical relationship between legal institutions and their mediations at the level of individual experience, see Thompson (1975), especially pp. 258–69. Thompson writes: "law was often a definition of actual agrarian *practice*, as it has been pursued 'time out of mind'. How can we distinguish between the activity of farming or of quarrying and the rights to this strip of land or to that quarry? The farmer or forester in his daily occupation was moving within visible or invisible structures of law" (1975: 261). See also Sugarman (1983), especially pp. 254–7. Cf. a remark by Walton concerning the relationship between formal legal arrangements and actual practice in the realm of water rights:

> The importance of legal institutions in water development has too often been overlooked. The development of water law must parallel and in many cases precede that of water works.
>   Cultural institutions, like legal ones, usually evolve slowly. They are shaped by religion, by history, by language and by the natural environment. Shared convictions about the relationships among individuals and between the individual and the group; assumptions regarding initiative and responsibility; concepts of justice; attitudes of fatalism or optimism toward the environment; policies regarding payment for water; and many other cultural precepts will determine whether any given institutional arrangement will succeed or fail.
>
> (1970: 34)

8 Trelease suggests that the common perception of "the British Isles as lush

and green, well watered, where people have managed for centuries with the
strictest form of the doctrine of riparian rights allowing almost no major
abstractions from streams" is essentially correct as a picture of British water-
use prior to World War II (1970: 41). The principal technological problem
in nineteenth-century English farming tended, in fact, to point in quite the
opposite direction from irrigation, since farmers were more frequently concerned with the problem of adequate soil-drainage. Caird (1967: 185–97), in
his still definitive survey of mid-century Lincolnshire farming, makes no mention of irrigation, though he does note the frequent use of drainage tech-
niques.

9 "Perhaps it was because *teaching* came *naturally* to Mr Stelling, that he set
about it with that uniformity of method and independence of circumstances,
which distinguish the actions of animals understood to be under the immediate
teaching of nature" (Eliot 1961: 122, my emphasis).
   Though not technically a chiasmus (as it would read if the final phrase
were the grammatically equivalent "nature's teaching") this sentence establishes both the general structure of irony and the syntactic pattern of balanced
and symmetrical repetitions which underlie the chapter as a whole.

10 The passage represents an *exchange* of traits in the fullest sense; it is not
merely that Tom loses certain traits and acquires others, but that his failure to
demonstrate even the minimal scholarly aptitude expected of him is contrasted
consistently with Maggie's *un*expected aptitude.

11 Mrs Tulliver laments that her sister "Mrs Deane, the thinnest and sallowest
of all the Dodsons, should have had this child [Lucy], who might have been
taken for Mrs Tulliver's any day" (Eliot 1961: 55). In discussing Philip with
Tom, Maggie says "I've read of very bad men who had good sons, as well
as good parents who had bad children" (ibid.: 158).

12 Wakem's rather neutral outlook on the whole affair is, presumably, altered
in retrospect when the return of the mill fails to advance his son's chances
with Maggie.

WORKS CITED

Baudrillard, Jean (1975) *The Mirror of Production*, trans. and Intro. by Mark
Poster, St Louis, MO: Telos Press.
—— (1976) *L'échange symbolique et la mort*, Paris: Gallimard.
—— (1981) *For a Critique of the Political Economy of the Sign*, trans. and Intro.
by Charles Levin, St Louis, MO: Telos Press. First published 1972.
Caird, James (1967) *English Agriculture in 1850–51*, 2nd edn, ed. and Intro. by
G. E. Mingay, Reprints of Economic Classics, New York: Augustus M. Kelley,
Bookseller. First published 1852.
Chambers, J. P. and Mingay, G. E. (1966) *The Agricultural Revolution
1750–1880*, London: Batsford.
Darwin, Charles (1968) *The Origin of the Species by Means of Natural Selection
or The Preservation of Favoured Races in the Struggle for Life*, ed. and Intro.
by J. W. Burrow, Harmondsworth: Penguin. First published 1859.
Eagleton, Terry (1976) *Criticism and Ideology: A Study in Marxist Literary
Theory*, London: Verso.
Eliot, George (1961) *The Mill on the Floss*, ed. with an intro. and notes by
Gordon S. Haight, Boston: Houghton Mifflin, Riverside. First published 1860.
Gilbert, Sandra, and Gubar, Susan (1979) *The Madwoman in the Attic: The*

Woman Writer and the Nineteenth-Century Literary Imagination, New Haven, Conn.: Yale University Press.

Hardy, Barbara (1970) "The Mill on the Floss," in Barbara Hardy (ed.) *Critical Essays on George Eliot*, London: Routledge.

Homans, Margaret (1986) *Bearing the Word: Language and Female Experience in Nineteenth-Century Women's Writing*, Women in Culture and Society series, ed. Catharine R. Stimpson, Chicago: University of Chicago Press.

Jacobus, Mary (1981) "The Question of Language: Men of Maxims and *The Mill on the Floss*," in *Critical Inquiry* 8(2): 207–22.

Jameson, Fredric (1981) *The Political Unconscious: Narrative as a Socially Symbolic Act*, Ithaca, NY: Cornell University Press.

Jones, Edgar (1985) *Industrial Architecture in Britain 1750–1939*, London: Batsford.

Knoepflmacher, U. C. (1968) *George Eliot's Early Novels: The Limits of Realism*, Berkeley: University of California Press.

Leavis, F. R. (1960) *The Great Tradition: George Eliot, Henry James, Joseph Conrad*, New York: New York University Press.

echi, J. J. (1855) "The New System of Irrigating Land by Means of Subterranean Iron Pipes," in Julius Stockhardt (ed.) *A Familiar Exposition of the Chemistry of Agriculture, Addressed to Farmers*, London: Bohm.

Miller, Nancy K. (1981) "Emphasis Added: Plots and Plausibilities in Women's Fiction," *PMLA* 96 (1): 36–48.

Moretti, Franco (1987) *The Way of the World: The "Bildungsroman" in European Culture*, London: Verso.

Spectator (1860) unsigned review of *The Mill on the Floss*, reprinted in David Carroll (ed.) *George Eliot: The Critical Heritage*, London: Routledge & Kegan Paul, 1971, pp. 109–14.

Sugarman, David (1983) "Law, Economy and the State in England, 1750–1914: Some Major Issues," in Sugarman (ed.) *Legality, Ideology and the State*, London: Academic Press.

Syson, Leslie (1965) *British Water-Mills*, London: Batsford.

Thompson, E. P. (1975) *Whigs and Hunters: The Origin of the Black Act*, New York: Pantheon.

Trelease, Frank J. (1970) "New Water Laws for Old and New Countries," in Corwin Waggoner Johnson and Susan Hollingsworth Lewis (eds) *Contemporary Developments in Water Law*, Austin, Texas: Center for Research in Water Resources.

Walton, William C. (1970) *The World of Water*, The Advancement of Science Series, London: Weidenfeld & Nicolson.

Chapter 5

Tess, tourism, and the spectacle of the woman

Jeff Nunokawa

Jeff Nunokawa's chapter takes as its starting point the school of feminist psycho-analytic film theory founded by Laura Mulvey's "Visual Pleasure and Narrative Cinema," a school that collates the subjectivity and subjection of women with their status as the object of a masculine gaze. However, it moves beyond Mulvey by historicizing a particular instance of the psychoanalytic scenario which has proven central to feminist theory in recent years. Nunokawa argues that Hardy's novel not only ratifies the perennial stationing of the feminine spectacle as the site of masculine violence, but also suggests that the historical particularities arranging this spectacle may surprise us. Tess's "to-be-looked-at-ness" results, at least in part, from her location in a tourist fantasy: the "pretty face and shapely figure" are illuminated as inhabitants of a traveler's panorama, an exotic vision of rural England, and of "underdeveloped" regions beyond, a scopophiliac pastoral sustained both by nineteenth-century sightseer's handbooks, and by a novel informed by them.

* * *

> I am ashamed to say that I saw a woman hanged . . . I remember what a fine figure she showed against the sky as she hung in the misty rain, and how the tight black silk gown set off her shape as she wheeled half-round and back.[1]

Hardy never got over his fascination with pictures like this: the by now well-known collusion between victimizing and visualizing women appears everywhere in his fiction, and especially in *Tess of the d'Urbervilles*, where the various meanings of apprehension have never been closer. As if to illustrate the grave power of men's eyes over the spectacle of femininity in this novel, Alec d'Urberville's praise for Tess's "pretty face and shapely figure," "set off with that tight pinafore thing," echoes Hardy's admiration for another "shape set off" by a "tight black silk gown" (Hardy 1987: 409). Everywhere in *Tess of the d'Urbervilles*, the figure of the hanged woman haunts the vision of femininity; she is never far from even the most casual of glances. D'Urberville dresses in workmen's clothes so that he can get near enough "to see" Tess while she labors, "nothing more. The smockfrock, which I saw hanging for sale as I came along, was an after-thought" (Hardy 1987: 432). And if the spectacle of Tess recalls the hanging that Hardy witnessed, it also anticipates her own spectacular execution, whose visible signs are witnessed by "riveted" "eyes," gazing from "an almost unlimited prospect." The death of Tess is a picture for an exhibition, one of a series of views, "landscape beyond landscape" which continue "till the horizon was lost in the radiance of the sun hanging above it"; it is a dramatic display that fronts "rows of short barred windows," and which culminates with the uttering of an "Aeschylean phrase" (ibid.: 48–9).

Hardy's account of Tess's death reveals the closest of connections between taming a woman and arranging her for show, between hanging her and hanging her; so does the novel's famous scene of sexual coercion: "upon this beautiful feminine tissue, sensitive as gossamer, and practically blank as snow as yet, there [was] traced . . . a coarse pattern" (ibid.: 119). To subjugate a woman in *Tess of the d'Urbervilles* is to enlist her for display, to frame her either as the object or the surface of an exhibition.

And not only there: the entanglement of women's subjection and their situation as spectacle is, as we know, business as usual for a scopic regime which extends at least from the Renaissance to post-modernism, from Shakespeare to Brian DePalma. But the very routineness of our recognition that the vision of women is a form of masculine power has worked to abbreviate our understanding of *how* the feminine comes to be cast as a spectacle. Even the most significant theoretical speculations about the fateful "to-be-looked-at-ness" of femininity have tended to confirm this reticence: the psychoanalytic investigations of the feminine spectacle inaugurated by Laura Mulvey's "Visual Pleasure and Narrative Cinema" have concerned themselves with the phallic violence visited upon this spectacle, rather than the conditions that enable it.[2]

Such reticence may result from the tautological relation that psychoanalytic theory often envisions between the "to-be-looked-at-ness" of femininity (Mulvey), and femininity, per se. Psychoanalytic theorizations of the feminine spectacle and the masculine gaze usually cast the sexual difference between seer and scene as synonymous with sexual difference itself – according to much of the work which has emerged from Mulvey's essay, the distinction between seer and seen coincides with the difference between male and female subjects.[3] The theoretical vantage point afforded by this collation has little to say about the sources of the feminine spectacle, in particular, because it sees the production of this spectacle as another name for the construction of femininity, in general.

But even if the "to-be-looked-at-ness" of femininity is coterminous with sexual difference itself, the agents that secure this aspect of women's subjectivity and subjection can surely be specified historically. The aim of this chapter is to isolate one of the cultural forces that draws Hardy's feminine "standard" (Hardy 1987: 141) into the killing fields of vision: as we have already seen, *Tess of the d'Urbervilles* ratifies the perennial stationing of the feminine spectacle as the site of masculine violence, but it also suggests that the historical particularities that arrange this spectacle may surprise us. I am going to argue here that Tess's "to-be-looked-at-ness" results, at least in part, from her location in a tourist fantasy: the "pretty face and shapely figure" are illuminated as inhabitants of a traveler's panorama, an exotic vision of rural England, and of "undeveloped" regions beyond, a scopophiliac pastoral sustained both by sight-seers' handbooks, and by a novel informed by them.

Everyone is always looking at Tess. Alec d'Urberville's fascinated gaze meets its match in the narrator's own obsessive eye. Hardy's insistent and lavishly detailed consideration of her "flower-like mouth," the "colour of her cheeks," and the "hundred" "shades" of her "large tender eyes" (ibid.: 140–1) surpasses mere admiration; it amounts to a compulsive preoccupation with her "aspect" (ibid.: 52). Like its villain, whose sight is "riveted" to Tess's "pretty face and shapely figure," the narrative is unable to keep its eyes off this "most . . . finely-drawn figure of them all" (ibid.: 138). It's not for nothing that all parts of Tess "seemed to be endowed with a sensitiveness to ocular beams – even her clothing – so alive was she to a fancied gaze which might be resting upon her" (ibid.: 385). Such sensitivity reflects the constant presence of a fancying gaze within the novel, as well as the fancied gaze – the fictional gaze – of the novel itself.

But if everyone is always looking at Tess, this may be because there is nothing else to do. The novel casts all aspects of the "most finely-drawn figure of them all" as *aspects*; it makes everything about her available for viewing – not just the "flower-like mouth," the "colour of her cheeks," the "hundred" "shades" of her "large tender eyes," but also all kinds of things that are normally invisible. Tess's voice, her past, her psyche – all of these are sights to see. She "sp[eaks] so brightly that it seem[s] as though her face might have shone in the gloom surrounding her" (ibid.: 144). "Phases of her childhood lurked in her aspect still. As she walked along . . . you could sometimes see her twelfth year in her cheeks" (ibid.: 52).

> Her affection for [Clare] was now the breath and life of Tess's being; it enveloped her as a photosphere, irradiated her into forgetfulness of her past sorrows, keeping back the gloomy spectres that would persist in their attempts to touch her – doubt, fear, moodiness, care, shame.
> (ibid.: 260)

Fittingly, Clare's love for such a spectacle assumes shape as a means of illumination, as the energy of "radiance" (ibid.: 311), and his idealiz-

ation of her consists in imagining her "a visionary essence of woman –
a whole sex condensed into one typical form." Conversely, his disillusion-
ment with this "visionary essence" (ibid.: 187) doesn't eclipse the spectacle of Tess; it merely alters it. With the revelation of the "dark vista"
(ibid.: 260) of her past, "the picture of life . . . changed for him" (ibid.:
332).

Tess is part of a wider view; this "visionary essence of femininity"
inhabits a spectacular world, where winter days "harden in colour,"
(ibid.: 366) where summer evenings are luminous with the vanishing light
of "quicksilvery glaze on rivers and pools" (ibid.: 249). Everything here
is spectacular, from "the holiday gaieties of the field – the white gowns,
the nosegays, the will-wands, the whirling movements on the green," to
the "yellow melancholy of [a] one candled spectacle," (ibid.: 57) to the
mangled body of a dead horse, whose "blood . . . assum[es] the irides-
cence of coagulation," and displays "a hundred prismatic hues" (ibid.:
71). If Tess's speech takes form as light, the angelic "notes" that she
hears "in the attic above her head" assume another spectacular shape,
"wander[ing] in the still air with a stark quality like that of nudity"
(ibid.: 178). And it's not only Tess's psychic life that the novel makes
available to the eye: the "subjective experience" of any "peasant" is "a
new aspect" for the "acute sojourner" from the city:

> It was amazing indeed, to find how great a matter the life of the
> obscure dairy had become to him. . . . Many besides Angel have learnt
> that the magnitude of lives is not as to their external displacements,
> but as to their subjective experiences. The impressionable peasant
> leads a larger, fuller, more dramatic life than the pachydermatous
> king. Looking at it thus he found that life was to be seen of the same
> magnitude here as elsewhere.
>
> (ibid.: 213–14)

Tess of the d'Urbervilles does all it can to make the "life that was to
be seen here" available to us, not only by incessantly mentioning it, but
also by instructing us how best to see it. "[A]cquaintance" with "the
beautiful Vale of Blakemore . . . is best made by viewing it from the
summits of the hills that surround it" (ibid.: 48); "to the side was the
milk-house door, through which were visible the rectangular leads in
rows. . . . At the further end the great churn could be seen revolving"
(ibid.: 174); "The highway . . . dipped into a valley, across which it
could be seen running from edge to edge" (ibid.: 473).

Advice like this frequently attends the novel's view of Wessex, but it
gathers especially around the spectacle of the woman who has "imbibed
the essence of her surrounding, and assimilated herself with it" (ibid.:
138). "[T]he muslined form of Tess could be seen standing still, unde-
cided" (ibid.: 92); "you could sometimes see her twelfth year in her

cheeks" (ibid.: 52); "a person watching her might have noticed that . . . Tess's glance flitted wistfully to the brow of the hill" (ibid.: 139). In the following passage, Hardy counsels a spectator who might care to have a more detailed look at Tess's sorrowful eyes, transformed into a landscape vista:

> "[T]was a thousand pities that it should have happened to she, of all others . . ." . . . It was a thousand pities, indeed; it was impossible for even an enemy to feel otherwise on looking at Tess as she sat there, with her flower-like mouth and large tender eyes, neither black nor blue nor grey nor violet; rather all those shades together, and a hundred others, *which could be seen if one looked into their irises –* shade behind shade – tint beyond tint – around pupils that had no bottom.

> (ibid.: 140–1, my emphasis)

A "hundred shades," "tint beyond tint" that surround lake-like "pupils that had no bottom," "could be seen if one looked into their irises." The pathos of *Tess* (and Tess) often gives way to a concern for the best access to these views.

While the instructions lodged in this passage are ultimately related to Tess's tragedy, they are immediately associated with a genre more mundane than "Aeschylean," a genre we can begin to recover by recalling that the final scenes of the novel occur in places that were popular tourist attractions at the time Hardy wrote. After his return from South America, Clare catches the "last train" (ibid.: 462) to find Tess in "a fashionable watering-place" (ibid.: 463) Hardy calls Sandbourne. Improvements in the rail system and the increase of middle-class leisure time afforded by the passage of legislation such as the Bank Holiday Act of 1871 enabled the development during the late nineteenth century of a mass domestic tourist industry, which supported the "glittering novelty" (ibid.) of such resort towns.[4] Stonehenge, where Tess is finally apprehended, was fast becoming a tourist trap by the end of the nineteenth century. Direct railway service from London to Salisbury was introduced in 1857, making access to the "heathen temple" (ibid.: 484) easy for city dwellers, and the result was a Victorian version of Waikiki beach. A cartoon in *Punch* depicts tourists wandering around the "Temple of the Winds" (ibid.), or playing cards on the stones; *The Times* worried that the volume of sightseers who visited Stonehenge would "vulgarize it out of all recognition, and certainly out of all its venerable charms" (Chippindale 1983: 117).[5] Arriving at night, Tess and Angel were apparently able to beat the crowds.

More generally, various parts of the English countryside, like the region that Hardy called Wessex, were popular destinations for sightseers during this period, sightseers such as the "three young men of a superior class" who spend "their Whitsun holidays in a walking tour" (Hardy 1987: 52–3), and encounter the perennial tourist spectacle of vanishing aboriginal rites: "The forests have departed, but some old customs of their shades remain . . . linger[ing] only in a metamorphosed or disguised form. The May-Day dance, for instance, was to be discerned on the afternoon under notice" (ibid.: 49). Clare and his brothers trace the most familiar path of the nineteenth- and twentieth-century tourist, what Louis Turner and John Ash call

> an invasion outwards from the highly developed metropolitan centres into the "uncivilized" peripheries. . . . The tourist comes from a highly developed urban culture, and . . . seeks . . . the exotic and the simple. The pursuit of the exotic is directed towards other cultures (distant in time or space). The pursuit of the simple is directed towards the other cultures in so far as they are seen to be more *primitive* than the home culture. . . . The tourist travels from his metropolitan home to the world of antiquity, to picturesque, pre-industrial cultures and the unspoilt animal kingdoms of African game reserves.
>
> (Turner and Ash 1976: 129)[6]

The gaze that admires Tess at Talbothay's dairy, the gaze that "rises out of the past as . . . a long regard of fixed, abstracted eyes" (Hardy 1987: 169), first encounters the "visionary essence of femininity" as a tourist attraction.

And Hardy's novel is a kind of handbook for this spectacular theme park. Guides for travelers, which appeared in England and the continent early enough to assist medieval pilgrims on their pious excursions, gained enormous popularity as the tourist industry developed in the years that followed. When John Murray III began to publish his famous series of handbooks for travelers in 1836, he was entering an already heavily populated field, and by the middle of the nineteenth century handbooks such as his were sufficiently popular to be a common object of high cultural scorn. At the center of the tourbook industry in England during the latter half of the nineteenth century was the ubiquitous Karl Baedeker. Introduced to the English-language market in 1861, the Baedeker handbook eventually achieved the hegemony there that it already enjoyed on the continent. According to Edward Mendelson, "[b]y the end of the [1860s] . . . 'Baedeker' was becoming a synonym for a guidebook" (Mendelson 1985: 394).[7]

For his part, Hardy apparently relied on Baedeker handbooks to guide him on his vacations, recording in their margins his own assessments of the sights that he visited at their direction (Millgate 1982: 306). In turn, the handbooks took their revenge for these intrusions by taking up residence in his prose. Baedeker's presence in *Tess of the d'Urbervilles* can be literally documented: Hardy's description of Sandbourne, whose official name is Bournemouth – a "fashionable watering place, with its eastern and its western stations, its piers, its groves of pines, its promenades, and its covered gardens" (Hardy 1987: 463) – appears to draw on Baedeker's account of this resort town in *Great Britain: England, Wales, and Scotland . . . Handbook for Travellers*, published in English four years before *Tess*:

> a fashionable watering-place and winter resort of recent growth, with 17,000 inhab., owes much of its salubrity to the luxuriant pine-woods in which it is embosomed. It lies mainly on two small hills, flanking the sheltered valley of the Bourne, the banks of which are laid out as public gardens, with pleasant walks. The sandy beach affords excellent bathing, and two Piers provide agreeable marine promenades.
>
> (Baedeker 1887: 86)

Language like this echoes more generally throughout *Tess*; Hardy's descriptions of local landscape often reproduce the combination of neutral informational purposiveness and colorful metaphor which marks Baedeker's handbooks – d'Urberville's estate, to mention one example, dwells next to a "soft azure landscape," "a truly venerable tract of forest land, one of the few remaining woodlands of undoubted primeval date" (Hardy 1987: 77).[8]

Hardy's first look at Wessex shapes Tess's native habitat as tourbook landscape:

> The village of Marlott lay amid the north-eastern undulations of the beautiful Vale of Blakemore or Blackmoor . . . an engirdled and secluded region, for the most part untrodden as yet by tourist or landscape-painter, though within a four hours' journey from London. It is a vale whose acquaintance is best made by viewing it from the summits of the hills that surround it – except perhaps during the droughts of summer. An unguided ramble into its recesses in bad weather is apt to engender dissatisfaction with its narrow, tortuous, and miry ways. This fertile and sheltered tract of country, in which the fields are never brown and the springs never dry, is bounded on the south by the bold chalk ridge that embraces the prominences of Hambledon Hill, Bulbarrow, Nettlecombe-Tout, Dogbury, High Stoy, and Bubb Down. The traveller from the coast, who, after plodding northwards . . . is surprised and delighted to behold, extended like a map beneath him, a country differing absolutely from that which he has passed through. Behind him the hills are open, the sun blazes down upon fields so large as to give an unenclosed character to the landscape, the lanes are white, the hedges low and plashed, the atmosphere colourless. . . . The atmosphere . . . is languorous, and is so tinged with azure that what artists call the middle distance partakes

also of that hue, while the horizon beyond is of the deepest ultramarine. Arable lands are few and limited; with but slight exceptions the prospect is a broad rich mass of grass and trees, mantling minor hills and dales within the major. Such is the Vale of Blackmoor. The district is of historic, no less than of topographical interest.

(Hardy 1987: 48–9)

The standard features of the tourbook gather in this passage, rendering it almost indistinguishable from a Baedeker: the guide to access ("a vale whose acquaintance is best made"); the thumbnail local history ("The district is of historic, no less than of topographic interest"); the sketch of local resources ("Arable lands are few and limited"). So recognizable is the tourists' guide in these lines that we may be tempted to regard its warning that "[a]n unguided ramble . . . is apt to engender dissatisfaction" as an exercise in self-interest.[9]

If, when Hardy wrote about them, places like "the beautiful Vale of Blackmoor" were "for the most part untrodden as yet by tourist or landscape-painter, though within a four hours' journey from London," his tourbook novel helped ensure that this obscurity wouldn't last for long. In the "General Preface to the Wessex Edition" the author speaks with slight pride of the "interest" that his novels had already inspired in the "scenes" where they take place (Hardy 1987: 494). He could have had no idea of their drawing power in the years that followed. Numerous Hardymaniac guidebooks, with names like *The Landscape of Thomas Hardy* and *Thomas Hardy's Wessex Scene* document his vast contribution to the tourist trade in his region of rural England. One such guidebook speaks of the masses of tourists who

make a pilgrimage to satisfy their curiosity about Casterbridge and Bulbarrow and Egdon Heath; and by no means are these British pilgrims only. In any summer, and particularly during one of the Hardy Festivals, you will find Americans, Japanese, Europeans taking snapshots of the birthplace at Higher Bockhampton, visiting the Hardy family graves in Stinsford Churchyard, wandering through Dorchester or Weymouth, going on conducted tours of some especially evocative and relevant parts of "the Hardy country."

(Edwards 1966: 13)[10]

Handbooks to "the Hardy country" often lend "eloquence" to their accounts of the "colour" and "shape" of this landscape by quoting from the novels, and thus turn themselves into inverted reflections of the work whose author they admire.

But whatever its ties to the English countryside, Hardy's tourbook novel doesn't merely describe the landscape that inhabits his text: it creates this luminous spectacle. "[T]he traveller" mentioned in the novel's first survey of "Wessex," is the reader of *Tess*, the reader who, crossing the bar marked by the cover of the book, is "surprised and delighted to behold" a figure for the text he reads in "a country differing absolutely from that which he has passed through"; in an "atmosphere . . . so tinged with azure that what artists call the middle distance partakes also of that hue," and in the valley "stretched like a map beneath him," stretched, in other words, like the often azure maps that fold out of Baedeker's handbooks (fourteen of which festoon the 1887 *Handbook to Great Britain*).

Hardy furnishes another figure for his tourbook text in the transistorized landscape that the tourist encounters, where "the world seems to be constructed upon a smaller and more delicate scale." This survey will recall Hardy's readers to his defense of the small scale of his novels in the "General Preface to the Wessex Edition:"

> I would state that the geographic limits of the stage here trodden were not absolutely forced upon the writer by circumstances; he forced them upon himself from judgement. I considered that our magnificent heritage from the Greeks in dramatic literature found sufficient room for a large proportion of its action in an extent of their country not much larger than the half-dozen counties here reunited under the old name of Wessex, that have throbbed in Wessex nooks with as much intensity as in the palaces of Europe . . .
>
> (Hardy 1987: 492)

As Hardy suggests here, the textual landscape of his novel contains within its confines a wealth of things from elsewhere; and if this wealth consists of "our magnificent heritage from the Greeks in dramatic literature," and "the domestic emotions," it consists as well of all the various versions of the sightseer's pastoral: Hardy's novel is a generic handbook for the tourist, gathering together in one volume the "antique, ethnic and pristine" landscapes that form the object of his attraction.

The ethnic natives of England's underdeveloped periphery, "with [their] fast-perishing lumber of superstitions, folk-lore, dialect, and orally transmitted ballads" (ibid.: 61) are merged here with the "fast perishing" natural landscape that surrounds them. These pastoral peoples are in turn joined with England's ancient history: in a Shakespearean cloning operation that literalizes the cult of noble savagery, the Durbyfields are cast as d'Urbervilles in pastoral garb.

Moreover, the "extinct" culture that the novel describes includes the ancient and aboriginal regions of what is now known as the third world, already popular destinations for tourists by the middle of the nineteenth century.[11] Hardy country features a "swarthy" (ibid.: 79) Alec d'Urberville, who displaces Tess's idealized anticipation of him, an equally "oriental" vision of "an aged and dignified face . . . furrowed with incar-

nate memories representing in hieroglyphic the centuries of her family's
and England's history" (ibid.). "Ethiopian scorchings browned the upper
slopes of the pastures" (ibid.: 207), at Talbothay's dairy, and the patrons
of Rolliver's inn "deposited their cups as they stood in the road and
drank, and threw the dregs on the dusty ground to the pattern of Polyne-
sia" (ibid.: 63). Flintcomb-Ash contains "zebra-striped" fields and is
inhabited by "two Amazonian Sisters" (ibid.: 366); the engine-man who
works there "strayed into . . . this region of yellow grain and pale soil,
with which he had nothing in common, to amaze and to discompose its
aborigines" (ibid.: 404). When the milk train casts its light on "the native
existences" of Wessex, Tess herself is illuminated as part of a third world
landscape: "No object could have looked more foreign to the gleaming
cranks and wheels than this unsophisticated girl, with the round bare
arms, the rainy face and hair, the suspended attitude of a friendly leopard
at pause" (ibid.: 251).

In a recent investigation of anthropological rhetoric, James Clifford
observes the tendency of ethnographic texts to absorb "the vanishing
primitive" within its bounds. Ethnography, he argues,

> textualizes the other, and gives the sense of a reality not in temporal
> flux, not in the same ambiguous, moving *historical* present that includes
> and situates the other. . . . The other is lost, in disintegrating time
> and space, but saved in the [ethnographic] text.
>
> (Clifford 1986: 111–12)

The vanishing primitive is saved as well in *Tess of the d'Urbervilles*,
whose pages preserve an "extinct" world "of some interest to the local
historian" (Hardy 1987: 45). "The forests have departed, but some old
customs of their shades remain. Many, however linger only in a metamorphosed or disguised form" (ibid.: 49). If the "metamorphosed or disguised form" that lingers here is the spectacular Mayday ritual that the
tourist witnesses, it is also the nostalgic tourbook novel that Hardy's
audience reads, a novel whose universal landscape renders it a paradigm
for the handbook in general.

The generic language of the tourbook emerges into full view at the
end of the novel, when Hardy describes the site of Tess's death in "the
city of Wintoncester . . . a foretime capital of Wessex." Having supplied
directions to a good view of the execution ("From the western gate . . .
the highway . . . ascends a long and regular incline of the exact length
of a measured mile, leaving the houses gradually behind"), the narrative
details the panorama afforded by "this almost unlimited prospect":

> In the valley beneath lay the city . . . its more prominent buildings
> showing as in an isometric drawing – among them the broad cathedral
> tower, with its Norman windows and immense length of aisle and

nave, the spires of St Thomas's, the pinnacled tower and gables of the ancient hospice, where to this day the pilgrim may receive his dole of bread and ale. Behind the city swept the rotund upland of St Catherine's Hill; further off, landscape beyond landscape, till the horizon was lost in the radiance of the sun hanging above it.

Against these far stretches of country rose, in front of the other city edifices, a large red-brick building, with level grey roofs, and rows of short barred windows bespeaking captivity, the whole contrasting greatly by its formalism with the quaint irregularities of the Gothic erections. It was somewhat disguised from the road in passing it by yews and evergreen oaks, but it was visible enough up here . . . From the middle of the building an ugly flat-topped octagonal tower ascended against the east horizon, and viewed from this spot, on its shady side and against the light, it seemed the one blot on the city's beauty. Yet it was with this blot and not with the beauty, that the two gazers were concerned.

(ibid.: 488–9)

And if Hardy sounds like Baedeker here, the "two gazers" who observe the scene that he describes look like tourists, stopping a while to take in a view, before moving to the next. The "speechless gazers" "remain a long time, absolutely motionless," to absorb the aspect of this scene that concerns them particularly, "a black flag," but "[a]s soon as they had strength they arose, joined 'hands again, and went on" (ibid.: 489–90). This is the conclusion of *Tess of the d'Urbervilles*; Hardy's tourbook prose prepares us to imagine it also as the end of the novel in the other sense of the term: it prepares us to imagine that the appreciation of a spectacle is the aim to which the text is directed, as well as the act with which it is concluded.[12]

By casting his final description of the landscape of the novel as a look, Hardy emulates and exposes the characteristic vantage of the tourbook, which insistently frames the various elements of the region it describes (architectural, historical, anthropological, geographic, and geological) as *views*. The tourbook's definition of sites as sights thus participates in the general construction of tourism that was consolidated in the west during the eighteenth and nineteenth centuries, a construction alive today in our own sense that tourism and sightseeing are two ways of saying the same thing.[13]

This ocular bias prevails everywhere in the tourbooks: when they are not actually surveying sights to be seen, they busy themselves furnishing background information that will enable or enhance the tourist's view of them. Whether it be reports of roads in rural England, "charming walk[s] or drive[s], affording a series of varied and beautiful views," or suggested strategies for the most effective exploitation of the "importunate

Beduins" who will transport the tourist to the top of the Pyramids, where "the VIEW is remarkably interesting and striking," the prospect defines the aim of the nineteenth-century tourist's guide (Baedeker 1887: 401–2; 1914: 128).[14] Historical digests, specimens of local folklore, road maps, brief language lessons, architectural guides, ethnographic accounts, geological and geographic surveys, hotel and restaurant ratings – all of the elements of the Baedeker handbook arrange themselves with this view in mind, instructing its reader to appreciate what he will see, advising him how to get there, and informing him where to stay and eat when he does.

We have already apprehended the tourbook aspect of *Tess* in the novel's inclination to cast everything that inhabits it as views, and to instruct the reader how to gain access to them. Baedeker's voice speaks through Hardy when he tells us what we, or others, "could" see, and where we can best see it; when he explains how to see things like the vale of Blackmoor "best discovered from the heights around" (Hardy 1987: 159); or, more significantly for us, when he directs our eyes to those of Tess, whose "hundred shades . . . could be seen if one looked into their irises." Hardy's handbook vision of Tess appears most extensively and explicitly in the following passage, a painstaking guide to what one sees, and can see, and where, and when:

> This morning the eye returns involuntarily to the girl in the pink cotton jacket, she being the most flexuous and finely-drawn of them all. But her bonnet is pulled so far over her brow that none of her face is disclosed while she binds, though her complexion may be guessed from a stray twine or two of dark brown hair which extends below the curtain of her bonnet. . . . A bit of her naked arm is visible between the buff leather of the gauntlet and the sleeve of her gown. . . . At intervals she stands up to rest, and to retie her disarranged apron, or to pull her bonnet strings. Then one can see the oval face of a handsome young woman with deep dark eyes.
>
> (ibid.: 138)

Here Hardy accentuates the ancestry of the spectacle of Tess by casting it in the present tense that characterizes the sightseers' handbook, an absolute present that bathes the view and the viewer that it arranges in a timeless synchronic glow: "Derwentwater . . . is perhaps the loveliest of the English lakes. Its compact form enables it to be taken in at one view"; "An admirable view of the town is obtained as we approach it from the railway-station, but it is seen to greatest advantage from a boat in the bay" (Baedeker 1887: 401, 122).

The present tense of the tourbook's eye surfaces all over Hardy's novel; it appears, for example, as a slight grammatical infelicity lodged in the midst of Hardy's account of the fields where Tess labors:

> Along one side of the field the whole wain went, the arms of the
> mechanical reaper revolving slowly, till it passed down the hill quite
> out of sight. In a minute it came up on the other side of the field at
> the same equable pace; the glistening brass star in the forehead of the
> fore horse *first catching the eye* as it rose into view over the stable.
>
> (Hardy 1987: 137, my emphasis)

The eye as well as the object that catches it are exempted from the past
tense that governs this passage, and cast in the permanent present of
the ablative absolute.

As if registering the pressure of the guidebook that inhabits it, Hardy's
spectacle of femininity is lodged generally in the present tense, or, more
precisely, the present Tess, the "visionary essence of woman – a whole
sex condensed into one typical form." The "luxuriance of aspect" that
aggravates Alec d'Urberville is an image that transcends the cycle of birth
and death, proceeding from an earlier generation ("she had inherited the
feature from her mother": (ibid.: 82)), and passed on to the younger
sister, "a tall budding creature . . . a spiritualized image of Tess . . .
with the same beautiful eyes" (ibid.: 488); elsewhere, this "finely drawn"
figure is the perennial spectacle of poetry or mythology. For Alec d'Urberville, who "used to be quite up on that scene of Milton's" (ibid.: 431)
Tess is Eve; her mouth "force[s] upon [Clare's] mind" "the old Eliza-
bethan simile of roses filled with snow" (ibid.: 209); "he called her,
Artemis, Demeter" (ibid.: 187). Elsewhere still, the spectacle of Tess is
the persistent primal scene of her author's imagination: the vision of the
hanging that Hardy saw "as a young man," dwells in the "pretty face
and shapely figure" "set off" by "that tight pinafore-thing," a limitless
vista that more than one man holds dear.

The paradox here is worth remarking: the persistently contemporary
aspect of the female spectacle in Hardy's novel may be read as a symptom
of its historical character, marking as it does one of the discursive prisms
through which visions of femininity, and especially visions of the feminine
body, were refracted at the time that Hardy wrote. If spectacular femininity appears to rise above the limits of history in *Tess of the d'Urbervilles*,
and enter the precincts of eternal presentness, this is partly because it is
informed by a nineteenth-century rhetoric whose habit it is to make such
visions always new.

R. Talbot Kelly's guide for the Middle East tourist, *Egypt – Painted
and Described* (1901) pronounces the faith that silently inhabits the present tense of the travellers' handbook: "The Nile valley and the temples
remain the same, and no vicissitudes of circumstance can ever serve to
rob Egypt of the glory of its sunlight" (Kelly 1901: 233). No vicissitudes
of circumstance can ever serve to rob Tess of the glory of *her* light,
either, stationed, as she is, in the endless visionary fields of the nine-

teenth-century tourbook. The spectacle of femininity that falls under masculine eyes in Hardy's novel draws its radiance from a genre whose purpose is, in the words of another of its most illustrious practitioners, "before all, to make you see" (Conrad 1925: xiv).

NOTES

I would like to thank Richard Moran, Ginger Strand, Sasha Torres, and Linda Shires for helping me with this chapter.

1 Letter to Lady Pinney, 20 January 1926 (Hardy 1988: vol. 7, 5). The hanging itself took place on 9 August 1856.
2 Mulvey (1975). Mulvey invokes film as an exemplary instance of the anxious reign of the phallic gaze: cinema is "an advanced representation system," which "poses questions of the ways the unconscious (formed by the dominant order) structures ways of seeing and pleasure in looking." According to Mulvey's generative scenario, the sometimes lethal disciplining of the feminine spectacle in the field of the phallic gaze arises out of a constitutive masculine anxiety: as the pleasure of seeing this spectacle slides into the problem of identifying with it, the delights of scopophilia give way to the terrors of castration. To contain this threat, the feminine spectacle is fetishized (cast as a visible sign of the phallus) or punished. For an especially sophisticated variation on, and critique of Mulvey's account, see Rose (1986).
3 This collation of sexual and scopic difference is often most explicit when feminist psychoanalysis takes up the problem of the female gaze. Thus, for example, Mulvey casts the female spectator as a kind of transvestite in "After-thoughts on Female Pleasure." In "Film and the Masquerade: Theorizing the Female Spectator" (1982) Mary Ann Doane characterizes the problem of female spectatorship as an overidentification with the image. See also Doane (1988–9). Such theorizations draw from various distances on the speculations of Luce Irigaray, which work in different ways to cast the feminine as spectacle and the masculine as the gaze. See, for example, Irigaray (1977) especially p.74 and Irigaray (1985). I do not mean to cast these brief remarks as a complete, or even representative account of the complex career of feminine spectatorship theory. For a recent review of this terrain, see *Camera Obscura* 1989.
4 On the growth of domestic tourism in England during the nineteenth century, see especially Turner and Ash (1976: 129–48). See also Pimlott (1948) and Swinglehurst (1982).
5 For a later return to the theme of Stonehenge's ruination at the hands of sightseers, see *National Lampoon's European Vacation* (1985), in which an inept American tourist (Chevy Chase) succeeds in destroying the temple with his rented car.
6 Turner and Ash note that this is only one version of tourism: "The North Atlantic Community's veneration for the past is not shared by other societies" (1976: 132). Dean MacCannell characterizes tourism as an exemplary instance of the staged confrontation between "modernity" and the "aboriginal" (1976: 57). On the cultural arrangements by which other cultures are cast as primitive, see Fabian (1983).
7 For a contemporary report of the ubiquitous influence of the tourist's guide-book during the latter part of the nineteenth century, see Leslie Stephen's

complaint in *Cornhill Magazine* about tourists who conform unthinkingly to the directions of Murray (Stephen 1869: 209). See Vaughan (1974) and Buzard (1988). Buzard notes that Stephen's complaint against Murray was already a commonplace by the time he wrote it.

8 Prose such as this may be characterized as instances of what Edward Mendelson denominates as the "Baedeker parenthesis": "One of its many functions was to juxtapose, without irony, the poetical and the practical" (Mendelson 1985: 397).

9 The language of the tourbook underwrites "the model of the filing system of a disinterested observer" that characterizes the organization of tourism, generally, according to MacCannell: "Attractions are usually organized . . . on the model of the filing system of a disinterested observer . . . the tourist world is complete in its way, but it is constructed after the fashion of all worlds that are filled with people who are just passing through it" (1976: 51). Mendelson draws attention to a similar moment of tourbook self-interest in Baedeker (Mendelson 1985: 393).

10 See Holland (1948), Kay-Robinson (1984) and Hawkins (1983). For a very recent version of tourbook Hardymania, see Hardy (1990: 3).

11 On the identification of rural England and the third world, see Williams (1973), Hechter (1975), and Said (1989). For a brief account of the development of the third world as a tourist site, see Smith (1977: 33–47).

12 Dorothy Van Ghent may be correct when she asserts that "we do not believe that young girls make ameliorated lives out of witness of a sister's hanging" (Van Ghent: 87). On the other hand, we may also suspect that such a view would make a spectacular tourist attraction.

13 Historians and theorists of tourism often locate sightseeing as the object of attraction around which tourism is defined and organized. (See MacCannell; Turner and Ash). For an account of the transformation of tourism into sightseeing during the eighteenth century, see Turner and Ash (1976: 41–5). Fabricant (1987) describes the construction of country estates as tourist spectacles during the eighteenth century. The intense association of tourism and sightseeing is reflected in the paradigmatic place granted the former in theorizations of the spectacle and the "society of the image." See, for example, Boorstin (1961). Debord (1983) sees tourism as an exemplary instance of a social order which prefers images to the material reality to which they are supposed to refer. Fredric Jameson (1979) offers the "familiar example of tourism" to illustrate the displacement of the real by its image that, in his view, characterizes modernity. For a critique of the society of the spectacle which doubles as a tourbook, see Baudrillard (1989).

14 Baedeker contends that the view from the Pyramid may be beyond comparison: "There is perhaps no other prospect in the world in which life and death, fertility and desolation, are seen in so close juxtaposition and in such marked contrast." Presumably the writer had not read *Tess of the d'Urbervilles*.

WORKS CITED

Baedeker, Karl (1887) *Great Britain: England, Wales, and Scotland as Far as Loch Maree and the Cromarty Firth – Handbook for Travellers With 14 Maps, 24 Plans, and a Panorama*, London: Dulau & Co.

—— (1914) *Egypt and the Sudan – Handbook for Travellers with 22 Maps, 85 Plans, and 55 Vignettes*, 7th edn, London: T. Fisher Unwin.

Baudrillard, Jean (1989) *America*, trans. Chris Turner, New York: Verso.

Boorstin, Daniel J. (1961) *The Image: A Guide to Pseudo-Events in America*, New York: Harper & Row.

Buzard, James Michael (1988) "Forster's Trespasses: Tourism and Cultural Politics," *Twentieth Century Literature*, 34(2): 74–93.

Camera Obscura (1989) 20–1.

Chippindale, Christopher (1983) *Stonehenge Complete*, Ithaca, NY: Cornell University Press.

Clifford, James (1986) "On Ethnographic Allegory," in James Clifford and George E. Marcus (eds) *Writing Culture: The Poetics and Politics of Ethnography*, Berkeley: University of California Press.

Conrad, Joseph (1925) *The Nigger of the Narcissus*, New York: Doubleday.

Debord, Guy (1983) *The Society of the Spectacle*, Detroit: Black & Red Press.

Doane, Mary Ann (1982) "Film and the Masquerade – Theorizing the Female Spectator," *Screen* 23 (3–4): 74–87.

—— (1988–9) "Masquerade Reconsidered: Further Thoughts on the Female Spectator," *Discourse* 11 (1): 42–54.

Edwards, Ann-Marie (1966) *Discovering Hardy's Wessex*, London: Longman.

Fabian, Jonas (1983) *Time and the Other: How Anthropology Makes its Object*, New York: Columbia University Press.

Fabricant, Carole (1987) "The Literature of Domestic Tourism," in Laura Brown and Felicity Nussbaum (eds) *The New Eighteenth Century*, New York: Methuen, pp. 254–75.

Hardy, Susan (1990) "Walking in Hardy Country: from Village to Village in the English Novelist's Realm of Wessex, Casterbridge and *Tess*," *The New York Times*, Section D: 2 – 4.

Hardy, Thomas (1987) *Tess of the d'Urbervilles*, Harmondsworth, Middlesex: Penguin.

—— (1988) *The Collected Letters of Thomas Hardy*, Oxford: Clarendon Press.

Hawkins, Desmond (1983) *Hardy's Wessex*, photographs by Anthony Kersting, London: Macmillan.

Hechter, Michael (1975) *Internal Colonialism: the Celtic Fringe in British National Development*, Berkeley: University of California Press.

Holland, Clive (1948) *Thomas Hardy's Wessex Scene*, London: Longman.

Irigaray, Luce (1977) "Women's Exile," *Ideology and Consciousness* 1: 62–76.

—— (1985) *This Sex Which Is Not One*, trans. Catherine Porter with Carolyn Burke, Ithaca, NY: Cornell University Press.

Jameson, Fredric (1979) "Reification and Utopia in Mass Culture," *Social Text* 1: 54–82.

Kay-Robinson, Denys (1984) *The Landscape of Thomas Hardy*, pictures by Simon McBride, London: Webb & Bower.

Kelly, R. Talbot (1901) *Egypt – Painted and Described*, London: A. & C. Black.

MacCannell, Dean (1976) *The Tourist: A New Theory of the Leisure Class*, revised edn, New York: Schocken.

Mendelson, Edward (1985) "Baedeker's Universe," *The Yale Review* 74(3): 386–403.

Millgate, Michael (1982) *Thomas Hardy: A Biography*, New York: Random House.

Mulvey, Laura (1975) "Visual Pleasure and Narrative Cinema," *Screen* 16 (3): 6–18.

—— (1981) "Afterthoughts on 'Visual Pleasure and Narrative Cinema' inspired by *Duel in the Sun*," *Framework* 6 (15–17).

Pimlott, J. A. R. (1948) *The Englishman's Holiday: A Social History*, London: Faber & Faber.

Rose, Jacqueline (1986) "George Eliot and the Spectacle of the Woman," and "Sexuality in the Field of Vision," in *Sexuality in the Field of Vision*, London: New Left Books, pp. 104–22; 225–34.

Said, Edward (1989) "Yeats and Decolonization," in *Remaking History*, New York: Dia Books, vol. 2: pp. 3–29.

Smith, Valerie L. (1977) *Hosts and Guests: The Anthropology of Tourism*, Philadelphia: University of Pennsylvania Press.

Stephen, Leslie (1869) "Vacations," *Cornhill Magazine*: 209–20.

Swinglehurst, Edmund (1982) *Cook's Tours: The Story of Popular Travel*, Dorset: Blandford Press.

Turner, Louis and Ash, John (1976) *The Golden Hordes: International Tourism and the Pleasure Periphery*, New York: St Martin's Press.

Van Ghent, Dorothy (1953) "On *Tess of the d'Urbervilles*," in *The English Novel: Form and Function*, New York: Holt, Rinehart & Winston.

Vaughan, John (1974) *The English Guide Book 1780–1870: An Illustrated History*, Newton Abbot: David & Charles.

Williams, Raymond (1973) "The New Metropolis," in *The Country and the City*, New York: Oxford University Press, pp. 279–88.

Chapter 6

"To tell the truth of sex"
Confession and abjection in late Victorian writing

Marion Shaw

In this chapter Marion Shaw uses discourse theory and Julia Kristeva's notion of abjection to complicate Foucault's perceived link between confession and a compulsive search for the truth of sex in the nineteenth century. The confessional mode to be found so often in fiction of the late Victorian period serves not only to extract the truth of sex, Shaw argues, but also to summon and dispel horror and to engage with the fear of a total collapse of meaning. Specifically, Shaw studies *Dr Jekyll and Mr Hyde* and *The Island of Dr Moreau*, fictions which rely on gendered concepts of the "truth" of a perverse Darwinian sublime, in which the female represents the threatened indeterminacy of meaning which confession seeks to cancel out through a narrative constructed in the service of father-son bonding, a narrative of cultural legacy. To document this thread of the late Victorian cultural unconscious, Shaw contextualizes these fictions by examining the material practices of Freud and Havelock Ellis and the gruesome Whitechapel murders of 1888.

* * *

In the case of "Fraulein Elisabeth von R.," in *Studies on Hysteria*, Freud successfully practiced the pressure technique which he had recently substituted for the cruder hypnosis used by Breuer; in doing so he overcame his patient's sly resistance and "cured" her hysteria. In addition, at the end of the treatment he arrived at a psychoanalytic insight which he considered significant. This was that hysterical symptoms and linguistic usage are cognate, that they "alike draw their material from a common source" (Freud 1955: 181). Hysteria itself, he concluded, is not symbolization but rather its opposite, in that it restores an original sensation which language may have symbolized so that, for example, when a bereaved patient suffers from a psychosomatic chest pain, this hysterical symptom re-enacts the adrenalin-induced, physical pain experienced on betrayal, which is usually forgotten, except in the linguistic symbolization of the expression, "I was stabbed in the heart." According to Freud at this stage in his thinking – *Studies on Hysteria* was published in 1895 – hysteria is an attempt to remember sensations which in earlier times, so Darwin had taught, "had a meaning and served a purpose."

The hysterical body thus reveals not only a truth about an individual's repressed sufferings but also atavistic truths about human nature in general. The book that Freud alludes to in these conclusions is Darwin's *The Expression of the Emotions in Man and Animals*, published in 1872 and claiming, with Darwin's customary equanimity, kinship between humans and animals in the way they express emotion, and that in both, differing only in degree, there is an involuntary element depending on primitive physiological origins.

These Darwinian truths that Freud's hysterical patient reveals are discovered by an act of confession which is manifest in the confessor's (Freud's) laying on of hands by which pathogenic memories are, so to speak, *pressed out* of the victim. The nature of Fraulein Elisabeth von R.'s story confirms the confessional act in its narcissistic mixture of autobiography, affirmation, and expurgation, plus a desire, common to all confessionists, to unburden and lay bare the self, what Rousseau described as "a continual need to confide [which] is constantly bringing my heart to my lips." In the case of Fraulein Elisabeth, however, the confession is no Rousseauesque, spontaneous act of self-revelation but is exacted, under quasi-medical conditions, by an inquisitorial confessor. As Steven Marcus says, Freud becomes "a relentless investigator, a Sherlock Holmes of the psychic world in search of reality or truth of which there are giveaway signs" (Marcus 1984: 77). Confession has become a science, an expert practice, in which the confessionist is a patient who awaits but does not initiate deliverance. The deliverance involves the replacement of a hysterical symptom, itself a re-enactment of primitive impulse, by a "truthful" (as opposed to the oblique or displaced symbolization which unconfessed hysterics sometimes use) form of symbolization, by a narrative in which the symptom's origins are tracked and their development articulated. This narrative may be described as a hysterical text in that it too suffers from reminiscences; if the symptom remembers the original emotion, the narrative is committed to telling the truth of the symptom's causes, of explaining how and why it came to be. In Darwin's book, animal and human expressive behavior, such as purring or frowning, is traced back to a primitive usefulness now often physically superfluous. For Freud too, deeply impressed by Darwin at this stage, the symptom and its confessional narrative can be traced to an origin intrinsic both to the individual, Fraulein Elisabeth, and to general human nature. As Freud sees it, the truth that awaits deliverance through confession always has to do with sex. In the case of Fraulein Elisabeth, her hysterical symptom of hyperalgesia of the thighs is converted into a confessional narrative in which her crime is perceived as a transgressive desire for her brother-in-law; her expiation is to be brought to tell the truth of sex, and her absolution

– or punishment – in Freud's wistful, secular world, is to be given away
in marriage to a man who is neither her brother-in-law nor Freud:

> In the spring of 1894 I heard that she was going to a private ball . . .
> and I did not allow the opportunity to escape me of seeing my former
> patient whirl past in a lively dance. Since then, by her own inclination,
> she has married someone unknown to me.
>
> (Freud 1955: 160)

This is, as far as Fraulein Elisabeth is concerned, the end; her story has
been told and her cure-confession completed in the love-and-marriage
ending Freud writes for her. The psychotherapeutic confession has acted
as an *abreaction:*

> *It brings to an end the operative force of the idea which was not
> abreacted in the first instance, by allowing its strangulated affect to find
> a way out through speech; and it subjects it to associative correction by
> introducing it into normal consciousness.*
>
> (Freud 1955: 17; emphasis in original)

Two years after *Studies on Hysteria*, Havelock Ellis published *Sexual
Inversion*, the first published volume of *Studies in the Psychology of Sex*.
In collecting material for *Sexual Inversion* Ellis had collaborated with
John Addington Symonds, whom he knew to be homosexual. Symonds
was desperate to have Ellis's patronage; feeling himself threatened by
the Labouchère clause in the Criminal Law Amendment Act of 1885, and
obliged to live abroad to escape its reaches, Symonds wanted scientific
legitimation of his experiences and observations. He also wanted his
story to be told, his life's meaning (he was shortly to die, in fact before
the publication of *Sexual Inversion*) to be given the authority of a written
document, particularly one by a man of science. The result was a series
of homosexual confessions, many of them supplied by Symonds, in the
guise of a scientific study. The sample was selective, drawn mostly from
the upper middle classes and chosen to validate what Ellis already
believed, that homosexuality, or inversion as he preferred to call it, was
congenital. Although the terms "invert" and "inversion" were not his
invention – he claims they were used as early as 1871, and certainly
Symonds used the expression "sexual inversion" several times in his
essay, "A Problem in Greek Ethics" in 1882 – Ellis gave them coinage.
They were particularly appropriate to his conception of the homosexual
as a lonely, tragic figure, doomed from birth to an outcast existence.
Turned in upon his own kind, upon himself therefore, the invert reflects
one of nature's aberrant truths. "Unnatural acts," as they were called
in the trials of Oscar Wilde, nevertheless point to something natural;
like Freud's hysterics, Ellis's inverts reveal atavistic symptoms of what

"once had meaning and served a purpose" and their confessions are thus a search for origins.

Unlike Freud, Ellis did not theorize the confessions given to him, seemingly unwilling or unable to solve the mystery of his confessionists' stories, except to say that an individual is born with a constitutional abnormality in which his sexual instinct is turned toward persons of the same sex. Ellis's confessions are inconclusive, with the patients uncured and their narratives unplotted; he is less successful than Freud as a story teller or romance novelist and his confessions remain simply a number of myth-like fragments, typified in this extract from History XXI, that of "a successful man of letters":

> I dreamed that I saw my own father murdered by a gang of ruffians, but I do not remember that I felt any grief, though I was actually an exceedingly affectionate child. The body was then stripped of its clothing and eviscerated. I had at the time no notion of anatomical details; but the particulars remain distinct to my mind's eye, of entrails uniformly brown, the colour of dung, and there was no accompaniment of blood. When the abdomen had been emptied . . . I was seized . . . and was laid between the thighs of my murdered parent; and from there I had presently crawled my way into the evacuated abdomen. The act . . . caused me extreme organic excitement . . . The dream had no outcome; it seemed to reach its goal in the excitement it caused.
>
> (Ellis 1936: 145)

These early cases of Freud and Ellis are paradigmatic of the scientific confessions which abound during the last years of Victoria's reign and in which dark, perverse, transgressive yet nevertheless true secrets are apparently discovered and brought into "normal consciousness." Foucault has commented on the development of the act of confession from an original penitential process to a late nineteenth-century compulsive *scientia sexualis* which undertook "the tasks of producing true discourses concerning sex . . . by adapting – not without difficulty – the ancient procedure of confession to the rules of scientific discourse" (Foucault 1984: 67–8). If Western man has become a confessing animal, this has resulted in a transformation in the literature of the age:

> Whence a metamorphosis in literature; we have passed from a pleasure to be recounted and heard, centering on the heroic or marvellous narration of "trials" of bravery or sainthood, to a literature ordered according to the infinite task of extracting from the very depths of oneself, in between the words, a truth which the very form of the confession holds out like a shimmering mirage.
>
> (Foucault 1984: 59)

Although Freud's and Ellis's cases read like fiction – a romance story and a Gothic fragment respectively – their confessional form guarantees truthfulness, although Freud had some misgivings on this score: "[It] still strikes me myself as strange that the case histories I write should read like short stories and that, as one might say, they lack the serious stamp of science" (1955: 160). Equally he might have commented that much of the fictional literature of the age carried "the serious stamp of science," not least because it assumed a confessional mode and thereby promised a truth extracted from the depths of the self. The psychic secrets of *Heart of Darkness*, the "invert" truths of *De Profundis*, the demonic innocence of *The Turn of the Screw*, or the necrophiliac fantasies of *Dracula*, all these guarantee their truthfulness about human nature by adopting confessional modes: letters, a journal, or, as in the case of *Heart of Darkness*, an obsessional eyewitness account.

In some respects, Freud and Foucault are right in that the confessional element in these accounts has to do with sex; but there is more to the horror they invoke than sex, or sex is only a symptom of the horror. The truth that is sought seems to be a perverse Darwinian sublime, a reaching out to the limits of the human state, what lies beyond the rational and civilized, the point where not only sexual proprieties disappear but meaning itself collapses:

> A massive and sudden emergence of uncanniness, which, familiar as it might have been in an opaque and forgotten life, now harries me as radically separate, loathsome. Not me. Not that. But not nothing either. A "something" that I do not recognize as a thing. A weight of meaninglessness, about which there is nothing insignificant, and which crushes me. On the edge of non-existence and hallucination, of a reality that, if I acknowledge it, annihilates me. There abject and abjection are my safeguards. The primers of my culture.
>
> (Kristeva 1982: 2)

In their confrontation of uncanniness, the confessional texts of the late nineteenth century can be seen as assuming a burden which is both "repellent and repelled, a deep well of memory that is unapproachable and intimate" (Kristeva 1982: 6). In doing so, they both summon and dispel the horror; the symptom of a forgotten, Darwinian life is transformed into a story, the perverse confessional narrative: confession as abreaction, "commonplace and public at the same time, communicable, sharable . . . Narrative as the recounting of suffering: fear, disgust, and abjection crying out, they quiet down, concatenated into a story" (ibid: 145)

In this chapter I wish to look at two perverse confessional fictions of the late Victorian period in which horrific truths about human nature are not merely Gothic thrills or primitivistic warnings but appear also to intimate a sickening collapse of meaning and of limits of the kind Kristeva means in her use of the term "abjection." The two fictions are R. L. Stevenson's *The Strange Case of Dr Jekyll and Mr Hyde* and H. G. Wells's *The Island of Dr Moreau*. In both of these, truthfulness is assured by the apparatus of confession: letters, journals, confidential documents, and interviews, and, above all, the pressing need of the raconteurs to disburden themselves of the truths they have realized. Both these stories are about doctors and partake of the "sexual climate of gloom, frustration, fear, muted despair, and moral uncertainty and bafflement" (Marcus 1984: 9) that characterizes medical writing in the latter part of the nineteenth century. As Sherlock Holmes was made to say (in 1892), "When a doctor does go wrong he is the first of criminals. He has the nerve and he has the knowledge" (Doyle 1981: 185). *The Strange Case* and *The Island of Dr Moreau* also have in common the fact that women, or the female, are almost absent and that each story is dominated by male acts of creation and each features confrontational dialogues between men in an unequal relationship in which the more powerful male figure is in possession of perverse knowledge. As Kristeva suggests, there is in the perverse "something which is deposited to the father's account [*verse au père – père-version*]." Certainly, in these late Victorian confessional dialogues it is, as it were, a Darwinian father who conveys the truth of origins to an intimidated son, and in so doing causes the irreparable damage to them both. In their grotesque enactment of perverse paternal influence these stories posit the collapse of limits and meanings, yet at the same time, in being narratives, especially in being confessional narratives, they bring about a concatenation, a quietening down, of fear and disgust.

First, however, it is as well to look at an actual symptom suffered by the hysterical body of late Victorian society, perhaps *the* perverse symptom of the period and one which constituted the most thrilling and horrifying threat to notions of human identity and social order. Between August and November 1888, two years after *The Strange Case of Dr Jekyll and Mr Hyde* and eight years before *The Island of Dr Moreau*, and bridging Darwin's essay of 1872 and Freud's interpretation of it into psychoanalytic terms in 1895, there occurred seven murders of women in the Spitalfields, Whitechapel, area of London which bore the mark of the same killer, Jack the Ripper, as he became known in the extensive and sensationalist reporting of the cases. The hallmark of the murders was their extreme brutality, but they had other features in common; each of the women was impoverished and working-class, and, at the time of her murder, a prostitute. The case of the last victim, Mary Jane (or Anne) Kelly, aged twenty-four, good-looking and fond of drink, was a summation of all the others. She had moved into Dorset Street with her "husband," who had then left her, since when she had earned her living, and that of a six-year-old child, by street-walking. Dorset Street was a poor area with most of the buildings being common lodging-houses, full every night with as many as 300 people in one house. This was the kind of populace that Beatrice Webb described in her diary for 1885:

> A drift population of all classes and races; a constantly decomposing mass of human beings; few arising out of it but many dropping down dead, pressed out of existence by the struggle. A certain weird romance with neither beginning nor end.
>
> (Webb 1971: 271)

Webb noticed that the lodging-house rooms were painted "in the same dull, dead-red distemper, unpleasantly reminiscent of a butcher's shop" (ibid: 269), and it was in such a room that the butchery of Mary Jane Kelly took place, her murderer emerging unobtrusively from the violent culture in which she lived and disappearing back into it unnoticed. On the night of her murder Kelly was heard singing "Sweet Violets"; the next morning her naked body was found with her throat cut "from ear to ear, right down to the spinal column." Her ears, nose and breasts had been sliced off, and her liver and uterus removed. Many witnesses and suspects were questioned but apparently no trace of the murderer was found although theories about his identity abounded (and still do abound), favoring at the time someone with anatomical knowledge, a butcher travelling on the livestock boats, perhaps, or a medical man.

Were these sexual murders? In an obvious sense they were but there was an excess of violence to them which seemed, at the time, to go beyond sexuality to pose essentialist questions concerning human identity. The vocabulary of reporting of the crimes charted a wild uncertainty about their significance, as to what they were confessing about human nature. The crimes were described, variously and often in the same paragraph, as "bestial," "demonic," "monstrous," "primitive," "diabolical," "barbarous," and, of course, "inhuman." In the murders themselves and in the reactions to them (including mobbings and persecutions), it seemed as if Victorian society spewed out its disgust and perplexity with its own condition, a hysterical symptomization of what was "radically separate, loathsome . . . unapproachable [yet] intimate" and which sought in the narratives of the period a "way out through speech."

If the murders had occurred two years earlier it would have appeared that *The Strange Case of Dr Jekyll and Mr Hyde* was written in response to them. As it was, Stevenson's story predated them, perhaps even called them into being; certainly there are uncanny echoes of the story in the murders, particularly in the persistent suspicion that the murderer was a doctor. A woman interviewed immediately after Kelly's death described how she had been accosted by a man wearing "a black silk hat, a black coat, and speckled trousers," who carried "a black shiny bag about a foot in depth and a foot and a half in length" (*The Times*, Saturday 10 November 1888: 7); this is how Jekyll would have appeared, a mysterious and even sinister figure, particularly to those whose poverty kept them awed and in ignorance of medical practice.

The conception of *The Strange Case of Dr Jekyll and Mr Hyde* was, in its way, as bloody and violent as the murders it foretold. A grotesque reworking of Romantic narrative motifs, the story originated in a nightmare from which Stevenson was woken by his wife. He wrote down the story "with feverish activity," and then rewrote it in even greater haste, all the while hemorrhaging so badly that he could not speak and had to communicate his wishes by means of a slate and pencil. The written text which was expelled, abjected, one might say, with such inspirational violence from its author, poses, as its title suggests, both a medical problem and a detective puzzle. It is also a confessional document which undertakes, as Foucault puts it, the "infinite task of extracting from the depths of oneself, in between the words, a truth . . . like a shimmering mirage."

Stephen Heath has pointed out that Hyde's two victims are the sacred figures of purity and reverence of the Victorian moral scene: a little girl "of maybe eight or ten" and "an aged and beautiful gentleman with white hair" (Heath 1986: 93). The other casualty of Hyde's breaking out is the civilized male companionship that Jekyll, Utterson, and Lanyon have enjoyed: "pleasant dinners . . . all intelligent, reputable men, and all judges of good wine" (Stevenson 1924: 17). By the end, only the appropriately named Utterson, safeguarded, apparently, by being "backward in sentiment . . . lean, long, dusty, dreary [and therefore] somehow lovable," remains alive to tell the story; Jekyll and Lanyon, lusty men given to concealed "irregularities" in their respectable lives, are destroyed, victims of the hypocrisy, the "profound duplicity," that Stevenson claimed was the story's moral:

> The harm was in Jekyll, because he was a hypocrite – not because he was fond of women . . . The hypocrite let out the beast in Hyde – who is no more sensual than another, but who is the essence of cruelty and malice, and selfishness and cowardice: and these are the diabolical in man – not this poor wish to have a woman . . . But the sexual field and the business field are perhaps the two best fitted for the display of cruelty and cowardice and selfishness. That is what people see; and they confound.
>
> (Maixner 1981: 231)

In 1887 Stevenson wrote an article for the *Contemporary Review* which provides a gloss on the strange case he had fictionalized a year before. Entitled "The Day After Tomorrow," it is an attack on socialist thinking, not simply the flag-waving variety of Hyndman but what Stevenson calls "the stall-fed life of the successful ant-heap," that is, interventionist welfarism which flies in the face of Darwinian principles:

> Our race has not been strained for all these ages through that sieve of dangers we call Natural Selection, to sit down with patience in the tedium of safety; the voices of its fathers call it forth. Already in our society as it exists, the bourgeois is too much cottoned about for any zest in living; he sits in his parlour out of reach of any danger, often out of reach of any vicissitude but one of health; and there he yawns.
> (Stevenson 1924: 477–8)

In this state of boredom, humanity will resort for its excitement to "the pleasures of intrigue and sedition," to a gratuitous violence such as the Whitechapel murders displayed. The moral is clear: polite, civilized behavior, particularly bourgeois behavior, will break out, as it has done in the figure of Mr Hyde.

The Strange Case of Dr Jekyll and Mr Hyde is, therefore, in the manner of Freud's cases, a "hysterical" text which searches, through the act of confession, for an atavistic truth about human nature which is discovered, with apparent certainty, in the ape-like hands of Mr Hyde and his tigerish mauling of the elderly man of science, whom, with fitting retribution, he murders. "Let the ape and tiger die," Tennyson had written nearly fifty years earlier, but here they are alive and well and dwelling in the streets of London and the dispensaries of respectable doctors. But the problem with this discovery is that it is a curiously hollow one, indeed, as the quotation from Tennyson illustrates, an old-fashioned one, belonging to a previous age of humanist disillusion. There is also the question of what Hyde actually does that is so terrible; when his crimes are scrutinized, they appear either few and simple or so unspecified as to be meaningless: "What he told me in the next hour I cannot bring myself to set on paper" (Stevenson 1924: 49), says Lanyon, registering an inadequacy that, as Heath has pointed out, Stevenson's contemporaries were puzzled by. It was left to life, in the particulars of the Whitechapel murders, to fill in the details of the "diabolical in man" that Hyde represents.

What nevertheless makes *The Strange Case of Dr Jekyll and Mr Hyde* a compelling story is the confessional mode in which it is cast, the process of uncovering the secret, what Foucault calls "the slow surfacing of confidential statements," a peeling away of meanings, a dance of the seven veils of human depravity which leads to no consummation but, like the dream of Ellis's invert, "seemed to reach its goal in the excitement it caused." Like Kurtz's "horror" in *Heart of Darkness*, the secret itself is nothing, or at least not anything that the mind can be brought "to set on paper"; what is important is the journey to the secret, the act of confession itself. Just as Hyde wears clothes made for a much larger man, so his crimes are mystifyingly enlarged by a confessional narrative structure in which time, place, and utterance replicate themselves in lingering disclosure and uncanny repetition. *The Strange Case* is a story of doubles, of there being two of everything or of things being told twice over: there are two doors to Jekyll's house, and two crimes; there are always two men – Utterson and Enfield, Utterson and Lanyon, Utterson and Guest – in dialogue; there are two written confessions, Lanyon's and Jekyll's; and when Utterson and Poole break into Jekyll's cabinet to discover his suicide, as they search for him what they see is

> the cheval-glass, into whose depth they looked with involuntary horror. But it was so turned as to show them nothing but the rosy glow playing on the roof, the fire sparkling in a hundred repetitions along the glazed front of the presses, and their own pale and fearful countenances stooping to look in.
>
> (Stevenson 1924: 46)

It is a hall of mirrors in which Henry Jekyll discovers, when he looks upon Edward Hyde, that "This, too, was myself," an exquisitely solipsistic exercise in which the confessionist both asks the questions and gives the answers, is both father and son: "I saw my life whole," says Jekyll, "from the days of childhood, when I had walked with my father's hand [to] the damned horrors of the evening [and] the crowd of hideous images and sounds with which my memory swarmed against me." In the notebook jottings which he makes in the weeks before his death, the words "double" and "total failure" repeatedly occur and these seem less to point to an ultimate depravity as to recognize an absence where the horror should be and around which the confession is woven.

Stephen Heath says that, despite Stevenson's disavowal, and their minimal place in the story (primarily as street-walkers), it is women, and what they make men do, that creates the need for Hyde's existence; in other words, sex is not only perverse itself but also the cause of the even greater perversity of hypocrisy. But this too simply explains a story which is at pains to defer explanation and which finally denies the perverse Darwinian sublime it has all along promised. When Poole and Utterson break into Jekyll's cabinet they find Hyde dead and his secrets with him; they also find three documents: a letter directing Utterson to a document he already has, a sealed packet to be read after the first document has been read, and a will in which Hyde's name has been replaced by Utterson's and by which Utterson becomes Jekyll/Hyde's beneficiary and heir, like Conrad's Marlow, the one to whom the legacy of confession is entrusted, burdened by its mystery and tainted by its implications. If the shadows of women flicker in the margins of *The Strange Case*, they do so not as a source of moral evil but as a threatened indeterminacy of meaning which confession strives to expel. To confer meaning is the *raison d'être* of confession, a self-identifying, father-son exchange of cultural values in which women serve a marginal purpose. Though it courts oblivion more overtly, this is as true of an admittedly perverse confession such as *The Strange Case* as it is of "normal" confessions; particularly in such a text, women remain out in the streets, behind doors, or concealed in "irregularities." " 'Once . . . I heard it weeping,' " says Poole, " 'Weeping like a woman or a lost soul,' " but what the weeping meant, or even what "it" was, and what relation it bore to the mutilated body of Mary Jane Kelly – all this remains secret behind the closed door of Jekyll's laboratory. *The Strange Case* transforms "it" into an abject confession in which "an opaque and forgotten life . . . Not me. Not that," has become "a primer of my culture."

Like *The Strange Case of Dr Jekyll and Mr Hyde, The Island of Dr Moreau* (1896) is a double confession, a confession of knowledge and power (Moreau's) enfolded within the narrative of a naïve and accidental confessionist, Prendick, who is beguiled and infected by the horrors he has learned. The background to the story is the passing of the Cruelty to Animals Act of 1876 whereby licenses for animal experimentation came under the control of the Home Office. The Act contained, amongst other matter, a clause which stated that all experiments were subject to the pain rule, which prohibited "severe pain which is likely to endure." As was pointed out by the anti-vivisectionists, this rule was open to considerable abuse and it is as its blatant abuser that Dr Moreau has been expelled from England and now has his own island with its House of Pain where, by subjecting them to torturous surgery, he attempts to turn animals into men.

The story is, of course, written under the shadow of Darwinian theories (there is even a Dr Moreau mentioned by Darwin in *The Expression of the Emotions in Man and Animals* as one of his predecessors in animal physiology) and Moreau is a kind of Darwinian God: "so irresponsible, so utterly careless," and also incompetent, a God who has been dissatisfied with instinctual behavior yet has been unable to replace it with a creature of true rationality:

> First one animal trait, then another creeps to the surface . . . I can see through it all, see into their very souls, and see nothing but the souls of beasts, beasts that perish – anger, and the lusts to live and gratify themselves.
>
> (Wells 1962: 112–13)

Moreau's confession is different from Jekyll's in that it is not an admission of crimes but a confession in the sense of being a declaration of belief. Like Jekyll's, however, it is exacted under pressure from an outsider demanding explanation, who learns an unpalatable truth, in

Prendick's case that there is not only an ineradicable link between humans and animals (as Darwin had repeatedly pointed out) but that any process which attempts to refine the link has involved, has to involve, suffering: "Each time I dip a living creature into the bath of burning pain, I say, This time I will burn out all the animal, this time I will make a rational creature of my own" (ibid.: 112). It is apparent that by 1896, the date of *The Island of Dr Moreau*, the full horror of the Darwinian message had been imaginatively ingested, as Dr Moreau's appearance suggests. He too is a venerable figure of the Victorian scene, not unlike the gentlemanly scientist whom Hyde murders, not unlike Darwin: "a white-faced, white-haired old man, with calm eyes [who] might have passed muster among a hundred other comfortable old men" (ibid.: 114). In Dr Moreau's calm eyes, as in Darwin's calm prose, is spelled out the epistemological import of a theory of Natural Selection which entails, in Darwin's words, "Divergence of Character and Extinction of less-improved forms" (Darwin 1968: 459). The story also brings into focus a recognition that unless governed by fear of retribution, the (literal, in the case of Moreau's humanoids) construct we call human inescapably reverts to animality.

Yet, like Hyde's crimes, the actual substance of Moreau's revelations is hardly new, as the story's strong debt to a precursor text, *Gulliver's Travels*, suggests. Like *The Strange Case* it is the confessional wrappings of *The Island of Dr Moreau*, and the absences they both intimate and conceal, which contain its fascination. The encasing confession, Prendick's, is, like Jekyll's and Lanyon's, now a dead man's message to the future, and his too is a confession of despair, of an ordinary man alienated from human society so that on his return to London, the urban poor strike him as similar to the humanized animals he has left on the island, and his final words place the future in a devitalized, ahistorical cosmos:

> I see few strangers, and have but a small household. I spend many of the clear nights in the study of astronomy. There is . . . a sense of infinite peace and protection in the glittering hosts of heaven . . . in the vast and eternal laws of matter [where] whatever is more than animal within us must find its solace and its hope.
>
> (Wells 1962: 191–2)

Apart from Prendick's confession, the only traces of Moreau's experiments on the island are a few "curious white moths . . . and some peculiar rats." We are told this at the beginning of the story and we are also told that Prendick is dead so that the "truths" Moreau tells of the evolutionary struggles of existence are uncannily distanced, letters from the dead past of humanity. Moreau's disquieting disclosures are also diluted by a double process of confession, Moreau's impatient explanation to Prendick, which is followed by Prendick's filial echo of this explanation in his baffled and nihilistic confession. The alternatives the story finally offers are either the necessary suffering and cruelty of Moreau's prescription or its passive version in the cloistered hopelessness of Prendick's conclusion.

But what these alternatives foreclose and negate is a moment of outrage, a glimpsed breakdown of the perverse alliance of strong father and victim son in the challenge presented by Moreau's latest tortured victim, almost the only female on the island, the puma. Her cries of pain are "as if all the pain in the world had found a voice" (ibid.: 54), and in her mutilated body is summarized both the eviscerated, breastless body of Mary Jane Kelly and Kelly's undiscovered, unconfessed murderer: a retributive meaninglessness, an escape from or confusion of categories. Prendick's sighting of the puma is of

> an awful face rushing upon me, not human, not animal, but hellish, brown, seamed with red branching scars, red drops starting out upon it, and the lidless eyes ablaze . . . swathed in lint and with red-stained bandages fluttering about it.
>
> (ibid.: 141)

When Moreau's dead body is discovered, "one hand was almost severed at the wrist, and his silvery hair was dabbled with blood. His head had been battered in by the fetters of the puma" (ibid.: 151). But though Moreau is dead, his own power to tell or write his message finished, and his venerable figure besmirched, the abreactive potency of his words is disseminated through the secondary confession of his weak Darwinian son, Prendick.

"The meaning of woman is to be meaningless," Otto Weininger was to write in 1903, eight years after *Studies on Hysteria* and seven after *The Island of Dr Moreau*, in *Sex and Character*, the weirdly confessional (and suicidal) document that is a final leave-taking of the nineteenth century:

> [Woman] represents negation, the opposite pole from the Godhead, the other possibility of humanity. [Thus] is to be explained the deepest fear of man; the fear of the woman, which is the fear of unconsciousness, the alluring abyss of annihilation.
>
> (Weininger 1906: 298)

Weininger's book is a desperate attempt to shore up the crumbling structures of nineteenth-century thought, to be a "primer of culture" in offering what he calls "the germs of a world scheme . . . allied most closely with the conceptions of Plato, Kant and Christianity" (ibid.: xi). His advice is that although women are intrinsically without morality or will or sense of self, the "germ of good" must be assumed by men to be present in them; for this to happen both men and women must give up their sexual selves so that women will cease to be womanly. In giving this advice, his book "may be considered as the greatest honour ever paid to women" (ibid.: 339); if Freud's confessions implicate women the more thoroughly in the passivity of heterosexual romance, Weininger is the new man who denies the heterosexual relationship altogether. But for both men, women must be explained and confessed, their hysterical symptoms the "dark continent" or "unlimited negation" that impels the abreactive function carried out by the confessional narrative. If, as Weininger says, woman "herself is the sin which is a possibility in man," and that sin is "the abyss of annihilation," then male confessions of that sin of meaninglessness are exercises in abjection, self-sustaining, and self-justifying, question and answer. The female presences in *The Strange Case* and in *The Island of Dr Moreau* are, as Stevenson intimated, not a cause of the horror but its symptom, which the act of confession seeks to soothe and smoothe away. Whilst two men, father and son, keep the confidential dialogue flowing, even, or particularly, a dialogue of perversion, the "world scheme" is kept in place.

WORKS CITED

Darwin, Charles (1921) *The Expression of the Emotions in Man and Animals*, London: John Murray. First published 1872
—— (1968) *The Origin of Species by Means of Natural Selection or The Preservation of Favoured Races in the Struggle for Life*, Harmondsworth: Penguin. First published 1859.
Doyle, Sir Arthur Conan (1981) *The Adventures of Sherlock Holmes*, London: Penguin. First published 1893.
Ellis, Havelock (1936) *Studies in the Psychology of Sex, Volume II, Part Two, Sexual Inversion*, New York: Random House. First published 1897.
Foucault, Michel (1984) *History of Sexuality: Volume I. An Introduction*, Harmondsworth: Penguin.
Freud, Sigmund [and Breuer, Joseph] (1955) *The Complete Psychological Works, Volume II: Studies on Hysteria*, London: Hogarth Press. First published 1893–5.
Heath, Stephen (1986) "Psychopathia Sexualis: Stevenson's *Strange Case*," *Critical Quarterly*, 28 (1 and 2): 93–108.
Kristeva, Julia (1982) *The Powers of Horror: An Essay on Abjection*, trans. Leon S. Roudiez, New York: Columbia University Press.
Maixner, Paul (ed.) (1981) *Robert Louis Stevenson: The Critical Heritage*, London, Boston and Henley: Routledge & Kegan Paul.
Marcus, Steven (1984) *Freud and the Culture of Psychoanalysis*, Boston: Allen & Unwin.
Stevenson, Robert Louis (1924) *The Strange Case of Dr Jekyll and Mr Hyde. Fables, Other Stories and Fragments*, London: Heinemann. First published 1886.
Webb, Beatrice (1971) *My Apprenticeship*, Harmondsworth: Penguin. First published 1926.
Weininger, Otto (1906) *Sex and Character*, London: Heinemann.
Wells, H. G. (1962) *The Island of Dr Moreau*, Harmondsworth: Penguin. First published 1896.

Chapter 7

Reading the Gothic revival
"History" and *Hints on Household Taste*

Christina Crosby

Noting the nineteenth-century rage to make all knowledge historical and to make history the origin and end of man, Christina Crosby turns her attention closely to the Gothic revival in order to argue that history is not only in style, but style is itself history. Crosby, who draws on theories of Derrida, Schor, Kant, and Marx, takes seriously the Victorian interest in material history, some *thing* both palpable and concrete. Investigating texts by Pugin, Ruskin, and Eastlake, she argues that in the historicist aesthetic of the Gothic revival (which sees commodities as false and history as true) history nevertheless itself becomes a commodity and a fetish. In thinking to establish a masculine history and in reforming taste, the revival also forms "woman," associating the feminine with unredeemed commodification, ornament, commercial value.

* * *

History, as those who study Victorian culture know, was very much in style in the nineteenth century. Historical novels and narrative histories, Pre-Raphaelite art, antiquarian and archaeological research, the restoration and preservation of old buildings, a revival of Gothic architecture and Gothic design, all were in fashion during Victoria's reign. These phenomena are part of a move to make all knowledge historical, to make something called "history" the origin and end of "man." Indeed, history in the nineteenth century is endowed with remarkable explanatory powers, for a certain concept of history becomes the truth of "man" – itself a newly conceptualized category, said to be universal because historical. Man, it is said, has his ends in a history which is both the mark of his limits, his finitude, and the guarantee of his ongoing life, the *telos* of mankind. As Carlyle writes in his essay, "On History,"

> [We] do nothing but enact history, we say little but recite it: nay, rather, in that widest sense, our whole spiritual life is built thereon. For strictly considered, what is all Knowledge too but recorded Experience, and product of History, of which, therefore, Reasoning and Belief, no less than Action and Passion, are essential materials?
> (Sheridan 1971: 51)

Given the profound significance of history so conceived, its foundational status, what might be the consequences of the Victorian stylization of history? For in nineteenth-century Britain history is not only in style, but, as I will argue, style is history. Vocabulary and grammar, the disposition of details, the effects of their order, their arrangement in space, become history. This is not to trivialize history or the nineteenth-century investment in it. On the contrary, it is to take seriously the Victorian production of history as some *thing* which is visible, palpable, and concrete, materialized in the stones of Venice, its grand palaces, for example; and spoken by the "grammar of ornament," the shape of a sideboard, the pattern in carpets, the design of wallpapers. "History" is the foundation of "our whole spiritual life"; history is a matter of fashion and furnishings. This history, one could say, is "a very queer thing, abounding in metaphysical subtleties and theological niceties," as Marx observes of the commodity, that crucial sign of capitalism (Marx 1967: 71). Reading some of the texts of the Gothic revival is one way to approach this problematic "history," for in the historicist aesthetic of the revival, style is fetishized and history is commodified – indeed, history "itself" is a commodity fetish.

The Gothic revival has been differently periodized, but may loosely be said to stretch from Walpole's "Gothick" elaborations of Strawberry Hill through the Arts and Crafts movement at the end of the nineteenth century. My concern is not, however, with large questions of periodization or patterns of influence within the movement, but with specific texts – A. Welby Pugin's *An Apology for Christian Architecture in England* (1843), John Ruskin's *The Stones of Venice* (1851), Owen Jones's *The Grammar of Ornament* (1852), Charles Eastlake's *Hints on Household Taste in Furniture, Upholstery and Other Details* (1869) and his *History of the Gothic Revival* (1872) – their categories of analysis, the truths they declare, the articulation which binds together the profundities of Ruskin with the practical advice Eastlake proffers to "housekeepers or others about to furnish." These various texts are all concerned with beauty, style, and taste; all call for aesthetic reform along historical principles; all comment more or less critically on the corrupting influences the modern market-place exerts on art. Theirs is an historicist aesthetics in which beauty and truth, the truth of beauty, the truth of buildings from foundation to spire, are to be known as historical beauties and truths.

"The history of architecture is the history of the world," Pugin declares in his *Apology*; architecture embodies history, is the representation of history (Pugin 1969: 4). "Architecture is the material expression of the wants, the faculties, and the sentiments, of the age in which it is created,"

Jones writes nine years later (Jones 1982: 5). By 1862 the idea is a truism, a reference any writer on architecture could assume. So in an essay in the *Builder*, Mellard Reide wonders how the antiquary of the future will ever make sense out of nineteenth-century London, declaring:

> he will be sorely troubled to [illuminate] the history of the English nation from its writings in brick and stone. If the history of architecture be the history of the human mind, his researches will indicate a very chaotic mental state of the present generation.
>
> (Bright 1984: 17)

Middle-class Victorians and the Victorian elite, conscious of their own efforts to read the architectural "writing" of innumerable archaeological digs at home and abroad in the empire, worried in the future anterior, wondered what their buildings will be thought to have said about them, asked the question of the hour, "A New Style: How Can It Be Found?" (Bright 1984: 17)

Style is the legibility of architecture, "the form that expression [of the wants, the faculties, and the sentiments of the age] takes," as Jones says (1982: 5). Style is thus of paramount importance, for it speaks the truth of the historical "age," expresses the epoch. According to Ruskin, buildings speak; one of the "practical duties" of a building is "talking, as the duty of monuments or tombs, to record facts and express feelings; or of churches, temples, public edifices, treated as books of history, to tell such history clearly and forcibly" (Ruskin 1867: I, 35). Such talking is done through the disposition of details, the ornaments which are the vocabulary of a building and which make up its particular style. Ruskin finds that the stones of Venice speak to him, telling of the rise and fall of a great mercantile city: "as she was in her strength the centre of the pure currents of Christian architecture, so she is in her decline the source of the Renaissance," a corrupt style correspondent with the "national criminality" of a Venice driven by "her commercial interest" and devoid of religious feeling (ibid.: I, 24, 6–7). This Venice is a warning to England, another great commercial power whose architecture is, according to Ruskin and many others, sadly in need of reform.

For Ruskin, the Christian architecture of Venice in its glory is recognizable by the "moral elements" expressed in Gothic style, that is "1. Savageness. 2. Changefulness. 3. Naturalism. 4. Grotesqueness. 5. Rigidity. 6. Redundance" (ibid.: II, 151). A savage, changeful, natural, grotesque, and rigid redundance characterizes the Gothic, makes up the Gothic style of exfoliating details, distorted yet naturalistic ornament, proliferating points and spires. Foundations, walls, roofs are functional, and must serve their functions well – which is why Ruskin begins his book on architecture by explaining these basic parts – but he finds that a building speaks most eloquently through its ornamentation, through the design given to basic structures. Ornament, then, more than plan or elevation, is what makes a building intelligible and makes legible the history not only of the building itself but of its whole epoch. The design of a capital, of a door jamb, of ornamental sculpture, the vaulting of a roof and turn of a drip-spout are to be read, for each detail tells the truth of its historical moment.

Ornament is essential to style, is a matter of detail, in the case of Gothic style, a matter of extravagant, expansive, terrific details dispersed over the whole building. The changefulness and redundance, the apparent endlessness of the Gothic is what attracts Ruskin, and what attracted Hegel before him. Naomi Schor, in her remarkable study of the aesthetics of the detail, observes that Hegel was drawn to the apparent inexhaustibility of the Gothic. She turns to his *Aesthetics*, in which he writes of the Gothic cathedral:

> everything is lost in the greatness of the whole. It has and displays a definite purpose; but in its grandeur and sublime peace it is lifted above anything purely utilitarian into an infinity in itself . . . particularization [Partikularisation], diversity, and variety gain the fullest scope, but without letting the whole fall apart into mere trifles [Besonderheiten] and accidental details [Einzelheiten].

> (Schor 1987: 28–9)

Schor argues that this is an aesthetics of "definalized details," that is, details "not having a finality, a goal, a *telos*." Such details have no end, no goal, no function or purpose of their own, but are "sublimated," as she puts it, "by the totality into which they are absorbed" (ibid.: 29). The transcendental endlessness of beauty which lacks mundane purpose has since Kant been understood as an essential feature of art; Hegel's praise for the Gothic, and Ruskin's too, celebrate this lack, this loss of an endpoint which signifies participation in infinity.[1] So Ruskin writes of the Gothic that

> the vital principle is not the love of *Knowledge*, but the love of *Change*. It is that strange *disquietude* of the Gothic spirit that is its greatness; that restlessness of the dreaming mind, that wanders hither and thither among the niches, and flickers feverishly around the pinnacles, and frets and fades in labyrinthine knots and shadows along wall and roof, and yet is not satisfied, nor shall be satisfied. . . . the work of the Gothic art is fretwork still, and it can neither rest in, nor from, its labour, but must pass on, sleeplessly, until its love of change shall be pacified for ever in the change that must come alike on them that wake and them that sleep.

> (1867: II, 181)

Such beauty has nothing to do with satisfaction, is defined as beautiful precisely because it is endless, definalized. Yet definalized details, while without a goal of their own, nonetheless are sublimated into a whole as they pass on to an infinity. Thus definalized details are not trifling or accidental, even as they are without purposiveness.

This aesthetic can, as Schor says, "[praise] dispersion and [recognize] the beauty of the parcellary" while declaring, in Hegel's words, that "the majesty of art brings back into simple unity everything thus divided up and partitioned" (1987: 29).[2] Organized yet without purpose, the Gothic is a wonderful instance of "finality without end," a style celebrated by an aesthetic discourse which makes lack (the lack of an end) central to its assertion of wholeness, the absolute of infinity (Derrida 1987: 61).

Schor reads in the Hegelian aesthetic a fetishistic refusal to decide between division and unity, for Hegel both recognizes and disavows "the parcellary." The definalized yet sublimated detail is a fetish, invested with so much meaning as a prophylactic against the anomie of difference and divisions not subject to some last word, some organizing principle. The detail as fetish protects against disordered proliferation, against elements which may be stylized yet illegible, incoherent. This fetishizing of the detail is at work in Ruskin's text, for there ornament ensures the full legibility of buildings, their stylistic and therefore historical significance.

One can read the same logic at work in Owen Jones's *Grammar of Ornament*. This book is dominated by luxurious colored plates which reproduce hundreds of designs, from Egyptian friezes to Persian mosaics, Figi tattoos to Gothic tracery. Proper ornament is vital to architecture, Jones maintains, for ornament makes architecture art rather than engineering:

> ornament . . . is in all cases the very soul of an architectural monument; and by ornament alone can we judge truly of the amount of care and mind which has been devoted to the work. All else in any building may be the result of rule and compass, but by the ornament of a building we can best discover how far the architect was at the same time an artist.
>
> (1982: 82)

So persuaded is Jones of the significance of ornament that he barely mentions buildings in his study, never pictures them, lavishes all his attention on the soul of architecture. Yet he also qualifies his devotion to decorative detail, insisting that it "is most properly an accessory to architecture, and never should be allowed to usurp the place of proper structural features, or overload and disguise them . . ." (ibid.). Having warned against usurpation and lawless elaboration, Owen may then sanctify ornament and discover in decoration the soul of the building and of the builder, too – the evidence of his "care and mind."

Ornament is good, then, insofar as it is art, and it is art insofar as it does not pursue an end of its own, but is an integral part of the building, lifted up "into an infinity in itself" (Hegel). The logic of sublimation is here at work, producing particularity only to subsume it into generality, producing specificity, the particularity which is a definable style, only to insist on infinity. Legible as style, architecture is always detailed, historically specific, embodying a certain historical moment and representing man's historical life; as Ruskin says, it is "born of his necessities and expressive of his nature." Yet that "moment" is never an end in itself, but part of unending historical time (just as man is), a universal History stretching toward infinity. "History" is thus both specific and universal, particular and general, the first always subsumed in the second, just as beautiful ornament is both profusely particular and incorporated into an encompassing totality, the accessory and the soul of architecture. This is history as a Gothic cathedral: "particularization, diversity, and variety gain the fullest scope, but without letting the whole fall apart into mere trifles and accidental details" (Hegel); "the vital principle is not the love of *Knowledge*, but the love of *Change*" (Ruskin).

The endlessness of art (finality without end) and the ends of man in history converge in the revival's celebration of Gothic as the most aesthetic and most historical of all architecture. Extravagantly detailed, adorned with savage and grotesque ornaments designed from nature, Gothic buildings are thought to represent most fully man's finite being, his particularity, his mortal imperfections, *and* his capacity for the infinite, his participation in an all-inclusive history.

Architecture, then, is expressive of man's historical nature, and the "soul" of a building, its ornament, is the measure of the architect's devotion to his work. Indeed, work is of crucial importance in the writings of the revivalists; it is in man's nature as an historical being to labor, they say, and evidence of labor bears witness to this distinguishing human feature. "Care and mind," as Jones puts it, must be visible in the design and execution of a builder's work, for only then can one judge it beautiful and declare the architect an artist.

So in his *Grammar of Ornament* Jones is at pains to ensure that his book will be used properly, that the "rising generation" of architects who are his intended audience will prove themselves equal to their historical task. He warns repeatedly that the hundreds of designs from ancient epochs and remote civilizations collected and reproduced in his "grammar" are assembled

> not that they should be slavishly copied, but that artists should, by an attentive examination of the principles which pervade all the works of the past, which have excited universal admiration, be led to the creation of forms equally beautiful.
>
> (Jones 1982: 156)

Copying is forbidden, for then imaginative elaboration is foreclosed, art becomes mechanical repetition and the artist but a slave to patterns not of his invention or era. The labor of imaginative effort alone can produce a properly historical, timely, and timeless style.

Ruskin's text famously takes up these questions, making mental and physical labor the source of artistic value:

> All art which is worth its room in this world . . . is *art which proceeds from an individual mind, working through instruments which assist, but do not supersede, the muscular action of the human hand, upon the materials which most tenderly receive, and most securely retain, the impressions of such human labor.* And the value of every work of art is exactly in the ratio of the quantity of humanity which has been put into it, and legibly expressed upon it for ever.
>
> (1867: I, 381; emphasis in original)

On these grounds Ruskin builds his defense of Gothic as the architecture which is most fully endowed with humanity, which affords the widest scope to the imaginative labor of the artisan, which is most human. And on these grounds Ruskin attacks the nineteenth-century system of manufacturing which "enslaves" laborers in order to produce standardized objects, the "accurate mouldings, and perfect polishings, and unerring adjustments of the seasoned wood and tempered steel" which furnish "this English room of yours": "If you will have that precision out of them, and make their fingers measure degrees like cog-wheels, and their arms strike curves like compasses, you must unhumanize them" (ibid.: II, 162, 161). Christianity, and the architecture of Christianity which is the Gothic, was free of such degradation in medieval times, Ruskin declares. "[H]aving recognized, in small things as well as great, the individual value of every soul," Christians create a correspondent style: "they thus receive the results of the labour of inferior minds; and out of fragments full of imperfection, and betraying that imperfection in every touch, indulgently raise up a stately and unaccusable whole" (ibid.: II, 160).

Imperfect by mechanical rule, Gothic architecture is *"capable of perpetual novelty"* (ibid.: II, 153; emphasis in original), the artist never copying either a pre-ordained design or exactly imitating a natural object, but fertilely inventing and executing. In Ruskin's view, the decorative accumulation of Gothic has nothing to do with the profane accumulation of the market-place, for there both art and men are made the means to an end, and objects are created for the sole purpose of being sold. Ruskin would revive the Gothic – if not in copying medieval style, then in returning to its principles of organization – declaring that the "evil" of his age can be met only by a right understanding, on the part of all classes, of what kinds of labour are good for men, raising them, and making them happy . . . and by . . . determined demand for the products and results of healthy and ennobling labour.

(ibid.: II, 165)

Ruskin attacks manufacturing and the division of labor, the mechanical production and reproduction of buildings and furnishings, of commodities of all sorts, on the grounds that objects so produced have no soul and thus little beauty. Pugin, in his *Apology for the Revival of Christian Architecture in England* is equally appalled at a "wretched state of things" in which architects are driven by the demands of the market, submit to the whim of their employers, and pick up styles from all times and places: "Styles are now *adopted* instead of *generated*, and ornament and design *adapted to*, instead of *originated by*, the edifices themselves" (Pugin 1969: 2). This, he says, is "the *carnival* of architecture: . . . the Turk and the Christian, the Egyptian and the Greek, the Swiss and the Hindoo, march side by side, and mingle together" (ibid.). For instance, the new cemetery companies "have perpetrated the grossest absurdities": the entrance gateway to the cemetery is designed not to encourage reflection on man's temporal and spiritual ends, but

for the grand display of the company's enterprise and taste, as being well calculated from its position to induce persons to patronize the undertaking by the purchase of shares or graves. This [gateway] is generally Egyptian, probably from some associations between the word catacomb, which occurs in the prospectus of the company, and the discoveries of Belzoni on the banks of the Nile; and nearly opposite the Green Man and Dog public house, in the center of a dead wall (which serves as a cheap medium of advertisement for blacking and shaving-strop manufacturers), is a cement caricature of the entrance to an Egyptian temple . . . while, to prevent any mistake, some such words as "New Economical Compressed Grave Cemetery Company" are inscribed in *Grecian* capitals along the frieze.

(ibid.: 12)

Pugin ascribes the incoherence of architecture to the ascendancy of material over spiritual ends, which produces the jumbled styles of nineteenth-century buildings. Such eclecticism, is, according to his revivalist logic, anti-historical, for every element of the structure pursues its own end stylistically, and all together pursue the degraded function of advertising a commodity, economical compressed graves. There is no finality, no legible stylistic order to the details; there is no endlessness, no "unaccusable whole" which imperfectly but nobly realizes the infinite. To combat this profanation of art requires the revival of what Pugin recognizes as historical architecture expressive of man's true ends. Pugin, perhaps even more explicitly than Ruskin, articulates together in an indissoluble bond the endlessness of the aesthetic and the endlessness of history, both profoundly in opposition to the profane ends of exchange, as man himself is said to be opposed. Here the commodification of architecture, as much as the commodified ornaments and furnishings Ruskin reads as "signs of slavery in our England" are said to interpose between man and his proper ends, degrading men and the works they make.[3]

In 1851 "The Great Exhibition of the Industry of All Nations" opened in a vast 14-acre "Crystal Palace" made of glass and iron. Thirty-two nations had displays in the hall, though fully half of the building was devoted to British goods. In the British half, visitors passed clocks and globes, locomotives set on tracks, dioramas of cities, displays of furs and fabrics, tools and machinery, sculpture and furniture, finding themselves at last at the opening of a remarkable little enclosure, a "Mediaeval Court" designed by Pugin. What is Pugin doing setting up in Babylon, in the midst of a positive carnival of commodities, a spectacular display promiscuously mingling together goods and styles from the world over?

Like all the revivalists, he is trying to educate the English, and Pugin's Court, no less than his *Apology* or Ruskin's *Stones*, is an effort to reform society by reforming taste. "If I could obtain the public ear," Ruskin writes,

> and the principles I have advocated were carried into general practice, porphery and serpentine would be given [to architects] instead of limestone and bricks; instead of taverns and shop-fronts they would have to build goodly churches and noble dwelling houses, and for every stunted Grecism and stucco Romanism, into which they are now forced to shape their palsied thoughts, they would be asked to raise whole streets of bold, and rich, and living architecture.
>
> (1867: I, 379)

Such must be the promise of Pugin's medieval enclave, standing as a reproach to the very Crystal Palace in which it is enclosed. Such certainly is the premise of his *Contrasts: or, A Parallel between the Noble Edifices of the Middle Ages, and Corresponding Buildings of the Present Day: Shewing the Present Decay of Taste* (1841; Pugin 1973).

Yet despite the revivalist polemics against the dehumanizing effects of mechanized production, the degradation of art by exchange, and the corruption of taste by the dictates of fashion – and despite the supposedly elevating example of the Mediaeval Court – the historicist aesthetics of the revival are unwittingly inscribed within the very logic of commodification it opposes. The Court indeed takes its place among the 14,000 other booths of the Exhibition and contributes to the commodity spectacle, not because it is overwhelmed by its surroundings but because it, too, offers something for consumption, the "history" which it makes visible, palpable, graspable, *there*. That is, history is made available for consumption in the "pointed" architecture that Pugin so vigorously promoted, in the style of the structure and the design of its furnishings. Not that anyone could buy this history at the Exhibition; nothing was for sale there. But as Thomas Richards has argued in his study of Victorian commodity culture, the fact that one could only look further reified the goods displayed, directed the gaze of the beholder "to [their] immediate sensual attributes," endorsed their seemingly inherent value (Richards 1990: 38).

Stone by stone, ornament by ornament, detail by detail "history" is made concrete by the revivalists. This concreteness guarantees that history can be preserved, restored, constructed, and reconstructed, as in Pugin's work. And once history is conceptualized as some thing, it mingles with all the other things which are pouring into England from its empire, being manufactured at home in shops and factories, and collected for display in the Crystal Palace. There, as Richards notes, Victorians found unity in diversity and in terms strikingly similar to the revivalist appreciation of the Gothic. The *Illustrated London News* judges that "the whole work comes well together, and, from whatever point it is viewed, the vastness of the structure, the extent of the arrangements, and the variety of objects displayed, all go to make one complete whole" (Richards 1990: 30). Perpetual novelty and abundance, a vast quantity of detail which nonetheless makes one complete whole: this is the effect of the commodity spectacle. The fetishism of commodities follows from the abstractions specific to capitalism, the generalization of exchange, the reduction of labor to labor-power, so that "the relations connecting the labor of one individual with that of the rest appear, not as direct social relations between individuals at work, but as they really are, material relations between persons and social relations between things" (Marx 1967: 73). Marx insists that the fetishism of commodities is no delusion or error, but the reality of capitalism, the reality of its representations. The Exhibition stages this reality; there the "uniform social status" of commodities produces the "one complete whole" of the show's enormous diversity.

What, then, of the revivalist enthusiasm for definalized yet sublimated details, the fetishistic investment in abundant and novel ornaments, all so different yet all the same – all speaking the truth of history? In this case the fetish is, as Schor says, a refusal to decide, a way of seeing and not seeing differences; it is a way of producing history as an expressive totality. This aesthetic fetishism is not the same as the fetishism of commodities, which as Marx insists is not an error, mistake, or delusion, but a process, a complex of relations to be read. The revivalists, of course, see commodities as false and history as true; they fetishize history and find in it the cure for commodification. Here is a world of difference separating revivalist historicism from *Capital*, for in Marx's text history "as such" never appears. For such a history can only repeat – not read – the abstractions of capitalism.

The revival thus produces "history" as both a fetish and a commodity. Here Pugin's career, represented by a few biographical details, may once more be instructive. His first work was making medieval designs for "Messrs. Randell and Bridge, the well-known goldsmiths" (Eastlake 1970: 147) and collaborating with the King's upholsterers in designing new furniture, in Gothic style, for Windsor Castle. Next he painted scenery at Covent Garden Theatre, distinguishing himself by his reproduction of medieval architecture in the scenes for an opera which was set in the feudal past. Pursuing architecture, he "embarked on sundry speculations by which he undertook to supply carved work in stone and wood to those who required it for the ornamental portion of their works," but was soon brought into "pecuniary difficulties," as Eastlake reports in his *History of the Gothic Revival*, and barely avoided debtors' prison (Eastlake 1970: 148). Finally, as a practicing architect and polemical author he had considerable success, from his collaboration with Barry on the ornament of the Houses of Parliament, to the building of numerous churches and country houses. Ornament, especially ecclesiastical ornament and church furniture – screens, altars, censers, and so on – was his passion. "The attention which he bestowed on ecclesiastical furniture has been the means of reviving the arts of wood-carving and embroidery – and of improving the public taste in the choice of carpets and paper-hangings," Eastlake declares. "[I]n truth Pugin's influence on the progress of art manufacture may be described as more remarkable than his skill as an architect" (ibid.: 153). Indeed, there is no distinguishing between art (properly endless) and commodities like carpets and wallpapers (made for exchange) when "history" is taken to be materially present in both – when, in fact "history" *is* the details which Eastlake says Pugin found so "beguiling."

Of course, Eastlake, too, is beguiled by details, as is evident in his *Hints on Household Taste in Upholstery, Furniture, and Other Details* (Eastlake 1869). This book is a compendium of commodities: door-knockers, tiles, chairs, tables, curtains and curtain rods, rugs and carpets, wallpapers, shelves, braziers, lamps and brackets and candlesticks, vases, chiffoniers, mirrors, picture frames, beds, dishes and knives, forks and spoons, jewelry; and a catalogue of shops which supply these goods –

tiles from Messrs Maw and Co. of Salop, parquetry from Mr Arrowsmith of Bond Street, lamps from Messrs Benham and Froud of Chandos Street, and so on. In fact, the book itself may be added to the list of goods, for as the *Morning Post* says, it "will be found exceedingly useful by any person who is furnishing, and when the house is furnished, this book will do for the drawing-room table. It is a very well got up book" (Eastlake 1869: "Opinions of the Press").

In this text, as in the vastness of the Exhibition, one is first confronted with the sheer profusion of things. And everything is destined for consumption. Eastlake often appeals to his readers in fully Ruskinian terms, at times waxes quite poetic and polemical, but always in the process of giving his readers "hints" about what to buy and where to buy it. He makes his appeals in revivalist terms, reviling the corruption of taste by fashion and the desire to consume inferior goods, despising imitation Renaissance decoration – "the fat gilt cupids, the sprawling half-dressed nymphs, the heavy plaster cornices and the lifeless types of leaves and flowers which pass for ornamentation" (ibid.: 175) – inveighing against "those qualities of mere elaboration and finish which are independent of thought and manual labour" (ibid.: 95), but always to encourage consumption of objects in a different style, in the style of the properly historical Gothic. This is history as interior decoration.

To imagine history as a Gothic cathedral is one thing, as interior decoration another. Yet the effects are the same. Ruskin's remarkable investment in ornament allows him to embrace particularization while seeing an "infinite whole"; Eastlake is transfixed by objects which he sees both as items for sale and as the stuff of history "itself." Should one ask the cost of this sublimation?

What of "women"? Reading *Hints on Household Taste* allows one to calculate a certain cost which is exacted through – what else? – sexual categorization. In reforming "taste," revivalism forms "women," associates the feminine with all that resists sublimation, with the corruption of pure consumption, with unredeemed commodification.[4] "Women," then, are antithetical both to historical man and to history, and an inviolable difference between the sexes is produced to entitle the "masculine" and the "historical." Eastlake opens his book with an attack on "Materfamilias," who is in charge of furnishing the home, the consumer who buys upholstery, furniture, and the multitude of other items Eastlake takes up. She thinks she has taste, but he knows better. For instance, she likes "modern furniture" which "is essentially effeminate in form." "The ladies like it best when it comes like a new toy from the shop, fresh with recent varnish and untarnished gilding" (Eastlake 1869: 74). Eastlake, however, knows that such furniture is "in an artistic sense, worthless." Artistic value is differentiated from commercial value, from the seductive embellishments of varnish and gilding, surface decorations which have their own ends: to attract the beholder, to sell. False ornamentation is adornment which seduces by its material attraction – those gilt cupids, that gilded furniture. Nothing but finery, such objects have no artistic value, are "effeminate" because excluded by design from the endless beauty of the aesthetic and the endlessness of history. Victorian sexual categorization and the extension of commodity culture makes explicit and embodies what remains implicit in aesthetics since Kant, the linking of the feminine and "women" with profane, material detail and the articulation of man with the transcendent sublimations of art.[5] All consumers are, by the fact of consumption, feminized, as are commodities themselves.[6] Eastlake insists on this, setting himself up as the masculine reformer of this feminine domain, the advocate of a style which he believes will reform – transform – taste, and with it the systems of production and consumption. Yet he is himself entirely incorporated by interior decoration. His name becomes a household word in the 1870s, when to redecorate a house, or to furnish one in the best fashion, is to have it "Eastlaked."

One might, in a coda, look to *Middlemarch* (1871–2), that masterpiece having everything to do with history, as critics never tire of saying. Yet household taste has a part to play, too.

The plot of the novel is constructed so as to compare the various trajectories of the characters, including that of the rather effeminate Ladislaw and the undeniably virile – "tallish, dark, and clever" – Dr Lydgate. One might wonder why Ladislaw gets Dorothea and a seat in Parliament, while Lydgate is trapped in a degrading marriage and dies young. Some may say that this is Lydgate's punishment for being too much of a man, for objectifying Rosamund. He sees in her

> perfect womanhood – felt as if already breathed upon by exquisite wedded affection such as would be bestowed by an accomplished creature who venerated his high musings and momentous labours and would never interfere with them; who would create order in the home and accounts with still magic, yet keep her fingers ready to touch the lute and transform life into romance at any moment; who was instructed to the true womanly limit and not a hair's breadth beyond – docile, therefore, and ready to carry out behests which came from beyond that limit.
>
> (Eliot 1909: II, 119)

Yet this fault is but the occasion for another:

> happening the next day to accompany a patient to Brassing, he saw a dinner-service there which struck him as so exactly the right thing that

he bought it at once. It saved time to do these things just when you thought of them, and Lydgate hated ugly crockery. The dinner-service in question was expensive, but that might be in the nature of dinner-services. Furnishing was necessarily expensive; but then it had to be done only once.

(ibid.)

What we see in this entertaining narrative detail is a Lydgate beguiled by commodities, of which Rosamund on the marriage market is but one. He falls for finery – Rosamund, the crockery, the furniture, "green glasses for hock" – is driven into debt and has to pay, according to the logic of the book, with his self-respect and manly studies, his participation in properly historical life. In short, he is feminized by consumption.

Ladislaw, on the other hand, may be light of hair and slight of figure, but he produces rather than consumes. He is a painter and an author, and Eliot is nothing if not consistent in setting art against commodities. In his aesthetic pursuits (one might recall that he thinks of Dorothea as a work of art, especially when he sees her in the Vatican museum) and his detached appreciation of beauty he is indeed historical, as the plot makes perfectly clear.

Might not readers become a little wary, then, of this "history," its grounds, its costs, its ends?

NOTES

1 As Michael Sprinker writes, "the inauguration of aesthetics as a systematic discipline and the hypostatization of the aesthetic as a distinct modality of cognition . . . can be located in Kant's grounding of aesthetic judgment in models of non-referentiality . . . and in Schiller's conception of the aesthetic as a supererogatory harmonizing of the cognitive faculties that transcends the conflicts which otherwise inhere in their ordinary, or non-aesthetic operation" (1987: 11). Naomi Schor, in her "archaeology" of the aesthetic also refers to the significance of Kantian concepts of beauty as taken up by Hegel (1987: 29–32). See Derrida (1987: 15–148) for a reading of Kant's aesthetics, and especially pp. 83–118, for his discussion of *pulchritudo vaga* (free beauty) and *pulchritudo adhaerens* (adherent beauty).
2 As Schor explains, "the parcellary" is "the particular in the etymological sense of the word" (1987: 29).
3 Walter Benjamin's famous essay, "The Work of Art in the Age of Mechanical Reproduction," is obviously pertinent here. He writes that original art has an "aura" which is "its presence in time and space, its unique existence at the place it happens to be" (Benjamin 1969: 220). Art which is reproduced loses its aura because "the technique of reproduction detaches the reproduced object from the realm of tradition." Such an object comes "to meet the beholder . . . in his own particular situation," which leads "to a tremendous shattering of tradition" (ibid.: 221). Thus the discoveries of Belzoni come to England; cement reproductions of ancient Egyptian architectural details there pursue their own ends, advertising economical compressed graves, shattering history

conceived as an expressive totality in which a work of art is an attribute of a particular historical moment. The aura of finality without end is gone. Benjamin reads this shattering of tradition as a loss and a gain, seeing in it the undoing of an historicism which he resolutely opposes. Pugin, obviously, sees mechanical reproduction only as the work of the devil.
4 See Schor (1987) for a comprehensive elaboration of the relation of the feminine to the detail.
5 See Derrida (1987: 37–82) for his reading of the supplementary ornament in Kant's aesthetics.
6 See Richards (1990), especially pp. 205–48, and Rachel Bowlby (1985) for work on the relation of women and commodities.

WORKS CITED

Benjamin, Walter (1969) *Illuminations*, trans. Harry Zohn, New York: Schocken.
Bowlby, Rachel (1985) *Just Looking: Consumer Culture in Dreiser, Gissing and Zola*, New York: Methuen.
Bright, Michael (1984) *Cities Built to Music: Aesthetic Theories of the Victorian Gothic Revival*, Columbus: Ohio State University Press.
Derrida, Jacques (1987) *The Truth in Painting*, trans. Geoff Bennington and Ian McLeod, Chicago: University of Chicago Press.
Eastlake, Charles L. (1869) *Hints on Household Taste in Furniture, Upholstery, and Other Details*, London: Longmans, Green, & Co.
—— (1970) *A History of the Gothic Revival*, New York: Humanities Press. First published 1872.
Eliot, George (1909) *Middlemarch*, 3 vols, Boston: Houghton Mifflin. First published 1871–2.
Jones, Owen (1982) *The Grammar of Ornament*, New York: Van Nostrand Reinhold. First published 1852.
Marx, Karl (1967) *Capital: A Critique of Political Economy*, trans. Samuel Moore and Edward Aveling, New York: International Publishers.
Pugin, A. Welby (1969) *An Apology for the Revival of Christian Architecture in England*, New York, Humanities Press. First published 1843.
—— (1973) *Contrasts: or, A Parallel between the Noble Edifices of the Middle Ages, and Corresponding Buildings of the Present Day: Shewing the Present Decay of Taste*, New York: Humanities Press. First published 1841.
Richards, Thomas (1990) *The Commodity Culture of Victorian England: Advertising and Spectacle 1851–1914*, Stanford, CA: Stanford University Press.
Ruskin, John (1867) *The Stones of Venice*, 3 vols, London: Smith, Elder, & Co. First published 1851.
Schor, Naomi (1987) *Reading in Detail: Aesthetics and the Feminine*, New York: Methuen.
Sheridan, Alan (ed.) (1971) *Thomas Carlyle: Selected Writings*, Harmondsworth: Penguin.
Sprinker, Michael (1987) *Imaginary Relations: Aesthetics and Ideology in the Theory of Historical Materialism*, London: Verso.

Chapter 8

Excluding women
The cult of the male genius in Victorian painting

Susan P. Casteras

Susan P. Casteras here examines narrative paintings as being intimately related to ideologies of gender in the social sphere. Closely analyzing examples of the painting genre of "male genius," Casteras demonstrates how, on one hand, the genre maintains a misogynistic myth about male genius in line with prevailing beliefs about sexed giftedness and, at the same time, supports the ideology of the angel in the house. On the other hand, she argues, the feminization of the boy genius also works to subvert the ideology of the powerless, passive female. While male bonding and the exclusion of women or their relegation to the domestic sphere serve as hallmarks of this genre, many paintings also feminize the boy genius. Stressing his innocence, these paintings are eager to locate his beginnings in domestic security while pointing to his growth in the masculine realm of history, action, and fame. In this regard, they also act as calls for a resuscitation of English art and as allegories of empire. But the association of the boy genius with the feminine nurture and creativity of the mother also points to the increasing responsibility and power of the female in the Victorian domestic sphere.

* * *

In the mid- to late Victorian period artists explored and extolled the myth of "great men in history." For the most part, painters concurred with reigning interpretations of history as dominated by powerful men who made events happen and who achieved unique status in the arts and other fields of endeavor, especially invention and exploration. Indeed, art as a profession was itself dominated by male exercises of power, both in terms of the sex of the vast majority of artists and in the point of view they perpetuated. The "establishment" institutions of the Royal Academy and the British Institution, as well as art academies, were run by men and largely served men. Those female artists who managed to find a market for their work usually endorsed the same visual myths as their male counterparts, rarely depicting women in as assertive a light as men and almost never selecting a talented female genius from history (aside from Joan of Arc or a royal personage) to enshrine as worthy of heroic stature. Women served, instead, as mothers, muses, or servants/ handmaidens to male talent, in real life and in art.

After an overview of the Romantic cult of the male genius, this chapter will examine several paintings of the historical genre where genius is represented in the figure of the male child. While male bonding and the exclusion or marginalization of women is a crucial element in these images, they do not rely merely on sexual difference as a structuring motif. In other words, while they do reproduce the ideology of separate spheres, they do so with a twist, since the most interesting of these paintings of the cult of genius feminize the male child. Male artists of the period, then, seem to take account of the power of the feminine, culturally associated with creativity, even while appropriating it for their own ends and shunting women aside. In selecting the boy – providing spectators with keyhole glimpses of both ordinary and extraordinary moments in the youths of exceptional men – these artists serve various cultural imperatives. They rely on contemporary philosophical and scientific notions of giftedness as sexed; they soothe contemporary anxieties about the need to regenerate the flagging state of British art; they create allegories of empire. Returning to the origins of genius, they travel the same road as so many other Victorians who are obsessed with beginnings; those of individuals, those of cultural institutions, and those of civilization itself.

The notion of genius approached a religion in its elevation of males gifted with this mysterious endowment to the status of gods, as historians of the nineteenth century have documented. Feminist art historian Linda Nochlin has exposed the myth of genius operative in the art world in her classic essay "Why Have There Been No Great Women Artists?" In the nineteenth century, she argues, this "semi-religious conception of the artist's role is elevated to hagiography" (Nochlin 1988: 155). Ordinary men, she explains, are awarded extraordinary, even dangerous powers. It is customary to find their origins embroidered with "the discovery by an older artist or discerning patron of the Boy Wonder, usually in the guise of a lowly shepherd boy . . . a stock-in-trade of artistic mythology ever since Vasari immortalized the young Giotto" (ibid.: 154).

Of course this myth evolved and was sustained by various cultural events. The rise of the qualified individual during the Enlightenment meant that men without wealth or social status could "challenge the existing hierarchical order by substituting innate creative ability" (Becker 1978: 56). In addition, the Romantics, as part of their emphasis on self-expression and individuality, idolized each other. They even made a virtue of eccentricity and madness and particularly extolled those who died young, such as Chatterton and Keats. Cults formed, in addition, around Blake, Byron, and Shelley, not to mention Wordsworth, who featured as an influence in so many Victorian writings. Indeed, the few exceptional women admitted into the privileged category of "genius" were often described by contemporaries in terms reflecting the darker side of individuality – namely, as unacceptable freaks or witches.[1] The legacy of Romanticism, however, included the assessment of genius as androgynous, with the feminized attributes of intuition, imagination, sensitivity, and "soul" grafted onto the harder male virtues (Battersby 1989: 5–7, *passim*). The sex of genius was thus absolute, if the gendering was somewhat ambiguous. Governing themselves by the powerful ideology of separate spheres, the Victorians reinforced the idea of a genius as male and connected it with the harsher realities of history. Yet they also continued to associate the feminine with creativity – so making room for the feminine in art through the child figure, while concurrently excluding the female.

In the Victorian masculinist tradition of history, represented by Thomas Carlyle's 1841 text *On Heroes, Hero-Worship, and the Heroic in History* (Carlyle 1880), the genius is a male adult. Forays into the childhoods of Dante, Johnson, Rousseau, Burns, and others assume only a brief importance. Setting the stage for a seeming obsession with "great men," both native and foreign, Carlyle argues that the genius, omniscient and omnipotent because of a direct link to the Godhead, affords the possibility of leadership and superiority to his generation and to his culture. To Carlyle, however, the lionizing hero worship of the previous century was mistaken and inadequate; he believed instead that a genius was potentially a savior of society, not a mere romantic curiosity or rebel. The obsession with great men was to continue and thrive in spite of advances made during the 1850s and 1860s in feminism (by women and by men alike).

The history of science and the science of origins also supported a notion of exclusive male genius.[2] Scientific treatises such as Francis Galton's *Hereditary Genius* (1865) and Charles Darwin's *Descent of Man* (1871) strengthened rather than overturned prevailing sexual stereotypes, maintaining, as Christine Battersby explains, that the main difference between man, animal, and savage was man's genius (Battersby 1989: 3). Later in the century, Havelock Ellis's psychological profiles of sexual character in *Man and Woman* (1894) and *A Study of British Genius* (1901) continued a tradition of positive pronouncements on men's abilities, at the expense of women.

The young genius, the "child of gold" derived from the Platonic ideal, also reflected changing attitudes towards the importance and validity of childhood as a distinct period of growth, meaning, and potential. During the Victorian era in particular the child came into his or her own, and there was a generally increased individualization and commercialization of the child's needs and nature.[3] Children became an industry in themselves, as increased production in children's literature, magazines, and playthings also attested. A proliferation of child-rearing handbooks from the late 1840s onwards advised mothers on how to care for children and prepare them for their future roles in society. In addition, the growth of interest in developmental child psychology, speculations about early signs of male and female personality structures, and theories on childhood narcissism all burgeoned in the mid-to-late nineteenth century.

The confirmation of male genius and the emphasis on the child were inextricably connected with a desire for messianic "men of letters" to resuscitate English art, too. One might argue that, at least prior to the House of Parliament competitions for artists in the early 1840s and the subsequent galvanizing impact of the Pre-Raphaelite Brotherhood in 1848, the state of art in Britain in the 1830s and 1840s was stagnant, pervaded by a feeling of national mediocrity. A writer for the *Westminster Review* in 1844, for example, suggested that nothing less than a revolution needed to happen in the arts, "and we only wait the hand of a man of genius and originality enough to set the example and point the way that we may all follow him" (*London Review* 1861: 640). Another contemporary critic pointed to other civilizations as worthy of emulation, urging

It is high time that . . . the stigma of mediocrity which has so long lain on British art . . . be removed. We are in the stage of national existence when excellence in the fine arts might naturally be expected, in which Athens raised the matchless portico of the Parthenon, and Rome the stately dome of the Pantheon, and modern Italy gave birth to Raphael and Domenichino. Unless something be done now, and that, too speedily, we shall arrive at the stage of the corruption of taste before we have passed through its excellence. . . . we shall be rotten before we are ripe. . . . Now, then, is the time, before it [corruption] has yet arrived, to give it [our national arts] a refined and classic direction, and afford some ground for our boasted refinement by producing and encouraging works in the fine arts.

(*Westminster Review* 1844: 80)

Other critics also addressed the national inferiority complex about English art and specifically probed the underlying issue of the condition of genius in British society. John Eagles, an influential writer for *Blackwood's Edinburgh Magazine*, remarked in 1836 about the desirability of fostering genius on native soil:

To make a great, truly a great painter, requires as powerful and original a mind as to make a great statesman, or poet, or orator. It requires the ardent disposition, the *feu sacre*, which, early fixing the desire on the great achievement, disregards all labour, endures all fatigue in its prosecution.

(*London Review* 1861: 640)

Eagles argued that a man with such super-human abilities could prove himself in any arena, for he possessed a mind that could rival "the greatest of his age. Michael Angelo, Leonardo da Vinci, Rubens, or Titian would have been illustrious in any line of life." Authors such as Eagles conveyed a sense of real urgency that the Victorian era itself, indeed the entire nineteenth century, was a proving ground for British art – either of its "ripeness" or its "rottenness," its genius or creative deficiencies.

In addition to creating a high level of quality that future generations would admire, competing with previous eras became a goal worth promoting in the arts as well as in other fields. In their musings about how subsequent ages might assess them, the Victorians may well have considered their paintings to be an agent of salvation, especially art that edified and enlightened the public.

The art of Victoria's long reign was diverse in scope, but the general popularity of genre scenes of everyday life was nothing short of phenomenal. Scores of paintings self-consciously mirrored the deeds, heroes, look, and feel of contemporary life by stressing familiar systems of meaning through the use of elaborate, symbolic detail. History paintings, chronicling the private aspects of "great men," readily fit with such a devotion to realism and symbolism. The historical, the everyday, and the universal mixed easily in such art.

In some respects the Victorian fascination with artistic genius underscored the era's desire to draw comparisons between their own heroes and those of the past, as well as to make the past live again. Artists romanticized and, above all, personalized history to make it accessible, human, and exciting. In depicting gifted boys whose place in history was already guaranteed, artists could literally embody the myth of genius and point, as well, to the future growth and greatness of the empire.

One of the more fascinating examples of these ideas at work is to be found in William J. Grant's 1854 Royal Academy picture, *The Requiem* (Plate 1), accompanied with a text stating that "The last hours of Mozart were devoted unceasingly to his composition, all the efforts of his wife being unavailing to turn his attention from the work he loved so fervently" (Graves 1906: 299). The same theme of the young composer's last moments was also treated by Richard J. Lewis in 1847 and by Henry Nelson O'Neil in 1849. In Grant's visual interpretation, a lovely woman (Constanza, the wife of Mozart) is present to hold the famous composer's hand and tend to his sickroom needs, but the great genius forsakes emotional attachment and does not look up from his bedside labors and the disarray of papers and musical instruments. Instead he chooses to compose music (the pages are imprinted "Benedictis" and suggest the final blessing of his talent) unto his last breath. His noble soul, once freed from its moral casing, seems ready to depart through the nearby

Plate 1 William J. Grant, *The Requiem—Mozart on his Deathbed.* 1854. Oil on canvas. 28" × 34". Photograph courtesy of Christopher Wood Gallery, London.

open window. Grant's painting offers the ultimate refinement of genius; distilled into its most ethereal essence, Mozart's music can at last blend with a celestial harmony, the invisible music of the spheres towards which his earthly compositions have aspired.

Although understated, the female presence here conveys a definite impact and impression. In dress and feeling Constanza looks very much like a Victorian lady and modern madonna in art, not one of the eighteenth century, hovering over Mozart like a solicitous mother tending a sick child. On his deathbed even the great composer is reduced to dependency, like an infant needing constant attention, but he does not even look into the gentle face that has tended him so devotedly. Nor does he acknowledge the comfort she has created for him, bringing him food, warm shawls, and love along with her faith in him. Yet although Constanza is shut out, she has already played her part; her fidelity has enabled Mozart to write music and has inspired him, while her selling family goods and making do with less were also supportive gestures. Despite the fact that the great genius seems to ignore his helpmate and her nurturing efforts, she reinforces her presence and support by the human touch, extending her right hand onto his left one.

More common than representations of the premature death of the young artist, however (notably Henry Wallis's *Chatterton* of 1856, Tate Gallery) are paintings which reconstruct imagined incidents from the childhoods of gifted men.[4] Marcus Stone's 1862 Royal Academy (RA) entry, *A Painter's First Work* (Plate 2), illustrates the young painter's father and a friend coming upon the artist's first chalk drawings which have marred an oak press. A contemporary art review describing the scene relies on a stereotyping of gender and class traits as it links ignorance with the female servant and power and brilliance with the middle-class males. It awards control to the father, genius to the child, and intuitions of genius to the older man:

> The subject of the picture is the old, old story of the early manifestations of genius, and the misapprehension and opposition they are apt to encounter from parents and guardians. Our little incipient painter . . . has been left at home in an empty room. We may fancy that he has looked long and often at the Lely-like portrait of a lady hanging against the wall till, now in the solitary room, with no eye to observe and no hand to check, the irresistible imitative impulse, or rather the first o'ermastering inspiration of genius, prompts him to seize the chalk and copy what has so long held him under a spell. He does so, and, as a first work, even this rough chalk sketch has abundant indication of a special natural gift and faculty. Just as he has finished his outline and drawn some similar objects, which, being evidently executed from memory are not so good, the father returns, probably

Plate 2 Marcus Stone, *A Painter's First Work* (engraving by unknown artist), 1862. Reproduced in the *Illustrated London News*, 40, 1862: 576.

unheard at first. Entering the room and seeing the panels of the oak press scrawling all over and disfigured with chalk, he turns to scold the little fellow, for, as he thinks slovenliness and idleness, and to threaten him with the consequences of a repetition of the offence. The boy, surprised and detected, stands abashed; but still, as if conscious of having been incited by something pure and noble, his look of timid deprecation is mingled with the trace of a wish to justify himself. This is not needed, however, for he has already found a defender. The older gentleman, the grandfather of the boy, or the father's friend . . . sees in the rough chalk work the germs of what may bear glorious fruit; and he at once checks the father's inconsiderate anger. It is cleverly indicated that the old gentleman is either an artist himself or a lover of art, by the portfolio under his arms. The waiting-maid entering the room is not absolutely essential to the story, yet she contributes to its completeness by her goodnatured thoughtless and ignorant smile.

(*Illustrated London News* 1862: 576)

The sexual politics in this scene are a bit more complicated, however. The commentary on this 1862 painting on public display underlines one of the most provocative conventions of gendered representations in Victorian art – that of the early signs of genius, the struggle for acceptance, and the apocalyptic discovery by others of his talent. This brief description includes some revealing, indeed stereotypical, traits ascribed to the boy genius. He is among the rare souls who have been touched by "something pure and noble," and this unique endowment excuses his rebelliousness and disregard of ordinary rules, expressed here by his naughtiness in making a mess. Yet his actions in some ways trace the transition from childhood to adulthood, from ignorance to knowledge, from feminine to masculine domain. The child has initially acted within the feminine, domestic sphere, raiding the closet full of linen, clothing, and women's shoes in order to get pillows to stand on so he can draw. This scheme did not serve his purpose very well, so he then removed several books (emblematic of worldly masculine knowledge) and put them on a chair to achieve his ends. His defiance also creates a chaos that in itself is also gendered, for the boy has rather triumphantly challenged feminine teachings about the importance of neatness (perhaps he has already learned as well the corollary that invariably a female picks up after males). The boy's art includes various scrawls on the wall, ranging from a crudely drawn house and animal to an attempt at drawing the female figure. Significantly, his cartoon female portrait is among his very first paintings, an imitation of older male artists and of traditional subject matter of the female (the woman as an object of male art and the masculine gaze).

In this painting and in some subsequent examples the realm of art is completely male, with female creativity alluded to only vaguely by the inclusion of decorated pillows and other domestic accessories. The feminine is located here in the past – in the child (who has left behind feminine influence) and in his art (the female subject of the portrait). In terms of physical presence, the female is a mere intruder or onlooker, in this case a servant whose character is reduced to a smiling cipher of mindlessness. She may have entered the room where male talent (and conflict) emerges, but she never really belongs to that world. In fact, her feeble, placid domesticity is replicated in dozens of canvases in which the female – whatever her social class – remains at best an observer. In the iconological subgenre represented by this work, the identification of genius with the male sex is total, and a reversal of this pictorial situation is unthinkable. The message is binary and biased: the creative behavior and potential of boys and men signal energy, assertiveness, ability, and persistence, while girls and women are clearly associated with subservience, ignorance, and domesticity. In this clear sexual division of labor and talent, the young artist must subconsciously decide whether to cling to identification (as he does to the chair with the pillow) with his mother (his feminine side) or to bond instead with his father and critic (his masculine side). Success in the world would indicate the latter as the best choice. The boy seems both proud and worried about what he has done; he seems somewhat ashamed, yet also proudly sneaks a glance at what he has wrought. Yet there is a feminized ambivalence to his character and demeanor: his slight build and his pigeon-toed, inward-turning stance are not very assertive, and he seems rather diffident or shy overall. Likewise, there is some ambiguity in the father's evidently harsh reaction, and to modern eyes he seems more perturbed and questioning than furious. Another important element of the male response exists in the apparent hint of male bonding in Stone's picture. While the patriarch seems upset, the other man recognizes the child's precociousness. Perhaps he will – as fellow artist, or collector, or connoisseur – become a supporter of the youth, a parallel to Nochlin's myth of the older figure (a surrogate father?) or patron "discovering" and sustaining the Boy Wonder and thereby sharing, as well as basking in, some reflected glory.

Some related ideas recur, for example, in Edward Matthew Ward's 1849 RA painting, *Benjamin West's First Effort in Drawing* (Plate 3); the identical subject was also treated by Charles Compton the same year. As in the case of *A Painter's First Work* and in various subsequent examples, a significant figure from English history, indeed often from the history of art itself, has been selected to personify the virtues of the boy genius, in this case Benjamin West, a former President of the Royal Academy.[5] In this intimate glimpse of painterly precociousness, Ward alludes to West's American origins and childhood in Pennsylvania by

Plate 3 Edward M. Ward, *Benjamin West's First Effort in Drawing*, 1849. Oil on canvas, 39.7 cm × 47.6 cm. Dunedin Art Gallery, New Zealand.

including various American Indian objects, including a pair of moccasins and blanket at the right and a decorated feather fan on the floor. On the windowseat are a Bible and an hourglass, the latter a well-known symbol of time and its passage. A thriving plant on the windowsill, a favourite Victorian pictorial device, attests to the healthy state of the occupant.[6] According to the accompanying text, "Little Benjamin was placed with a fly-trap in his hand to watch the sleeping infant of his eldest sister, while his mother gathered flowers in the garden. As he sat by the cradle, the child smiled in sleep; he was struck with its beauty, and seeking some paper, drew its portrait in red and black ink" (Graves 1906: 129). The young artist, having flung down the peacock fan (an object perhaps alluding to youthful vanity), gazes intently at the baby and seems totally absorbed in the creative act. He has, on the one hand, rejected "women's work" of babysitting to create art, "men's work," yet he has used the domestic and the female domain of baby-tending as an important source of inspiration. Master Benjamin's intelligence is conveyed in part by his large head and high forehead, phrenological signs of ability that would have been readily understood by Victorian audiences. He literally lowers himself onto his knees to (almost worshipfully) study the baby, in doing so "returning" to his own infancy and dependency and evoking the idea of the adoration of the Holy Child even as he transforms this into a work of art. In fact, he gazes at the baby as intensely as a mother might, turning this bonding experience into a source of genius. Nurtured by an atmosphere of comfort, peace, and sustenance (there is even a tray of bread, cheese, fruit, and tea on the table against the wall), he produces his first work of art amid the womb-like security of home. Outside two women gather flowers to adorn and enhance their homey environment, the sacred hearth hailed by Ruskin as the "place of Peace". Moreover, an unspoken contrast is set up between the non-intellectual pursuits of these females and the cerebral creativity and contributions of males.

Pictures of this sort multiplied and were often placed on public view for judgment and approbation. Another emblem of boyish neglect of duty and a thwarting of maternal rule is found in John Absolon's slightly later RA picture *Opie, When a Boy, Reproved by his Mother* (Plate 4) of 1853. Here the mother plays a more involved role in her artistic son's fate, yet in some respects she is an adversary of male genius, scolding him for the untidiness he has wrought in his attempts to create a work of art. There is no adult male champion present, although in the background, left, a boy stands with his back to viewers. He seems to be examining the portrait produced by a young John Opie, and the lad's thoughtful gaze suggests some degree of male-to-male understanding of genius. The mother's face, in contrast, seems tinged with sadness. Perhaps she is acknowledging to herself and to her son John that this sign

Plate 4 John Absolon, *Opie, When a Boy, Reproved by his Mother*, 1862 version. Oil on canvas laid on board. 22½″ × 18½″ (56.6 cm × 47 cm). Photograph courtesy of Sotheby's, London.

of genius signals a necessary rupture in their relationship: he must leave her and take his genius to the world beyond. The child clings to her, with downcast eyes, perhaps fearful of leaving the safety of the snug cottage haven created by his mother. His lack of aggressiveness, indeed his seeming fear, hesitancy, and vulnerability are "feminized" attributes, yet they contrast with his mother's strength at this moment of realization. As in Ward's painting, the boy has disobeyed or flaunted female authority, but the mother here seems to be trying to disengage her son from her, opening her arms in a gesture that simultaneously points with one hand to his palette and with the other to the future and the world outside. She has played a crucial role in her son's life and formation and now realizes that her importance must be displaced by that of masculine principles and realities.

As many of these paintings suggest, despite their influence and import-ance to the nurture of young genius, women function as eternal outsiders in this rarefied realm of intellect and talent. For example, in Ebenezer Crawford's *Childhood of Mozart* (ex-Sotheby's, London) of 1873, the artist projects a vision of the prodigy as an intense little boy (feminized to some degree by his tiny frame, long hair, air of frailty, and huge eyes) seated, legs dangling, atop a pile of books and playing the piano. (Haydn's childhood also inspired, for example, Jessie Macleod's 1852 British Institution picture.) A bewigged gentleman of the Court, perhaps a music lover, teacher, or elegant visitor, towers over the child, but only physically, for the baby-like child was already an established *Wunderkind* by the Victorian era. Indeed, artists probably drew their inspiration from the often hyperbolic biographies that increasingly appeared in the nineteenth century chronicling the lives (especially the formative child-hood influences) of "great men." The only hint of a female presence in Crawford's scene is in the background doorway, where an older woman quietly, almost invisibly, sits and sews, not daring to enter or disturb the male creativity going on in the adjacent room. The invisibility of women in the presence of genius (despite the importance of maternal nurture in the early education and moral training of children) reaches somewhat comic proportions at times. In the realm of popular periodicals, a frontis-piece to the 1866 *Ladies Treasury* (Plate 5) depicts "The Childhood of Sir Walter Raleigh" in entirely masculine terms, with a supportive fath-erly figure, another encouraging, older boy, and the precocious (and rather precious-looking) hero himself. There is a female present, but whether mother or housekeeper, she is backgrounded to the extent that she is reduced to utter insubstantiality, a shadowy ghost who hovers but does not belong in this masculine bastion of intellect and achievement, symbolized here by piles of books, a globe, and maps. The young Raleigh appears like an effete forerunner of little Lord Fauntleroy, with stylish fancy-dress and lace collar. This boy too, having been "feminized" and nurtured by his mother or another female, moves on to other, masculine endeavors and principles.

Related messages about role-playing and female capacities covertly interact as well in Marcus Stone's undated *Watt Discovering the Conden-sation of Steam* (Plate 6). Here a female servant literally turns her back on Watt's tabletop experiments, also ignoring another boy in the background who is dealing with a customer. Watt's mother or sister

Plate 5 Unknown artist, "The Childhood of Sir Walter Raleigh", in *The Ladies' Treasury*, 1866. Photograph courtesy of the Yale Center for British Art.

watches him with some degree of interest, but she shows no signs of really comprehending what he is trying to explain or do, although she may none the less be encouraging him. An older man at the table also glances at the boy, but his rather phlegmatic expression is hard to analyze and seems more disapproving or puzzled than positive. (Popular biographies of Watt indicate that his father was an unsuccessful merchant whose reversal of fortunes caused young James to be briefly apprenticed

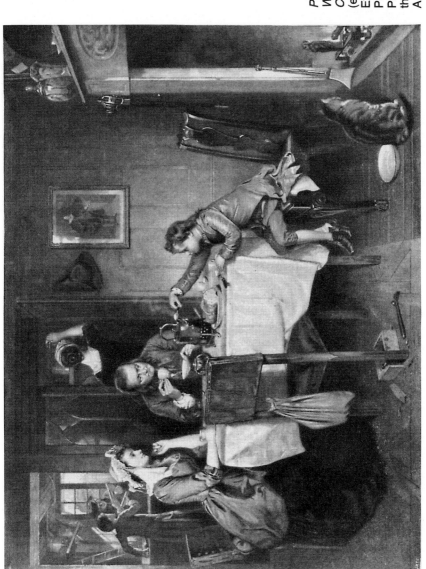

Plate 6 Marcus Stone, *Watt Discovering the Condensation of Steam* (engraving by Kurtz). Exact date not known. Private collection. Photograph courtesy of the Yale Center for British Art.

in his teenage years to an instrument maker. His famous condensing steam engine was not invented until later, although the artist here has imagined the germinal stages of the invention as conceived in childhood.) This element of either male or female opposition or lack of understanding underscores the essential "loner" role of genius, for even within his own family such a child is often misunderstood, ostracized, or criticized. Yet other meanings also seem embedded in the room, figures, and objects. The mother or sister, for example, sits directly opposite the young Watt, who is apart from her yet needs her approval. Like Ward's long-haired genius, Master James is still a "baby" in some respects. Here he dangles his feet over the chair edge and is engrossed in an experiment that looks like childish playing with food and cutlery. The setting is domestic, a room away from where commercial transactions take place, and although Watt sits beneath a male icon of the past (a portrait) and has masculine tools like a hammer nearby, for his experiments he is actually using objects with more feminine associations and usage – a teapot and kitchen utensils. Perhaps this is why the adult male is perplexed or unsettled: while the other boy assertively deals with the masculine realities of business and commercial transactions, young Watt has "retreated" to dream and think within the feminine world of the tea table. The feminizing impact has been displaced onto these objects and backgrounded to some extent, but this does not lessen the fact that the boy has appropriated the feminine (the support as well as the teapot) for his own ends.

Some of the same messages are conveyed in a different way in *Rembrandt's Studio* of 1867 (an 1869 version is in the City Art Gallery, York), one of several works by John Gilbert treating the theme of male genius. Here the sexual division of labor and the devaluation of females into subservient positions results in a curious pictorial asymmetry. The males and females in the composition seem almost to "line up" into sides: the left portion is occupied by an elderly woman and two younger females (one drawing and almost hidden by the huge easel), and the right by a young standing boy and two men, perhaps critics or patrons. Rembrandt himself proudly stands at center at his easel, and his work of art is visible only to the male onlookers. The counterpoint between this triumphant standing male poised in an act of creation and the seated young woman presumably "aping" male creativity and trying to create even though denied access to Rembrandt's is, to modern eyes, poignant, almost painfully pathetic. The boy child on the other side of this great divide is allowed to side with the adult males and watch the great master, but females are polarized into their own space. Excluded from the privileges enjoyed by the opposite sex, they exist only to inspire, serve, or amuse men. Once their functions as sources of security, inspiration, and help are fulfilled, they are put aside, here quite literally. This compartmentalization of female influence, as in some previous examples, once again shuts out females from the world of male power, which they presumably would not "understand."[7]

As might be expected, the overt inspiration of females in the cause of male genius (invariably paying homage to female pulchritude and little else) was a rather common and favorite motif, with women serving as muses, spectators, or admirers in myriad Victorian paintings. William Powell Frith, for example, suggested the power of feminine distractions in his (untraced) 1868 painting *Sterne and the French Innkeeper's Daughter* (the latter described in its accompanying text as a "slut . . . a cunning gipsy"), and in *Dr Johnson and Mrs Siddon* (untraced) of 1884 he also injected a strong dose of female charm and beauty into his pictorial biography of male intellect. Similarly, in Frith's 1881 RA picture *Swift and Vanessa* (untraced), the underlying story focuses less on male genius than on female rivalry (between Vanessa and Stella), with two women vying for Swift's attention. Another permutation of female inspiration, albeit on a higher plane, appears in John Frederick Lewis's dazzling 1838 watercolor entitled *Murillo Painting the Virgin in a Franciscan Monastery* (Minneapolis Institute of Arts). Aside from the necessary "intrusion" of the female and her baby to model for the artist, the occupants of the studio are all seated males. Only Murillo stands to "confront" and interact with his creation at the easel, seemingly unaffected by the presence of a crowd of onlookers who want to be in the presence of genius to witness (and perhaps, vicariously to experience) his creative act.

William Dyce portrayed the ultimate female muse in the form of the Virgin in a famous Pre-Raphaelite composition of 1857, *Titian Preparing to Make his First Essay in Colouring* (Plate 7). Amid the vivid hues and highly wrought details, a young Titian (according to an 1835–7 translation of Ridolfi's life of the artist) sits on the edge of a chair, his hand clutching some flowers onto the pages of his sketchbook. In Ridolfi's account, Titian's flower-gathering was not merely to bring a bouquet to honor a statue of Mary; instead, he crushes the blossoms and uses them as tints for his palette. All in all, to late twentieth-century eyes there seems to be a discernible tension between the immobile white statue and the contemplative child. There is even a hint of confrontation, for the young Titian does not respectfully stand or pray at this little shrine; instead he casually sprawls in a chair (perhaps dragged from home), his feet dangling and his demeanor generally almost flaunting a lack of respect for the Virgin. Are the flowers, hat, and walking stick intended to be read as offerings to the Madonna or, especially in the case of his personal belongings, are they deliberate encroachments and affronts to divine inspiration? Is he, as the *Illustrated London News* (1857: 44) suggested, showing here "the earliest indication of his future eminence as a colourist by drawing a Madonna which he coloured with the juices of flowers" or is something else happening? He rests his right hand on his sketchbook,

Plate 7 William Dyce, *Titian Preparing to Make his First Essay in Colouring*, 1857. Oil on canvas. 36″ × 27¾″ (91 cm × 70 cm). Aberdeen Art Gallery.

his own "Bible" of art, not on the Scriptures. It is not clear whether he gazes at the Child, Mary, or the two together, and it is a matter of speculation as to whether he also contemplates the circumstances and maternal relationship of his own childhood. Are the Christ Child and Titian somehow communicating – is this a representation of sacred inspiration or one of implied conflict between mortal and immortal powers and of heeding one's inner call above all else? The latter message may seem too audacious to ascribe to Victorian viewers, but to our eyes the child's expression, pose, and placement suggest something different from mere inspired adoration of the Virgin. In appearance, in fact, the boy is rather feminized, with a heart-shaped face, long hair, delicate features, pouty lips, and a tunic-like garment. Even his somewhat dreamy expression and isolation in a forest glen ally him to some degree with females, particularly with the scores of females awaiting suitors who appeared in countless Victorian courtship paintings.[8]

In fact, at its highest level, the portrait of the boy genius had covert Christian roots and implications, for the true "wise child" was the Christ Child. An obvious parallel to the worldly sage child is found in depictions of the young Jesus in the temple astonishing his elders with his divine wisdom, the subject of William Holman Hunt's *The Finding of the Saviour in the Temple* (Plate 8). Amid the priests and rabbis seated in the outer chamber of the temple, a young and beautiful Jesus (with feminized long hair, large eyes, and gorgeous gold garment) at about age twelve stands. As the *Athenaeum* critic remarked,

> The refinement, beauty, and dignity surrounding this personification of Our Saviour are only enhanced by the pathos which the action of the hand suggests to us. He is girding tighter the broad belt about his loins, as one who says, "I am ready to depart" . . . The idea of duty predominates above all.
>
> (Bennett 1969: 40)

The Perfect Child, the Holy Genius, accepts his mother's embrace even as he holds himself apart at least psychologically after his earthly parents have rushed in and found him. Unlike the young Opie in Absolon's painting, Jesus has already separated himself from his mother (and father) in order to come to terms with his own genius and mission. The magical or supernatural aura he generates both attracts and yet overwhelms people, and the rabbis accordingly seem to have pulled back somewhat from this source of great power and wisdom. The secularizing of these concepts in Victorian art substitutes the family parlor (or studio) for the temple, but the male bonding, the singular focus on exceptional youthful wisdom and precocity, the solitary mood and distancing of the boy genius from other people, and the awed incomprehension of adults who witness this phenomenal behavior are all shared aspects.

The contrast between male and female realms and modes of behavior, between active and passive gendered stereotypes, is apparent as well in representations of other, "lesser" cultures, nations, or people. In John Phillip's *Early Career of Murillo, 1634* (Plate 9), there is a "lusty peasant in red, who pushes forward in the middle, staring like a savage" (Palgrave

Plate 8 William Holman Hunt, *The Finding of the Saviour in the Temple.* Completed in 1860. Oil on canvas. 33¾″ × 55½″ (85.7 cm × 141 cm). Birmingham City Museum and Art Gallery.

Plate 9 John Phillip, *The Early Career of Murillo, 1634.* Oil on canvas. 72" × 100". The FORBES Magazine Collection, New York.

1866: 105). According to the accompanying script for this 1865 RA entry, the artist has chosen to portray a rare low moment in the history of genius – not boyish mischief or spotlit precocity, but instead the struggle to survive within hostile or uninformed surroundings. Thus, the youthful Murillo is "reduced to earn his daily bread by painting coarse and hasty pictures for the Feria (weekly fair) held in a broad street . . . [of a] venerable market" (Graves 1906: 121). Yet the handsome young genius at far left, forced to be a vendor of his art amid fruits and vegetables, seemingly has the attention and approval of some friars and a Dominican monk, whom one critic described as belonging to "an order also given to Art-patronage" (*Art Journal* 1865: 165). This enlightened or contemplative male response is counterbalanced by dark, rough, contentious types (mostly gypsies and muleteers) who crowd in behind, and in the foreground center by the coarsely amazed expression of a peasant woman with mouth agape. The young Murillo observes but does not become a part of, the energy and turmoil of the market-place, standing to one side behind a little barrier of chair and belongings that he has built to protect and separate himself from the crowd. The friars and the peasant woman and child also seem to erect a human wall or bulwark against the teeming masses in the Sevilla piazza. Murillo's easel and painting equipment in the left corner also seem to set up a visual contrast and contest in the composition between his artistic production and the natural still life of jugs and fruit on the opposite side.

Not only in Phillip's painting is the lower class portrayed as uncouth and untutored in the ways of art, but the main representative of this crude peasant mentality is predictably female, here almost a parody of the sublime concept of the mother and child. Her baby, having presumably been nursed and nourished at her partly bare breast, turns to one side to give grapes to another child. The young Murillo, nurtured by his own mother in the past and perhaps by the friars here, is, like similar genius progeny, oddly feminized, or at least androgynous, in facial appearance especially – with long tresses, refined features, and big eyes. His elegant attire, demurely shod and stockinged feet and legs, decorous stance, and sense of restraint, contrast markedly with the tumult of the crowd, the dirty faces and rags of the market-goers, and the bare feet of the astounded peasant woman.

Wishful thinking about actual or imaginary meetings among male geniuses was also plentiful, as evident in Eyre Crowe's *Pope's Introduction to Dryden at Will's Coffee House, the Strand* (ex-Sotheby's) of 1858.[9] Here the accompanying text cites a letter from Sir Charles Wogan to Swift, in which Pope as a child is introduced to Dryden in the presence of other eminent men of letters, a gathering akin in some ways to Christ among the elders. To this elite all-male club of geniuses belong such members as Johnson, Steele, Vanbrugh, Addison, Southerne, Dennis, and Congreve. The beautiful young child seems to be on display for their intellectual and physical delight and delectation. In fact, this group of mostly bewigged men in their typical eighteenth-century upper-class attire of silk stockings, high-heeled shoes, and elaborate coats may send some shudders through modern viewers, who on one level might interpret these literary lions and inquisitors as overly curious voyeurs who take delight in examining (and potentially exploiting) a pure child. Interestingly, the young Pope's mentor plays a maternal role in some respects, putting his arm around the boy, holding his hand, and generally comforting and nurturing him through these difficult moments. Although a genius and the mental equal of these men, the boy is still a rather frail-looking little child, and he appears small, helpless, and vulnerable amid this august enclave of intellect. He rather timidly leans on or shrinks back into his mentor's lap, seeming fearful of the imposing company and non-domestic surroundings (a commercial, urban coffee house) and perhaps longing for the safety of mother, home, and familiar settings.

The relationship between mentor and boy genius (in addition to possible latent homosexual interpretations) in Crowe's vignette is suggestive of the many myths of discovery, surrogate parenting, emotional bonding and identification, and "adoption" of boy wonders by older, protective males. Another work in this category is William Simson's 1838 RA picture *Cimabue and Giotto* (location unknown), which had the following exegesis:

> The humble birth and poverty [of the shepherd boy Giotto] seemed likely to condemn him to an obscure and miserable life; but nature inspired him with that talent which afterwards made him one of the great ornaments in his country. Cimabue, happening to pass one day, surprised the boy sighing over a rude sketch which he had traced upon a stone. . . . Cimabue felt instantly the desire to protect so happy a disposition; and being sure that he would leave to his country an heir worthy of his glory, he resolved to adopt this youth, a disciple of nature, and by doing so Cimabue acquired a new claim to the gratitude of Italy, which honours him as the restorer of painting and the master of Giotto.
>
> (Graves 1906: VII, 136)

Similar ideas resurfaced in the context of other historical eras, for example in Robert McInnes's (untraced) 1853 RA picture, *Metastasio, When a Child, . . . Discovered by Gravina Singing Extemporaneous Verses in the Streets of Rome*. In almost all these cases, a supportive older male not only recognizes fellow genius, but also (apocryphally) adopts – in spirit or in law – and strongly identifies with a younger, talented artist. In all these Victorian permutations a degree of self-glorification seems clear, for in these paintings (and in Stone's RA entry,

Plate 2), the older man, by acknowledging and fostering young genius, simultaneously protects a national resource, improves his own reputation, and increases national visibility and importance in the arts.

A different offshoot of these thematic concerns is represented by John Everett Millais's 1870 RA picture *The Boyhood of Raleigh* (Plate 10). The illustrious explorer, military and naval commander, and author is imagined as a youth sitting with his brother and held spellbound by the tales of a Genoese sailor, "one of those who were half pirates, half heroes, such as [Charles] Kingsley has delighted countless boys by describing" (Millais 1899: I 18). The boy on the right, whose "intelligence is not of the vision-seeing sort, but rather refers to the visions of others" (ibid.) lies on the ground, while the seated young Raleigh, his eyes full of wonder, holds onto his raised knees tightly as he listens to the storyteller's yarns. Perhaps, as one contemporary critic noted, the boy, with his

> fixed, dreaming eyes, seems to see El Dorado, the islands of the east and west, the "palms and temples of the south," as well as the Mexican and other monarchs he had read about. Ships, gold, the hated Spaniards, and (most brilliant of all) that special object of his life's endeavours, the "fountain of youth," were before his fancy.
>
> (ibid.)

As in the painting of Murillo's youth, a linking of genius and nationalism is suggested by an allusion to racial type: the child is contrasted with darker, swarthier people, here a sunburnt Italian sailor who points "over the blue sea of the Devonshire coast towards the far-off Spanish main" (*Illustrated London News* 1870: 487) and relates his own saga of adventure and woe. The rugged, brawny sailor with dirty feet is contrasted with the refined and pale young Raleigh, whose appearance is feminized by a frilly ruff on his neck, plumed hat, embroidered garments, beribboned shoes, and a general air of frailty and uncertainty.

The setting is very different from the domestic interiors in which most "boy geniuses" are placed. The figures sit on a stark rocky portion of the Devonshire coast, and the space they occupy is littered with signs of male conquest. The children's toy ship at left (partly cut off and "shipwrecked") alludes to Raleigh's later adventures and challenges as a commander, while the rusty anchor may have the traditional connotations of hope. At right near the anchor, various dead, stuffed birds lie on a rock, their skins a testimony to the plunder and ruin that explorers and conquerors cause (and to the market for such plumage to decorate ladies' hats). More than in any previous example, the absence of home and security, of domestic interiors and females signals a compelling shift of emphasis. Here Raleigh has left home to play near the sea, a choice that is intended to foretell his future greatness. But the austerity of the rocky setting, the appealing but frightening tales of the stranger, and the

Plate 10 John Everett Millais, *The Boyhood of Raleigh*, 1870. Oil on canvas. 42½" × 56". The Tate Gallery.

glittering seas symbolizing the unknown and uncharted are both fascinating and terrifying.

Not surprisingly, women artists also subscribed to many of these same stock images of famous boys, as attested to by the career of Margaret Dicksee, herself the offspring of a well-known (male) artist. The title of her first RA picture suggests a bolder approach and subject in *Miss Angel – Angelica Kauffman, introduced by Lady Wentworth, visits Mr Reynolds's Studio* (current location unknown) of 1892, but to modern eyes there is no novelty or celebration of female ability. Instead, this frothy costume piece is an embarrassing scenario with the accomplished eighteenth-century painter portrayed as just another elegantly clad female visitor and interloper – not an artistic colleague or equal – in a "great man's" world. The following year Dicksee painted *The Child Handel* (Royal Pavilion, Brighton), in which boyish conflict with the patriarch is dramatized.[10] The accompanying text describes how

> Handel's father, objecting to his son's absorbing devotion to music, forbade his following his bent, and banished all musical instruments to the attic, where, however, the little musician discovered them, and under cover of night resumed his beloved pursuit. The sounds thus produced, and the flitting of the little white-clad figure, started the notion that the house was haunted, until the truth was revealed.
>
> (Graves 1906: II 326)

The canvas captures a moment of discovery, when the golden child, not a ghost, is found defying paternal authority in order to pursue the inner dictates and drive of genius. Handel's singularity of purpose, his "divine" defiance in the cause of art, separates him physically as well as intellectually from the small crowd of amazed people who press into the room, and he is bathed in a pool of light. The setting is domestic, and Handel's mother rushes in to make sure her child is not harmed in any way. The child himself is feminized, not merely by being a sensitive genius, but also by the cap and long sleeping gown he wears, his large bright eyes, and his sweet face. The boy's slight build and dangling feet, which like those of other boy geniuses are not yet long enough to touch the floor, make him seem even younger, smaller, and more vulnerable. The seemingly frail, tentative Handel appears startled and defenseless against the noisy "invaders" into his private territory of music, but his mother will presumably protect and "rescue" him from any real danger.

As these various strands of imagery – coupled with the overriding reality of male cultural supremacy – all confirm, Victorian art projected a misogynistic myth about male genius in line with prevailing beliefs about giftedness. In these visual representations of inequality, females have no autonomy or control over events, and the clear demarcations of role, intellectual abilities, and separate spheres are strikingly mirrored in countless paintings. Yet their influence is nonetheless felt as a source of security and inspiration. Powerful in her own right, the female is backgrounded and her impact displaced onto the feminized boy geniuses whom she has helped to nurture. Her offspring, boy geniuses, are typically depicted as emotional, diffident, fearful or hesitant, and subtly feminized in appearance, usually within a domestic setting. In Ward's, Absolon's, and Stone's paintings and others, these feminized spaces ultimately serve as metaphors for creative endeavors that are made "safe" and comforting but which also hold the promise of national and international renown. Home, with its imprint of female domesticity, nurtures male genius and thus furthers the goals of the nation and empire, a message subtly conveyed in countless Victorian images, too.

Although the adult "great man" was also a popular subject, the figure of the child genius in particular offered viewers a privileged glimpse of the germinal stages of giftedness. In some respects he was perhaps, at least in art, a less threatening, more uplifting, visual role model than a mature male. In such paintings, as in literary fictions of the Boy Wonder, the Victorians could return again and again to the theme of the child as a locus of innocence and therefore renewal. Indeed, the very state of genius seems akin to many archetypal qualities associated with childhood and youthful conduct – willfulness, intense emotion, instinctive behavior, purity, even self-absorption and vanity. In the adult male some of these characteristics could be quite offensive, but in a handsome, even pretty, child they were prescient, individualistic, and acceptable. Whatever their age, these superhuman intellects were perceived as romantic rebels who listened to the "inner call" of genius without reservation, withstood social or parental opposition or rejection, and personified a masculine sense of power that mingled with feminine emotional attributes. But Victorian paintings rarely probed the darker sides of genius – the excesses (for example in sexual, neurotic, or bohemian behavior) or eccentricities – instead, mostly boyish promise is offered. Even adult male genius was filtered through rose-coloured glasses of perfection – caught in a moment of divine inspiration, poised on the threshold of the absolute while dying, nurtured by female inspiration, or in communion with other male talent.

These strands of imagery in Victorian vignettes glorified the history and superiority of past male heroes and simultaneously politicized the boy genius as a symbol of British achievement and potential. Much as a gifted child and his talents could enrich civilization and, in more localized English terms, make the empire even greater, so too could images of greatness improve the caliber of British art. The iconology of genius thus remains a lasting metaphor – not only of male cultural supremacy, but also as almost a propagandistic emblem of British culture, and, by extension, as a tribute to the entire nation and empire. Yet beneath these manifestos of masculine virtues and values lurks a subtext about femininity and the female role in sustaining genius. Even today these canvases imply how desperately the Victorian era and its artists wished to be perceived as a golden age of accomplishment, enhancing an image of youthful boldness and promise for future generations to ponder and, finally, to challenge.

NOTES

1 An outstanding book on the history of attitudes to male and female genius is Christine Battersby's *Gender and Genius. Toward a Feminist Aesthetic* (Battersby 1989).

2 For a modern analysis of scientific prescriptions of female creativity, see Flavia Alaya (1977) "Victorian Science and the Genius of Woman," *Journal of the History of Ideas* 5(38) (April-June): 261–80.

3 Among the many useful books that examine the phenomenon of childhood in the nineteenth century are Lawrence Stone (1979) *The Family, Sex and Marriage in England 1500–1800* (New York: Harper & Row); Philip Ariès (1962) *Centuries of Childhood: A Social History of the Family* (New York: Vintage Books); Joan M. Burstyn (1980) *Victorian Education and the Ideal of Womanhood* (London: Croom Helm); and Peter Coveney (1967) *The Image of Childhood* (Baltimore and Harmondsworth: Penguin).

4 While the individual genius from a humble background appeared as the hero in artistic depictions, his anonymous contemporary counterpart did not fare as well. Representations of lower-class urban or country lads drawing, painting, or sculpting are inevitably humorous in content, leaving audiences to smile at the childish efforts rather than to register awe or approval. William Hunt's *Neglected Genius*, for example (reproduced in the *Cosmopolitan Art Journal* 12 (1858): 283) portrays a lower-class city urchin holding up a slate with a stick figure and pokes fun at his limited abilities. In William H. Knight's *Grandfather's Portrait* (Tunbridge Wells Museum and Art Gallery) of 1860 and also Charles Compton's *The Young Sculptor's First Efforts* (ex-Christie's 1986 sale) of 1850, on the other hand, the rural onlookers watching the boy genius seem to laugh at the child more than to understand or praise his efforts.

5 Among the many examples of historical genre painting exalting the alleged greatness of British artists in their formative childhood years are Robert W. Buss's *Hogarth at School* (untraced) at the 1845 British Institution and Eyre Crowe's *Reynolds's First Sketch* (untraced) at the 1866 Royal Academy. According to its accompanying text, in Crowe's picture the formidable Reynolds is shown as "but eight years old . . . [when he] had made himself sufficiently master of Perspective, from the Jesuit treatise, to draw the school house according to rule, no easy matter, as the upper part is half supported by a range of pillars."

6 On this iconology see especially T. J. Edelstein (1980) "They Sang 'The Song of the Shirt,' The Visual Iconology of the Seamstress," *Victorian Studies*, 23 (Winter): 183–210.

7 Another striking example of the "shutting out" of female influence is found in William Simson's (untraced) 1844 painting, *Salvator Rosa's First Cartoon on the Walls of the Certosa*. The accompanying RA text described the sadly amusing (to our minds) female reactions of dumbstruck incredulity in the presence of male genius: " 'Santo Sacramento,' exclaimed . . . his mother,

with upraised hands and eyes. . . . 'Cosa stupenda,' re-echoed the simple
Signorina, his sister, as she gazed in stupid wonder at her brother's talent
and temerity."

8 On the motif of the waiting woman in the garden in Victorian art, see Susan
P. Casteras (1977) "Down the Garden Path: Courtship Culture and Its Imagery in Victorian Art," PhD dissertation, Yale University: 98–135.

9 Other permutations of this theme resurfaced, for example in Henry Wallis's
1865 RA entry *Introduction of Spenser to Shakespeare*, a lost work which
Francis Turner Palgrave, a contemporary critic, described in these terms:
"The older poet advances with a consciousness that he is in the presence of
the mightier genius; Shakespeare receives Spenser, on the other hand, with
the look of one for whom a long-cherished wish is at last fulfilling itself"
(Palgrave 1866: 15–16). Occasionally a single artist (such as John Gilbert)
produced several such examinations of greatness; another example is Solomon
Hart, who had on public exhibition in 1847 *John Milton Visiting Galileo* (a
popular theme treated by Charles Lucy in 1841 and others), *Benvenuto Cellini
Giving Instructions to his Assistant* in 1851, and *The Three Inventors of
Printing: Gutenberg, Faust, and Scheffer, . . . Discussing the Merits of Scheffer's Invention of Moveable Type* the next year. Victorian artists also portrayed
earlier artists paying homage to other "great men" in their profession, a
tendency manifested, for example, in Herbert L. Smith's lost 1844 RA work,
Michael Angelo, Zucchero, and Other Students (described in its text as a
painting in which "the great master summoned the bashful youth to receive
his approval"), Dante Gabriel Rossetti's 1852 watercolor, *Giotto Painting the
Portrait of Dante* (current location unknown), D. W. Deane's *Van Dyck and
Franz Hals* (untraced) of 1854, and Gilbert's (untraced) *Teniers and Rubens*
of 1858.

10 In addition, Dicksee painted in 1901 a fanciful representation of a similar
type that "reconstructed" Thomas Lawrence's first commission as a painter.
The accompanying text emphasized that Lawrence "early evinced his remarkable artistic talent, gaining as a very young child a considerable reputation
by taking portraits of the many travellers who stopped at the inn, on the way
to Bath." A photogravure of the image (Hartley Collection, Museum of Fine
Arts, Boston) reveals that this painting also depicts a domestic interior with
the Boy Wonder feminized and with his feet dangling from a chair. While
an elegant lady poses for a portrait, Lawrence's mother and a girl stand to
one side in awe. A gentleman traveller towers over the tiny innkeeper's son,
standing behind his chair and closely observing (as the females do not dare
to) as Lawrence's prodigious talents manifest themselves on paper.

WORKS CITED

The Art Journal (1865) "The Royal Academy" 27: 165.

Battersby, Christine (1989) *Gender and Genius. Toward a Feminist Aesthetic*,
London: The Women's Press.

Becker, G. (1978) *The Mad Genius Controversy, A Study in the Sociology of
Deviance*, London: Sage Publications.

Bennett, M. (1969) *William Holman Hunt*, Liverpool: Walker Art Gallery.

Carlyle, Thomas (1880) *On Heroes and Hero Worship*, London: Ward, Lock.

Graves, A. (1906) *The Royal Academy of Arts. A Complete Dictionary of Contributors and their Work from its Foundation in 1769 to 1904*, 8 vols, London:
Henry Graves & Co. and George Bell & Sons.

The Illustrated London News (1857) "Royal Academy Pictures," 34: 44.
—— (1862) " 'A Painter's First Work.' Painted by M. Stone," 40: 576.
—— (1870) "Fine Arts: Exhibition of the Royal Academy," 56 (7 May): 487.
London Review (1861) "Royal Academy Exhibition," 2 June: 640.
Millais, J. G. (1899) *The Life and Letters of John Everett Millais*, 2 vols, London: Methuen.
Nochlin, Linda (1988) *Women, Art and Power*, New York: Harper & Row.
Palgrave, F. T. (1866) *Essays in Art*, London: Macmillan.
The Westminster Review (1844) "The Progress of Art," 41: 80.

Chapter 9

Of maenads, mothers, and feminized males

Victorian readings of the French Revolution

Linda M. Shires

Arguing that feminist critics should examine the transplantation of symbolic representations from one geopolitical sphere and one political scene to another, Linda M. Shires takes up the image of the maenad. In the 1830s and 1840s in England, an era of rebellions and European revolution, that which threatens hegemonic dominance, as during the French Revolution of 1789, becomes imaged in the maenad. Yet the figure of female fury never exists alone, but gathers meaning as part of a cultural configuration including the mother as its other half and including feminized males. Shires analyzes the ideological contradictions inherent in the power of Victorian mothers by examining maenadic energy in women and the weakening of men in Anne Brontë's *The Tenant of Wildfell Hall* and Alfred Lord Tennyson's *The Princess*. Although one might think that the resurgence of the maenad and the anxiety about a powerful bourgeois mother-hood might have hampered English feminism, which was largely underground during the period, these ideological contradictions actually enabled the alternative of the woman who wishes to provide for herself, married or not, mother or not.

* * *

Feminist critics of culture need to attend carefully to the transplantation of symbolic representations and to their shifting meanings when moved from one geopolitical sphere to another. If we ought to assess the varied ideological ends such representations further, we also need to ask who uses them, how, and in what contexts. During the late eighteenth and early nineteenth century in both France and England the image of woman as unnatural, whether depicted as maenad, bacchant, or fury, becomes increasingly prevalent. At first, the image of the Unnatural Woman is associated by counter-revolutionaries and fleeing French exiles with the female activists of the French Revolution. Over time, however, and in other hands the image loses its connection with the particular historical and geographical events of the Revolution and, having attained the status of myth and symbol, becomes available for application to cultural situations which may bear only a slight resemblance to the original events. Thus the Owenite platforms of sexual equality in the 1830s or the call for British women's intellectual advancement in the 1840s would hardly seem to have a "historical" connection to the food riots led by women in 1789 and to Olympe de Gouges's drafts of a "Declaration of the Rights of Women." Yet in the 1830s and 1840s, as in the 1790s, that which threatens hegemonic dominance or the status quo becomes linked to the female who sexually stimulates others into a fascination with horror or a sublime exaltation.

The maenad, bacchant, or fury does not exist alone but always belongs to a cultural configuration which includes the mother as its other half (see Gallagher 1985: 194–5) and which also includes the feminizing of men. In this configuration the mother performs a double function. On one hand, she provides the antidote to ruinous maenadic energy. Both the Rousseauistic ideal of republican motherhood and the cultural division of separate spheres aim to keep woman firmly in her domestic place out of the public political arena. Busy raising the sons and daughters of empire, she is presumably not tempted to other forms of control. On the other hand, the mother wields increasing political power of her own, since during the Victorian period the domestic sphere acquires an ever-greater influence on public life. Politicized, the mother thus becomes powerful in her own right and can prove as frightening as a maenad to both men and women. With her increase in power, we concurrently find a feminization of the male.

This chapter aims to trace in an admittedly brief, but hopefully provocative, way the transplantation from France to England of the Revolutionary image of woman as Unnatural. In England the image of the maenadic fury, applied to both male and female French Revolutionaries, is later diluted when applied to mothers and to men generally. Yet as part of this cultural configuration and cultural anxiety, I argue, representations of the 1840s, especially, persistently indulge in portraits of feminized males. I am not claiming that such imagery or such hostility to female power was new to England (as a glance at *The Faerie Queene* or the late sixteenth-century wars of religion, for example, will confirm). However, I am arguing that it becomes reactivated in England, via France, during a period of widespread revolution and rebellion across Europe and, importantly, when a woman, Victoria, occupies the throne. The Unnatural Woman provides a locus for the intensified fears of revolution in an England which wants, at all costs, to preserve the stability of government.

Though we may think that such imagery would have hampered the feminist movement in England, which appears to be underground during the 1830s and 1840s, it actually furthered the movement's aims, as it had done earlier in France, by gendering the public sphere. To award such power to representations alone, of course, would prove naïve. The new imagery worked hand in hand with political and economic events.

Women were now explicitly barred from citizenship and its concomitant rights. Because of political actions, economic changes due to the Industrial Revolution, and cultural representations, gender assumed a new importance and worked with class, race, and religion as the most important social categories for delineating power lines.

After reviewing the actual social situation and the representation of women in the *ancien régime* and in the Revolution, I will look at British contemporary reactions to historical events and at the ways in which those events were narrated. I am chiefly concerned with the conservative response, initiated by Edmund Burke, sustained by many artists and writers, and attacked by Mary Wollstonecraft, who links the French Revolution with the oppression of women. In so doing, she establishes ideological ground for much of the British women's movement to follow in the succeeding century.

One of the major legacies of the French Revolution to the Victorians is the condensation of several cultural strands at the site of female subjectivity and sexuality. Those strands which come together in a fusion of the psychic and social include forms of male disempowerment, motherhood, female influence, and women's rights. Although Thomas Carlyle in his *History of the French Revolution* (1837), a major Victorian text on the subject, repeats the myths and the rhetoric of the counter-revolutionaries and of Burke, more unorthodox literary representations, written during 1848 and 1849, a time of renewed revolution in France and across Europe, work out a more ambivalent reaction to powerful women. Such texts as Alfred Lord Tennyson's *The Princess* and Anne Brontë's *The Tenant of Wildfell Hall* re-examine the myth of the woman as maenad while addressing anxiety about the influential mother. Though ultimately limiting the woman's independence they envision, these texts, following in the tradition of Wollstonecraft, also begin to create a viable cultural space for female power and thus establish important ideological ground for the feminist movement which re-emerges forcefully in the 1850s and 1860s.

Joan B. Landes has convincingly shown in her study of powerful French women before and during the Revolution that the collapse of the patriarchy and the silencing of the politically influential women of the *ancien régime* actually helped to create the bourgeois public sphere (Landes 1988). It is well known that before the 1789 Revolution, women held great power in the shaping of both public speech and action through their presence as leaders of intellectual salons. Indeed, as Landes proposes, the urban salon functioned as an alternative locus of cultural production which was accepted by but which also threatened the absolutist court. Such *salonnières* as Mme du Déffand, Mlle de Léspinasse, and Mme Géoffrin, for example, were known for shaping the careers of talented male authors and academicians. Yet in the political as well as the literary arena it was increasingly rumored that all favors men received actually were approved of by women in power. Even more worrying to members of these arenas, such women seemed to operate in an organized system quite apart from the King, as if they ruled their own mini-government within the larger one. Yet the salon was not separate from but virtually tied to the system of monarchy, aristocracy, and privilege. With the overthrow of Louis XVI, the overthrow of a feminized upper-class patronage system followed.

Women of all classes played many roles in the Revolution, from organizing women's political clubs such as the Parisian group "Amies de la Vérité" to catalyzing the sansculotte insurrection of Prairial in 1793, to joining the army in disguise (Anon. 1806; Higonnet 1989; Hufton 1989; Stephens 1922). Women were also influential in the press. The *Journal des Dammes*, run by women, supported both a classical version of republican motherhood (in opposition to the refined life of *salonnières*) at the same time that it promoted programs for women's rights (Landes 1988: 59–60). But political women leaders such as Claire Lacombe, Pauline Léon, Anne-Joseph Théroigné (who dressed as an Amazon), and Etta Palm, courageously argued for women's equality and were "uninhibited, often flamboyant in their demonstration of it, provoked hatred among the unshakably macho Jacobins and sans-culottes who, officially cherishing political women, preferred them respectful" (Williams 1989: xxxiii; see Levy *et al.* 1979, for French feminist documents). It is no surprise, then, that politically vocal women, who threatened the new masculinized bourgeois public sphere, did not escape censure for long as the feminism of the early Revolution was succeeded by virulent anti-feminism, including that by women themselves. Olympe de Gouges, a feminist even before the Revolution and well known for her law on contractual marriage and "Declaration of the Rights of Women," was guillotined in 1793. Others met similar fates of death or madness.

Although a number of men, notably the Marquis de Condorcet, following in the philosophic tradition of Montesquieu, Voltaire and others, argued for female citizenship, his views, along with those of the women feminists, remained marginal (Stephens 1922: 237–8). Instead, Rousseau's heavily publicized views on containing the frightening power of women, who like Eve proved weak yet corrupting, were more readily adopted by men and women alike. The Republican mother (developed on classical models) who would further civic virtue through her children but never exercise political rights in person was to be firmly admired (Reynolds 1987: 110–11). So the Republic buttressed itself by adhering to sets of principles, fears, and myths which progressively wrote women out of the public sphere they had eagerly appropriated and sometimes dominated. It consigned them to domestic space.

If we define the French Revolution, following François Fûret, as the "collective crytallisation of a certain number of cultural traits amounting to a new historical consciousness" (Fûret 1984: 45; see also Paulson 1983: 2), we make several major assumptions. We understand that the Revolution, enabled by the Jacobin overthrow of King and aristocracy, fostered a new kind of historical action and awareness. This disabling of the *ancien régime* first created a space encouraging the people, including women of all classes, to shape historical events. We must also see Jacobinism, however, as an ideology and practice which, flooding the country with a semiotic system of representations from liberty caps to statues of La France, offered specific boundaries for action. Political power was no longer to be wielded by women except as representations, never again as reality.[1]

Although the 1789 Revolution had strong supporters in England, the dominant and long-lasting reaction was indisputably conservative; overall perceptions were often narrow in scope. Most English observers, for instance, centered their attention almost exclusively on events occurring in Paris, rather than in the provinces, and frequently distorted those events to their own ideological purposes. With his publication of *Reflections on the Revolution in France* in 1790, Edmund Burke provided the formulations and rhetoric necessary to shape a conservative response both towards the French and towards the English radicals and reformers. He admits that he attacked the French Revolution as a symptom of an even more dangerous revolt within man against his own humanity. At first Burke views the upheaval as a marvelous "spectacle," but he quickly realizes its appalling nature as well. Although he depends on many sources for his metaphors and images, he follows French anti-Jacobins in his association of women with the revolutionary mob, with incoherence or madness, and with explosions of nature, calling the insurrectionists "the furies of hell in the abused shape of the vilest of women" (Burke 1987: 76).[2] The effeminacy of the Jacobins is particularly important. The point is not merely that women in the Revolution were likened to the fierce furies. Rather, the men were "reduced" to the state of female furies. Burke condemns all revolutionaries, mixing the sexes together, in his terms of utter condemnation and anxiety. He links them to chaos, to the breeding of utter foulness, to excrement, and to mothers and daughters:

> The revolution harpies of France, sprung from Night and Hell, or from that chaotic Anarchy . . . cuckoo-like, adulterously lay their eggs and brood over, and hatch them in the nest of every neighbouring state. These obscene harpies, who deck themselves in I know not what divine attributes, but who in reality are foul and ravenous birds of prey, (both mothers and daughters,) flutter over our heads, and souse upon

our tables, and leave nothing unrent, unrifled, unravaged, or unpol-
luted with the slime of their filthy offal.

(Burke 1869: 187)

Decking themselves out in the garb of seductive attributes, the revolutionaries nevertheless reveal themselves as spawned to ruin men of merit
and deprive them of control. David Bromwich has recently argued, correctly I think, that the terror they produce has much to do with their
effeminacy. At the same time, their feminization has much to do with
class position and gender position in the hierarchical grid of Burke's
society. In other words, the feminine sex of the harpies and furies points
to the subservient class positions they held before the Revolution and to
the anger they feel during and after the Revolution. (Bromwich 1990:
96). I cannot even begin to explore here the multilayered meanings in
Burke's allusions and metaphors, so often taken from the Bible, Milton,
and Shakespeare, but their resonance would have been felt profoundly
by his contemporary readers.

Burke was not alone in his masterful use of allusion and metaphor to
shape the narrative of revolution. As was recently indicated by the 1989
British Library exhibition of the English reaction to the Revolution, key
trends in representation created a one-sided view of the upheaval. The
guillotine, calling symbolic castration to mind, furnished the major
symbol of the Revolution for British printmakers. In addition, caricatures
featured the undifferentiated masses in all their grotesqueness instead of
individual Jacobins, whether French or English, in order to stress a loss
of humanity. "They became diabolical or mad, behaving like savages or
wild beasts in a state of nature" (Brewer 1989: 21). The Jacobins were
often shown as female, depicted as wolves or other dangerous creatures,
such as Medea, the furies, or Pandora, who could quickly destroy the
family or create an even more universal chaos.

At the same time, the English, again reading the Revolution in such
a way as to further their own need for a centralized masculine government and a stable family life, fostered a view of the French royal family
as ideal. Marie Antoinette was rehabilitated by Burke and others as a
heroine, forced to flee "almost naked" as if the brutal mob would have
raped her (Burke 1987: 76). Finally, numerous engravings, historical
paintings, and even mugs vividly illustrated the woeful separation of
Louis XVI from his family in order to promote domestic devotion,
rectitude, and unity while documenting their terrible destruction. Indeed,
these representations lent further support to the popular idea of the
beheading of the King as a criminal act against all of humanity rather
than merely against the crown. One of the main results of this propa-
ganda was to solidify further the English conservative's connection of

patriotism with the worship of ideal woman, and misogynism (Brewer 1989: 24).

In Mary Wollstonecraft's attack on Burke, *A Vindication of the Rights of Men* (1790) and in her *A Vindication of the Rights of Woman* (1792), she acknowledged the maenadic energy of some French women, and indicated that it might be better directed, but found far more reprehensible the oppression of women brought about by male worship of weak women. With this argument, she established the emancipation of women as a central issue in English political life. And she noted the wrongs against all classes of women which, though different, proved equally crushing. In addition, she most persuasively connected the oppression of women to the degrading of the male working class, thereby setting an agenda for the future of socialist feminism.

However, in spite of and because of Wollstonecraft's strong voice, in concert with radical Dissenting academies and Jacobin sympathizers, the 1790s saw the boldest defenders of women and revolution disgraced, exiled, or otherwise silenced. Anti-Wollstonecraft tracts such as *The Unsex'd Females* (1793), accused English women who promoted equality of a hardness verging on French female cruelty (Taylor 1984: 10). Yet the effect of such long-term and continuous representations of democratic women and pro-revolutionary men as maenads actually strengthened the connections between feminists and reformers and certainly made some feminists, such as the Owenites of a quarter-century later, even more committed to overthrowing entrenched institutions, such as state, church, and marriage. It also strengthened the public fear of sweeping alterations in the social fabric as somehow connected with women and equality. Militant female Chartists of the 1830s, for example, who were not feminists for the most part, still proved threatening by arguing vehemently for factory reform and a rebalancing of sexual power in the family (Taylor 1984: 268–9; see also Thompson 1984: ch. 7). It is well known that Chartists themselves shared in the iconography of the French Revolution by adopting both slogans and symbols, such as the liberty cap.

Memories of the 1789 Revolution, then, continued to haunt and to shape the English bourgeois imagination. Against a background of riots, rebellions, and revolts in the 1830s and 1840s, numerous books and pamphlets reinvoked and reinterpreted that moment in history which seemed to have firmly ended an era in Europe. We should note a distinction, however, between the treatment of the French Revolution by Victorian journalists and by that culture's imaginative bourgeois writers.

Most often, political commentators from journals such as *Fraser's*, the *Edinburgh Review*, or the *Quarterly Review* feature the series of French Revolutions from 1789 to 1848 as warnings to the English public about the dangers of weak leadership in a monarchy or in constitutional bodies and about the transgressive excesses of mobs who, in tearing down mortar, strike at the very fabric of established culture and society. They are careful to differentiate between the revolutions, including their own of 1688, which they consider to have been far better handled. And with their customary antipathy to the French, they point to national character as bearing the responsibility for the hotheaded and wanton acts of violence which characterize revolutions across the channel. Their essays and reviews rarely take up the issue of gender, unless it is to laud Marie Antoinette.

While journalists do not want to imagine that English social agitation, such as Chartism, could develop into a revolution, they still fear it as an irresistible and irrational force of nature which can come unbidden and quickly run out of control. The energy of the French Revolution of 1848 thus seems particularly inexplicable and frightening to mid-century journalists. Furthermore, its eruption reinvests their own historical moment with an anxiety experienced by many of the English during the Reign of Terror.

As we have noted, the 1789 Revolution elicited a reaction among the English which connected the mob with female excess. The later revolutions abroad reinvoked that link and elicited similarly contradictory responses. Many Victorian texts, assuming female power as a given, take up the intertwined issues of the nature, use, and cost of that power. Texts dealing overtly with political revolution, including Carlyle's massive and influential *History of the French Revolution* (1837), inevitably raise once again the issue of woman's participation in the public sphere. While few writers on the topic shared Carlyle's rhetorical skills, most adopted his association (inherited from Burke) of women with the revolutionary mob, with incoherence or madness, and with explosions of nature (Carlyle 1955: 272). His blending of female power and mad excess in the figure of the maenad, a Bacchant who tears flesh from her victims, was later transformed by Charles Dickens, also ambivalent about female power, into the passionate murderess Hortense in *Bleak House* (1852–3) or the bloodthirsty Madame DeFarge in *A Tale of Two Cities* (1859). That this association should persist during the reign of a female monarch, at a time when feminists are gathering strength, seems highly significant.[3]

In particular, the paradoxical position of the Queen determines the parameters for ideological confusion. On one hand, she is the most powerful woman in the world with an empire at her command. In this sense her position is revolutionary even though her government is stable. On the other hand, she is a domestic body, a woman who depends on her prime minister and her husband to advise and to rule because she believes that women should not hold such positions of power in government. Thus she herself conforms to her role of wife and mother and emotionally abdicates her throne and state power. And yet the very fact that she is a mother awards her immense power. What are Victorians to make of Victoria? Her position, sex, and person do not "match." One result surely was to further doubts and anxieties about powerful women, especially the power of mothers.

If Carlyle, in writing on the French Revolution had contributed to a fear of powerful women, other Victorian writers dealt more complexly with the connection of women, mad excess, and revolution. Their texts challenge the separate sphere ideology of male rule and female submission which either kind of revolution, class or gender, threatens to collapse. In "The Angel and the Strong Minded Woman" Elizabeth Helsinger, Robin Sheets, and William Veeder note the appearance of unorthodox heroines in fiction of the 1840s who vie with the dominant image of the angel in the house (see also Newton 1981). Such women are vital and yet also condemned by Victorians as "unnatural" because "strong minded" (Helsinger *et al.* 1989: III, 89). In their discussion, which features a close analysis of Jane Eyre and Princess Ida, Helsinger, Sheets, and Veeder suggest that during the middle decades of the century the feminine ideal was changing, and they imply that the debate about strong-minded women was new to Victorians.[4]

But I am arguing for a long iconological tradition behind this debate which runs back through Carlyle, Burke, and Wollstonecraft to representations of French women on the barricades and in radical clubs 1789–93 and to the effeminacy of French men. It is no coincidence that some of the very texts featuring unorthodox heroines, such as *Vanity Fair* and *Jane Eyre*, include plotlines or character traits which continue to target the French as both revolutionary and licentious. In the case of Becky Sharp, the sprightly rebel who throws Dr Johnson's *Dictionary* out of a coach window as she spurns English patriarchal rule, a youthful life with a French artist father is held partly accountable for her social and sexual subversiveness. Likewise, the French heritage of the love child and further double for Jane Eyre, Adèle, marks her as woefully in need of correction. Jane as good English governess must teach and mother this spoiled child of a courtesan. But the most obvious case is, of course, the Creole Bertha Mason, who like Burke's women from hell, acts as a "Fury" only "masked in ordinary woman's face and shape" (Brontë 1982: 212). She dies, with her long black hair like that of the virgin/ whore Liberty, "streaming against the flames," "waving her hands above the battlements" (ibid.: 431). It is as if the 1840s are still trying to make sense of revolutionary women, not only French women of the 1789 Revolution but also English women, placed in these fictions of 1847–8 at earlier historical moments of English rebellion and war, such as Waterloo and the Luddite rebellions.

Yet, pursuing Helsinger, Sheets, and Veeder's observations further, we also need to inquire what has remained and what has altered during the 1840s in the transplantation of the imagery of maenadic women.

Furthermore, what political power do such representations wield in their transformation of cultural material? The maenadic woman in these examples and others retains the connections we have already noted: gender and madness are used in the service of nationalism – the maenadic woman is alien to English propriety and containment. The site of excess is the sexual female body. The woman is suspicious to others because her sexual life is not "normal." She may be licentious, or she may be a prostitute, or she may bear guilt by association and be the child of a whore. In some cases, she errs too much in the other direction and is accused of manliness. She is engaged in some type of subversive activity, which directly or indirectly attacks the domestic circle and she still stands in opposition to the angel in the house.

In all cases the discourse of revolution takes as its object, not the Bastille or the factory, but the home. In the replacement of an open and public site of revolt by a contained, private one, these 1840s texts typify the coding of revolutionary discourse and gender in the mid-century. According to Nancy Armstrong, family scandal or sexual misconduct regularly stands in during this period for social rioting or class rebellion as a means of defusing social unrest (Armstrong 1987). She argues that "monstrous" women are brought into fiction in this decade only to be locked up, excluded, or killed off. Aberrant forms of desire, she points out, must be policed to restore normal households – thus, for instance, Bertha Mason must be killed off so that Jane may marry Edward Rochester.[5] Although Jane and Edward come from separate classes, their marriage, in uniting competing social and sexual forces, serves to dull the edge of class conflict through discourses of domesticity.

My point has been, however, that a threat of the rising influence of women in whatever arena they are allowed, rather than class conflict or industrial struggle alone, is displaced persistently during this period onto a maenadic figure and is read negatively, strongly, and yet vaguely – as subversive to cultural stability. Thus the female preacher, the feminist teacher, the mother can all be figured as maenadic.

But I want to stress three further points: first, gender, class, and race are used interchangeably in the period, so that a woman, a working-class man, and a black, say, are all at the bottom of a hierarchical grid (see Higonnet 1989; Kaplan 1988; Stallybrass and White 1986). So if I maintain that gender is the primary social category, I am hardly arguing for the unimportance of others. Each reciprocally constructs the others, as a closer analysis of Burke's anxieties about gender and class would also demonstrate.

Second, a telling alteration in the transplantation of the image is that the domestication of the maenadic woman not only pits her against the angel in the house/ideal mother, but demonstrates their indissoluble link. In the cultural imagination, one can easily slide into the other.

Third, the power balance in what Armstrong calls restored normal households remains strangely abnormal – the woman is still stronger, as if she has absorbed some of the energy banned from the text. The male is left weakened, with the result that we do not have a resolution such as we find in *Pride and Prejudice*, where Mr Darcy is chastened but remains dominant. Indeed, we are left with effeminate men.

If the French Revolutionary plot, as Paulson (1983) describes it, is one of Oedipal rivalry and cannibalism where the male aristocratic order is overturned by the bourgeoisie and lower-class "sons," these Victorian texts offer a different plot with variations for the story of a bankrupt patriarchy. The child, now not necessarily a son, does not overthrow the father to usurp position. In one prominent scenario the husband becomes childlike and the mother gains power over him, so increasing her influence and decreasing his in the public sphere. This scenario involves a blurring of age and thus dependency positions; in some cases, as in *Jane Eyre*, class positions are also blurred. In a different but related scenario, the wife who is afraid of the ability accorded her to rule a domain, awards the power gained from her motherhood to the father and psychologically abdicates her position. Finally, the opposite scenario also operates, where the husband appropriates the mother's power for himself and becomes the nurturer and educator as well as the breadwinner. In all cases, the father becomes feminized; in one he gives up power, in the other he accrues or seizes power culturally designated as female. This situation is distinctly unlike the Revolutionary plot where the stable father becomes unstable, is overthrown, and replaced by stable sons who will themselves be overthrown, while all the time the woman and mother remains marginal. In literary discourse of the 1840s, the roles and positions of the family members begin to collapse into each other.

Literary representations of the 1840s, as Armstrong argues, may attempt to erase class conflict through the introduction of a monstrous woman and the resolution of a marriage of "equals," as in *Jane Eyre*, but we also find a blurring of genders with manly women and effeminate men, a confusion of ages, and a uniting of ordinarily opposed cultural figures and spaces: filthy, whorish mothers who could let loose chaos on the world. Three contemporary historical crises meet in imaginative writing of the period – revolution, motherhood, and female independence.

With this in mind, it is important to recall the very famous, lengthy condemnatory review of *Jane Eyre* by Elizabeth Rigby, Lady Eastlake, printed in the *Quarterly Review* of 1848. It finely articulates what is implied, if not directly stated, in other reactionary cultural documents from these years. "We do not hesitate to say," writes Elizabeth Rigby, "that the tone of mind and thought which has overthrown authority and violated every code human and divine abroad, and fostered Chartism and rebellion at home, is the same which has also written *Jane Eyre*"

(Rigby 1848: 109–10). Influenced heavily by Jane's "liberty and equality" speech in chapter 12, this reviewer sees a dangerous connection being made in the novel between class and gender struggle and between state and domestic revolution. It is perhaps all the more ironic, since Charlotte Brontë was not a strong feminist, that her free-thinking literary character might actually seem dangerous to self-appointed preservers of culture. Jane's power as a negative model is reinforced by other reviewers such as James Lorimer who, in the *North British Review*, notes the influence of a "class of young ladies, of which she has been recognized as the type, and which consequently is now beginning to be known by the epithet of 'Jane Eyrish' " (Lorimer 1849: 487). The strong-minded, passionate woman who speaks of women's rights has now moved fully into myth.

We meet such a myth, almost a caricature of a powerful woman, in *The Princess* by Alfred Lord Tennyson. This poem, influenced by French socialist thinking, investigates the effect of female independence on gender relations by exploring the much-debated topic of granting women a university education. Progressive Princess Ida believes that she must resist marriage in order to found a woman's university. She defies both her father and her betrothed, Prince Hilarion, to do so. In order to win her, Hilarion and two of his friends cross-dress to gain entrance into her all-female enclave. Eventually they are discovered, a battle ensues, Hilarion and others are wounded, and Ida must confront her love for him. Tennyson's treatment of Ida is especially revealing, for it shows his ambivalence towards the powerful female who governs. Ida is torn between using her maenadic energy to the sole benefit of other women and settling down contentedly as an angel in the house. While she understands that to Hilarion and his men she and her free-thinking sisters seem "a kind of monster" (Tennyson 1987: III, 259), she prefers such a designation to that of unthinking angel. Yet if the poem offers a female fantasy of revolution and equality (thus gendering revolution itself as feminine) it also offers a male fantasy of female containment and submission by having Ida fall in love with Hilarion and nurse him back to health.

Tennyson presents an array of femininities which offer possibilities for Ida. She is particularly attracted to the ideas of two women who also happen to be mothers, but no longer wives. As her father tells Hilarion:

> Two widows, Lady Psyche, Lady Blanche;
> They fed her theories, in and out of place
> Maintaining that with equal husbandry
> The woman were an equal to the man.
> (ibid.: I, 127–30)

These two women, Lady Blanche "a tiger-cat/In act to spring" (ibid., II,

426–7) and sweet Lady Psyche, become her mentors and her followers. The fact that each mothers a daughter is important, for it illustrates the Victorian ideology of good motherhood. It is the poem's fervent hope that recalcitrance against cultural norms will not be passed on to the next generation. Neither of the daughters Melissa or Aglaia shows any indication of such revolutionary tendencies in spite of the views of their rebellious mothers.

The poem almost literally separates the intellects and the instincts of mothers – as if to make intellectuality a "role" akin to dyeing one's autumn tresses (which Blanche does). The result of female intellectuality and independence will not be felt by daughters in some chain of revolution, then, though the possibility is certainly voiced while in the process of being denied. Instead, the result will be women's faulty relations with men.

Because of the poem's insistence on sexual difference even while it proffers sisterhood, it is perhaps overdetermined that Ida should be attracted to mothers and mothering. So it comes as no surprise when she steals the child Aglaia from Psyche, who has betrayed the self-sufficiency of their community by knowingly hiding the three male invaders. It is also no surprise that Ida fully enjoys the warmth of mothering. In fact, the poem maintains that the maenad Ida is really a mother at heart, if not in body.

On one level *The Princess* explores whether or not traditional marriage and family arrangements can survive the fulfillment of woman's aspirations. Yet Ida proves a threat not only to the marriage relationship, but also to the male self-image which depends on the weakness of the female partner. Ida's gates have to be stormed, lest her own power become truly institutionalized. While the poem resists a too aggressive masculinity and a too aggressive femininity, it also resists a masculinity weakened by the power balance shifting to women.

To deal with this social problem of a powerful femininity and a weakened masculinity Tennyson tries to have it both ways. He grants power to both sexes and removes it from both. *The Princess* outlines the contours of what it insists is a new type of male/female relation – harmonious androgyny. But because of the dangers of the great female power which it imagines, the poem is forced to recuperate Ida, the figure of mad excess, into a compromise of marriage, though a very odd marriage indeed. For if Ida does not mother children, she mothers her husband. Hilarion's epileptic fits and his wounding in battle place him in the position of the child who requires and gets nurturance.

Contemporary reviewers of the poem, as Helsinger, Sheets, and Veeder have pointed out, found Tennyson's treatment of Princess Ida unambivalent. They enthusiastically approved of what they saw as an Unnatural Woman tamed into submission. She was variously dubbed a "she-man" (Howitt 1848), a "vengeful fury" (Kingsley 1850: 250) and "frozen" (Anon. 1848a). Only one reviewer praised Tennyson for Ida's feminist eloquence and announced her as an heiress to Mary Wollstone-craft (Anon. 1848b). It would take several more decades for the full contradictions of Tennyson's very popular poem to be appreciated, including the figure of the effeminate Prince Hilarion, whom mid-century reviewers primarily ignored except to dislike.

The Princess remains most interesting for exactly its ideological contra-dictions, rather than for its taming of Ida into a safe, heterosexual, royal wife at the close. In other words, radical gender constructions remain in play.[6] Though the ideologically acceptable male, he who is kingly material, is coded as heterosexual and military and the acceptable female is coded as domestic and maternal, we find a resulting mix that is hardly reassuring. Throughout the text, sexual difference is destabilized by male cross-dressing, female independence, and a vision of androgyny. In spite of the codings for proper social roles, as Eagleton (1978) reminds us, the Prince turns out to be no military conqueror and the Princess no angel in the house. Tennyson's critique of gender roles and the disturbance of power relations continues to disrupt the text. The gender mixings which emerge in *The Princess* serve hegemonic ideals while affirming the desire and need for female education, equal rights, and influence in the public sphere.

The Tenant of Wildfell Hall by Anne Brontë moves beyond the stress on containment in *The Princess* to detail the cultural misreading – especially one middle-class man's misreading – of the seemingly danger-ous woman. The novel is offered from a male first-person point of view framing a female first-person diary. Gilbert Markham's story documents Helen Huntingdon's rebellion against her husband Arthur and, in so doing, it recalls several eighteenth-century novels by Mary Wollstonecraft and Charlotte Smith. Yet it differs in that it counsels an inscribed male friend that what he may perceive as overly independent female behavior is a strong woman's only way to maintain integrity in a world where aristocratic male domination can easily slip into abusiveness. It is impor-tant that the text addresses a man, for the counter-hegemonic project of the text is not merely to expose a bad marriage but to teach patriarchy the value of female rebellion. Brontë's feminism, unlike her sister Char-lotte's, locates power in a female artist and mother who is forced to rebel against a licentious masculinity which has gone out of control.

Helen seizes on rebellion as a strategy when she breaks the laws of marriage and child-rearing, wrongly invoked by her unworthy, aristo-cratic husband Arthur. Repeatedly persecuted by this alcoholic, flir-tatious, and spendthrift husband, she flees the marital home with her son and sets herself up in the crumbling home of her birth from where she sends out paintings for sale. The connection of rebellion and female excess is doubly complicated in the text, however.

Unlike *Jane Eyre* or *The Princess* where anarchy is displaced onto Bertha or located in Ida, *The Tenant* encodes Helen as rebellious, but her husband is marked as dangerously anarchic compared to her more normal, moral behavior. In addition, his feminization marks him as akin to the eighteenth-century rake figure such as Lovelace. The book stages a historical progression which is also tied to gender so that the aristocratic male is feminized and killed off while the independent woman and mother survives with the goal of making her son act differently towards women in a future of changed relations between the sexes. Second, the rebelliousness which Helen practices is increased in importance by the frame narrative. Her new neighbors, unable to discover her secrets, quickly mark her as immoral. "If she were a proper person, she would not be living there by herself," remarks young Rose Markham, repeating the words of her own proper mother (Brontë 1986: 114). Cultural anxiety about a strong female subjectivity is immediately inscribed upon her body. Though many of her husband's dissolutions occur in Paris, it is she who is constructed by provincial neighbors as someone alien and threatening to cultural stability. As a newcomer who does not attend church or socialize, she is suspicious; as a mother who looks after her child closely, she is thought to be corrupting him (Brontë 1986: 55–8). Yet the ironic distance created between the "facts" of her life and the suspicions set into play effectively justifies her rebellion all the more. She is shown to be literally and metaphorically a tenant of "Wild" fell Hall. In other words the wildness and cruelty attributed to her (connected to a moral fall) are as limited as her tenancy.

Helen ends up married to her voyeuristic middle-class neighbor Gilbert, to whom she brings land and a fortune. Ideologically, this text, like *Jane Eyre*, promotes gender and class equality which it figures in heterosexual marriage. Yet nearly every man in the book is susceptible to appearances, sentimental romanticizing, cant, or corruption. Even Gilbert is ironized and made inferior to the wiser and more worldly mother-figure, Helen. Though not dissolute like the weakened Arthur, whom Helen eventually rejoins to nurse until he dies, Gilbert condemns himself rightly as a cosseted, spoilt son (Brontë 1986: 58). Like Prince Hilarion, Gilbert is feminized. He storms the barricades of the mysterious "Wildfell Hall" and its female occupant by ingratiating himself as a fellow nurturer for her little son. Yet, also like Hilarion, Gilbert himself is the boy child who wants to take possession of the mother. One is left grateful that Helen loses her first husband to death, but left wondering whether, like Ida, she is better married at all.

The hesitation about woman's need to marry centrally informs the feminism of this text; it is quite clear that Helen can manage on her own. *The Tenant of Wildfell Hall*, then, while still locating woman in the domestic and maternal sphere, alters that sphere and leaves questions about its perpetuation according to former models. Anne Brontë, like her sister Charlotte and like Tennyson, wishes to reduce the male to a child. When Gilbert Markham is aggressive, for instance, he is shown to be at his worst – he is far more acceptable in the text when he is weak and dependent, like Rochester. In softening the male, Tennyson and both Brontë sisters wish to exorcise an aggressive masculinity. Yet Anne's vision of male aristocratic domination, the need for female rebellion, and male disenfranchisement remains so intense that it rivals and even surpasses *Jane Eyre*. One can only speculate what Elizabeth Rigby might have made of this novel.

Revolution and female independence are indissolubly linked in these texts. Each, while in some sense recuperating the female subject into the safety net of the domestic, still manages to voice anti-English and anti-hegemonic sentiments: that men and women cannot always accept proscribed, ideal roles, that the domestic sphere is not necessarily a safety net or a neutral space. On a broader scale, the ideological contradictions of these texts voice a concern about female power, not just the power to rebel, but the power to rule. They address cultural concern about a powerful mother-figure who runs the nation, Victoria. One has to wonder whether the presence of a male monarch on the throne would have sustained quite so rigorously the politicizing of the domestic sphere. Yet these texts also address anxiety about the power awarded woman in the private sphere. This anxiety assumes somewhat different configurations in texts of a married husband and father such as Tennyson and a single, childless woman such as Anne Brontë. Finally, *The Princess* and *The Tenant of Wildfell Hall* voice unease about strong, eloquent women beginning to follow the path of Mary Wollstonecraft in the public sphere. For the 1850s, just around the corner, would see the start of a revitalized English feminism. Although these imaginative texts can be read as shutting down women's independent voices and actions, they should be read primarily as instrumental in enabling and promoting the next wave of revolutionary English feminism as they posit the alternative of the woman who wishes to think and provide for herself, married or not, mother or not.

NOTES

1 For a more detailed analysis of gender, verbal rhetoric, and visual symbolism during the French Revolution see Hunt (1984). Outram (1989) seeks to go beyond both François Fûret's emphasis on discourse and Hunt's treatment of discourse and visual symbolism in her own definition of political culture. She maintains that historians must attend to human behavior expressed concurrently both physically and verbally.

2 Burke draws not only on Homer, Milton, Shakespeare, and eighteenth-century predecessors such as Jonathan Swift and Alexander Pope, but also on the Bible for much of his rhetoric and imagery. See Paulson (1983: 57–73); also see Bromwich (1990).

3 Anna Jameson explores the influence of power on individual women rulers and the influence of women rulers on nations. Jameson's conservative position is clear from the choice of Madame Roland for her epigraph. "Women called to empire have been, in most cases, conspicuously unhappy," she writes, "or criminal" (1834: I, xv). Drawing on the discourse of ethics and of nature, she goes on to claim that the power belonging to a woman "is not properly, or naturally that of sceptre or sword" (ibid.: xv). Queen Victoria would echo Jameson's views. See the valuable discussion of her marriage and reign in Helsinger et al. (1989: I, 63–76). Victoria's description of her consort Albert reveals her ambivalence about wielding the sceptre or sword. Writing to her daughter Vicky, she describes a situation where the husband assumes all roles and both genders: "He was my father, my protector, my guide and adviser in all and everything, my mother (I might almost say) as well as my husband" (Fulford 1964: 112). For the relation of literary women and power to earlier monarchs, including Queen Anne, see Barash (1989).

4 As Armstrong notes, "Such well-known studies as Nina Auerbach's *The Woman and the Demon* and Gilbert and Gubar's *The Madwoman in the Attic* chart the literary manifestations of this figure. Finding no precedent for this woman in earlier fiction and recognizing the power of the figure, Auerbach attributes the appearance of the demonic woman to a myth that peopled the Victorian world with female demons and angels, while Gilbert and Gubar locate the source of the madwoman in the female author whose imagination was necessarily thwarted by a limiting repertoire of conventions for her self-expression" (1987: 165). There is much of value in both interpretations. But I also agree with Armstrong that the image of the monstrous woman which stands for deviant forms of desire is composed of cultural material having a history. We differ, however, in that I don't consider that history to be largely written; it is also verbal and visual. Nor do I view it as specifically connected to the British novel, although the British transform it to their own ideological ends.

5 For further analysis, see Cohan and Shires (1988: 142–8) where we isolate discourses of revolution and domesticity in order to show what is ideologically at stake in *Jane Eyre*'s discursive heterogeneity, in conflicting representations of the titular heroine's subjectivity, and in its recuperation of a unified subject in Jane Rochester.

6 For a more detailed analysis of this poem, which stresses ideological imperatives and sexual politics, see Shires (1990).

WORKS CITED

Anon. (1806) *The Female Revolutionary Plutarch*, 3 vols, by the author of *The Revolutionary Plutarch* and *Memoirs of Talleyrand*, London.

—— (1848a) "*The Princess*; by Alfred Tennyson," *Gentleman's Magazine*, 183: 131.

—— (1848b) "Tennyson's *Princess*," *Eclectic*, 4th series 23: 423.

Armstrong, Nancy (1987) *Desire and Domestic Fiction: A Political History of the Novel*, New York: Oxford University Press.

Barash, Carol (1989) "Augustan Women's Mythmaking: English Women Writers and the Body of Monarchy 1660–1720," Dissertation, Princeton University.

Brewer, John (1989) "This Monstrous Tragi-comic Scene," in David Bindman (ed.) *The Shadow of The Guillotine*, London: British Museum Publications, pp. 11–25.

Bromwich, David (1990) "Edmund Burke, Revolutionist (1795)," *The Yale Journal of Criticism* 4(1): 85–107.

Brontë, Anne (1986) *The Tenant of Wildfell Hall*, Harmondsworth, Penguin. First published in 1848.

Brontë, Charlotte (1982) *Jane Eyre*, New York: New American Library. First published in 1847.

Burke, Edmund (1869) *The Works of Edmund Burke*, 12 vols, Boston: Little Brown.

— (1987) *Reflections on the Revolution in France*, Buffalo: Prometheus Books. First published 1790.

Carlyle, Thomas (1955) *History of the French Revolution*, 2 vols, London: J. M. Dent & Sons. First published 1837.

Cohan, Steven and Shires, Linda M. (1988) *Telling Stories, A Theoretical Analysis of Narrative Fiction*, New York: Routledge.

Eagleton, Terry (1978) "Tennyson: Politics and Sexuality in *The Princess* and *In Memoriam*," in Francis Barker (ed.) *1848: The Sociology of Literature*, Essex: University of Essex Press, pp. 97–106.

Fulford, Roger (ed.) (1964) *Dearest Child: Letters between Queen Victoria and the Princess Royal 1858–1861*, New York: Holt.

Fûret, François (1984) *Interpreting the French Revolution*, trans. Elborg Forster, Cambridge: Cambridge University Press. First published in French in 1978.

Gallagher, Catherine (1985) "Response" to "Medusa's Head" in Neil Hertz, *The End of the Line, Essays on Psychoanalysis and the Sublime*, New York: Columbia University Press.

Helsinger, Elizabeth K., Sheets, Robin Lauterbach and Veeder, William (1989) *The Woman Question: Society and Literature in Britain and America 1837–1883*, 3 vols, Chicago, University of Chicago Press.

Higonnet, Margaret and Patrice (1989) "The Women and the Struggle," *Times Literary Supplement*, 19 May: 541–2.

[Howitt, William?] (1848) "Review" of *The Princess, Howitt's Magazine* 3: 28–9.

Hufton, Olwen (1989) "Voilà La Citoyenne," *History Today* 391 (May): 26–32.

Hunt, Lynn (1984) *Politics, Culture, and Class in the French Revolution*, Berkeley, University of California Press.

Jameson, Anna (1834) *Memoirs of Celebrated Female Sovereigns*, 2 vols, 2nd edn, London: Saunders & Otley.

Kaplan, Cora (1988) " 'Like a Housemaid's Fancies': The Representation of Working Class Women in Nineteenth Century Writing," in Susan Sheridan (ed.) *Grafts*, London: Verso, pp. 56–69.

Kingsley, Charles (1850) "Tennyson," *Fraser's* 42: 245–55.

Landes, Joan B. (1988) *Women and the Public Sphere in the Age of the French Revolution*, Ithaca, NY: Cornell University Press.

Levy, Darlene Gay, Applewhite, Harriet and Johnson, Mary (1979) *Women in Revolutionary Paris 1789–1795*, Urbana: University of Illinois Press.

[Lorimer, James] (1849) "Noteworthy Novels," *North British Review* 11: 487.

Newton, Judith Lowder (1981) *Women, Power, and Subversion*, New York: Methuen.

Outram, Dorinda (1989) *The Body and the French Revolution: Sex, Class, and Political Culture*, New Haven, CT: Yale University Press.

Paulson, Ronald (1983) *Representations of Revolution (1789–1820)*, New Haven, CT: Yale University Press.

Reynolds, Sìan (1987) "Marianne's Citizens? Women, the Republic and Universal Suffrage in France," in Sìan Reynolds (ed.) *Women, State, and Revolution, Essays on Power and Gender in Europe since 1789*, Amherst: University of Massachusetts Press.

Rigby, Elizabeth, Lady Eastlake (1848) "*Vanity Fair* and *Jane Eyre*," *Quarterly Review* 84 (December): 153–85; as reprinted in Miriam Allott (ed.) *The Critical Heritage*, London: Routledge & Kegan Paul, 1974, pp. 105–12.

Shires, Linda M. (1990) "Re-reading Tennyson's Gender Politics," in Thaïs Morgan (ed.) *Victorian Sages and Cultural Discourse*, New Brunswick: Rutgers University Press.

Stallybrass, Peter and White, Allon (1986) *The Politics and Poetics of Transgression*, Ithaca, NY: Cornell University Press.

Stephens, Winifred (1922) *Women of the French Revolution*, London: Chapman and Hall.

Taylor, Barbara (1984) *Eve and the New Jerusalem: Socialism and Feminism in the Nineteenth Century*, London: Virago.

Tennyson, Alfred Lord (1987) *The Poems of Tennyson*, ed. Christopher Ricks, 3 vols, 2nd edn, Berkeley: University of California Press.

Thompson, Dorothy (1984) *The Chartists*, London: Temple Smith.

Williams, Gwyn A. (1989) *Artisans and Sans-Culottes: Popular Movements in France and Britain during the French Revolution*, London: Libris.

Wollstonecraft, Mary (1790) *A Vindication of the Rights of Men in a Letter to the Right Honourable Edmund Burke occasioned by His Reflections on the Revolution in France*, 2nd edn, London: Joseph Johnson.

—— (1792) *A Vindication of the Rights of Woman with Strictures on Political and Moral Subjects*, London: Joseph Johnson.

Chapter 10

The "female paternalist" as historian
Elizabeth Gaskell's *My Lady Ludlow*

Christine L. Krueger

A patchwork of women's narratives long denigrated for its structural deformity, Elizabeth Gaskell's *My Lady Ludlow* affords Christine Krueger with an important example of an anti-totalizing representation of femininity. Krueger argues that Gaskell anticipates the dis-ease of modern feminists who resist the undermining of a theory of female oppression which a post-structuralist view of history often entails. Among the decentered histories of *My Lady Ludlow*, Gaskell provides one continuous history by a "female paternalist." Gaskell is thus able to examine a privileged woman's power within the patriarchy, noting where it produces contradictions in patriarchal ideology. The female paternalist marks an especially interesting site, yet is not privileged in a text asserting the diversity of both female desire and women's narratives of history.

* * *

Written in the aftermath of Gaskell's *Life of Charlotte Brontë* (1857), *My Lady Ludlow* (1858) shows the marks of an author wondering how history – particularly the history of women – might be written. Gaskell's biography had met with condemnation because it treated Brontë, not according to the repressive conventions of female biography, which would use women's lives to construct and enforce normative feminine behavior, but as a more fully realized subject.[1] So too after the publication of her novel *Ruth* (1853), dealing with the persecution of "fallen women," Gaskell was accused of immorality and indelicacy. Rather than retreating from the task of representing transgressive women, however, Gaskell took it up with even greater ingenuity in *My Lady Ludlow*. Here her aims are both to imagine a way of constructing historical discourse from the narratives by which women had created an ideologically diverse range of meanings in the past, and to critique totalizing accounts of female experience.[2] Representing the heterogeneity of women's histories enables Gaskell to examine the narratives' varied genealogies and to multiply the forms of resistance to hegemonic historical discourse, but also involves her in narrative and political contradictions that still engage feminists today.

For strategic purposes Gaskell seeks to preserve apparently incompatible narratives. She must negotiate between, on the one hand, stories that decenter the historical subject, disperse narrative authority, disrupt notions of progressive cause and effect, and, on the other, continuous history, specifically the romance, which posits continuity of the subject, consolidates the narrator's authority and claims to trace a linear historical plot.[3] She needs both kinds of narrative in *My Lady Ludlow* in order to uncover two varieties of what Foucault calls "subjugated knowledges." As Jana Sawicki analyzes Foucault's term, it refers both to experiences deemed unworthy of expert study and to the conflicts within history that totalizing historical discourses obscure (Sawicki 1988: 168). Gaskell represents the former category of subjugated knowledges by using marginalized female narrators, constructing several of the novel's stories in subordinate genres of historical discourse, and placing narrative detail on the same epistemological footing with structures of coherence. These strategies alone would meet with sympathy from feminist readers today. However, Gaskell's method for representing the conflicts obscured by continuist histories, as well as the conflicts within such discourses, has, I believe, resulted in the novel's exclusion from feminist analysis. For this purpose, Gaskell employs a peculiar variation on a master narrative: the romance of the female paternalist. Careful to avoid privileging Lady Ludlow's narrative over the other stories that make up this formally eccentric novel, careful as well to expose her character's affiliation with entrenched power structures, Gaskell nevertheless considers the representation of the female paternalist to be crucial. Rather than banish the paradoxical figure of the female paternalist from feminist history, Gaskell examines her power – political and discursive – within the patriarchy, noting where it has been complicit, but also showing where it produces contradictions in patriarchal ideology. That is, positioned where gender and class collide, the female paternalist's continuous history reveals sites where power creates resistance.

One tale among several narrated in this decentered novel, the romance of the female paternalist, like each story, narrator, and genre in *My Lady Ludlow*, invites us to observe how historical narrative is constructed and how it produces values in the present. In so doing, Gaskell offers feminist historians a revision of Foucaldian genealogy that neither deprives women of discursive strategies for theorizing pervasive male domination, nor entails our allegiance to any totalizing, normative account of femininity. She helps us to steer a course between on the one hand, what Isaac D. Balbus terms the Foucaldian "ban on continuous history," and on the other, what he argues is the only alternative: psychoanalytic mothering theory. Balbus claims that the Foucaldian ban

would make it impossible for women even to speak of the historically universal misogyny from which they have suffered and against which

they have struggled . . . [it] disciplines *women* by depriving them of
the conceptual weapons with which they can understand and begin to
overcome their universal subordination.

(Balbus 1987: 120)

As Jana Sawicki argues, Balbus presents a false dichotomy, since as an
instrument for critiquing theory rather than a theory in itself, Foucaldian
genealogy does not deny "the naming of patriarchy . . . but the attempt
to deduce it from a general theory and to privilege a single locus of
resistance" (Sawicki 1988: 170). Gaskell's use of the romance of the
female paternalist bears out Sawicki's contention: it is one representation
of women's experience among many, and a provocatively conflicted one
at that, whose fissures reveal, rather than conceal, the oppressive effects
of patriarchy. Deploying structures of coherence, particularly romance
conventions, as well as anti-narrative strategies of disruption, generic
heterogeneity, and destabilizing perspectives in *My Lady Ludlow*, Gaskell in fact provides women's history with an impressive array of discursive weapons, not only for resisting subordination, but also for redefining
the purposes of historical writing.[4]

Its female narrators and suggestive fissures make *My Lady Ludlow* a
rich text for feminist analysis. So too does its significant place in Gaskell's
career – immediately following the controversy stirred up by her biography of Charlotte Brontë, and the last lengthy work before her historical
novel, *Sylvia's Lovers* (1863). Yet, we have added little to the discussion
of the novel since Aina Rubenius treated of one of its characters, Miss
Galindo, as an example of a woman succeeding in the male-dominated
profession of clerking (Rubenius 1950: 125–8).[5] At the heart of this
exclusion, I would argue, is a misreading of the eponymous character,
Lady Ludlow. She is, *par excellence*, an instance of what Rosemarie
Bodenheimer has termed the "female paternalist" (Bodenheimer 1988:
21–5). Resolutely king and church, vehemently anti-Jacobin, Lady
Ludlow – who is treated sympathetically – apparently poses an embarrassing counter-example to any claims for Gaskell's feminism and progressive politics. Furthermore, the conventional romance plot of the story
Lady Ludlow narrates reinforces skepticism that this work, or for that
matter any of Gaskell's similarly structured social problem novels, such
as *Mary Barton, Ruth,* or *North and South* can be read as subverting
the patriarchal order.

The political dis-ease this story creates for feminist critics focuses the
issues at stake in our general neglect of Gaskell.[6] In her recent biography
of Gaskell, Patsy Stoneman attributes that neglect to the fact that Gaskell's writings have been "perceived as belonging either to the (masculine) preserve of the 'industrial' novel or the cosy world of the 'lady
novelists,' " and therefore thought to offer "nothing as promising as the

Brontë novels or George Eliot" (Stoneman 1987: 7). Feminist critics'
lack of interest in Gaskell as an historical writer generally, and in *My
Lady Ludlow* in particular, is unfortunate since, like feminist writers
today, Gaskell confronted the difficulties involved in imaging and enact-
ing female power in texts. Always a vexing problem for women writers,
it becomes particularly acute in historical narrative because, on the one
hand, female power can easily be marginalized, its historical impact
simply unrecognized ("the cosy world of the 'lady novelists' "), while on
the other hand, depictions of women assuming traditionally male-
dominated positions of power can be recognized and yet quickly subsumed into structures of oppression ("the [masculine] preserve of the
'industrial' novel"). Our period's successes in resolving this difficulty are
not always notably better than Gaskell's own. Rather than dismissing
My Lady Ludlow too hastily on the basis of its politics, we should look
to this work for enabling alternatives to our current discursive practices.

Having made these claims for Gaskell's project, I nevertheless
acknowledge its contradictions, comprehended by the term "female
paternalist." This category works towards refining earlier feminist analyses which characterize women in terms of either their gendered role in
patriarchy, or their class interests in capitalism. "Female paternalist"
insists on the frequent conceptual inseparability of gender and class
constructions of women's identities, granting neither a prior position. But
even this designation, with its implied accusation of complicity against its
subjects, too neatly opposes women's writing and paternalistic social
narrative. In discussing *My Lady Ludlow*, I wish to extend the apparently
oxymoronic term "female paternalist" to Victorian women writers who,
though their very status as authors challenged the patriarchal order,
nevertheless lend their support to social structures entailing dominance
and submission. Used by Rosemary Bodenheimer to denote heroines of
bourgeois social problem novels, the term helps to account for the many
novelists, including Elizabeth Gaskell, who at once locate the origin of
social evils in masculine competition, greed, and narcissism and yet
pattern their ideal society on the hierarchical model of the bourgeois
family.

Ultimately, Lady Ludlow's romance of the female paternalist – the
centered, conventionally plotted story she narrates – may prove incompatible with the novel's other disruptive voices, a regrettable capitulation
both to dominant ideology and to hegemonic historical discourse. After
all, though the aristocratic and middle-class characters of *My Lady
Ludlow* reform many of their prejudices, a version of the class structure
– newly benevolent, paternalistic, or, more accurately, maternalistic –
remains intact. Yet within the contexts of nineteenth-century politics and
discursive practices one can appreciate Gaskell's desire to retain the
voice of the female paternalist.

My Lady Ludlow suggests that our current way of thinking about the figure of the female paternalist needs refinement. Any term which classifies women writers as progressive or reactionary is of limited value in the context of eighteenth- or nineteenth-century politics because it ignores the feminist activity of women within conservative, patriarchal institutions, such as religious movements. Female preachers of the eighteenth and nineteenth centuries, for instance, are prime examples of women who uphold a patriarchal, paternalistic institution because, paradoxically, it affords them a cultural sanction for their radical appropriation of a privileged discourse. As Deirdre David has shown, two of the nineteenth century's most successful female writers, Elizabeth Barrett Browning and George Eliot, adopted the values of the landowning class in order to resist their subordination in a male-dominated society. (See, for example, Valenze 1985; Poovey 1988; and David 1987). This oppositional role *within* patriarchy is most obvious in women's histories of their own activities in such contexts, requiring them to reflect on the contradictory ideologies they must adopt for strategic purposes.

The historical narrative of the female paternalist must be put in the context of mid-nineteenth-century historical discourse in general. The coherent, centered narrative of the female paternalist (for example, what Bodenheimer calls the "romance of the female paternalist") can be seen as inevitably complicit with patriarchal structures of domination. But women writers needed not only to disrupt the rigid epistemological hierarchy and the transcendent, omniscient-appearing status of the historian in their culture's dominant discourses. At the same time, they needed to retain the authority to construct a counter-representation of women's history, where continuity of cause and effect still has a legitimate place. Women writing history often turned to the narrative flexibility of the novel as the most advantageous site to work out literary innovations that would help transform historical narrative (Doody 1980). The hegemonic designs of all narrative conventions notwithstanding, in the multiple voices of the novel women writers could simultaneously undermine dominant narratives and hold out the possibility that traditional literary conventions could advance feminist goals.

In *My Lady Ludlow*, Gaskell evolves a very eccentric narrative both to disrupt centered narrative and to suggest its qualified usefulness in writing women's history. She also betrays her dis-ease at the sometimes contradictory implications of these goals and at her own status as the author of this "de-formed" novel. It is not without cause that generations of critics condemned *My Lady Ludlow* for lacking "organic unity."[7] The novel, originally published in Dickens's *Household Words*, was in turn collected along with other pieces of both fiction and non-fiction Gaskell had done for the magazine in an eclectic volume she entitled *Round the Sofa* (1859). The only formal unifying principle of that work is the frame, in which characters gather around an invalid's sofa to entertain one another by relating everything from autobiographical reminiscences (*My Lady Ludlow*) to an anthropological treatise on the oppressed Cagots people of the Pyrenees (*An Accursed Race*). What readers disparaged as the narrative incoherence of *My Lady Ludlow* itself is, in fact, evidence of the range of strategies Gaskell employs in order to show how women might use and discard a variety of literary forms to represent their experience, and write their histories.

Told by multiple narrators using different generic conventions and interrupting each other's tales, the novel includes only one tale (told by Lady Ludlow but enjoying no privileged position in the work as a whole) which has anything resembling a conventional plot and closure. The novel is structured like a set of Russian dolls, with one woman's history set inside another's, each supplying a context for the others, and finally encasing a history of the French Revolution. *My Lady Ludlow* is framed first by the narrator of *Round the Sofa*, a young girl who has been sent to Edinburgh to be treated by a doctor. Ostensibly she writes *My Lady Ludlow* as a composition exercise, recording the life story of her physician's aging sister, Margaret Dawson. Margaret Dawson is literally at the center of the narrators of *Round the Sofa* as the invalid around whom they gather. Yet her story is the biography of another woman, the late Lady Ludlow, the person who most influenced Margaret as a young girl. The contradictions in the character of Lady Ludlow, a doctrinaire church and king aristocrat who nevertheless endows a paupers' school and tolerates bastards and Dissenters out of loyalty to friends, can only be understood in terms of formative experiences during the French Revolution. That narrative is given in Lady Ludlow's voice and constitutes an historical romance within the larger context of the novel revealing, as we shall see, a complex mix of the rational and sentimental origins of Lady Ludlow's politics.

The most striking similarity between the unnamed narrator of the frame of *Round the Sofa* – the young girl in the care of Mrs Dawson's brother – and Mrs Dawson, the narrator of Lady Ludlow's history, is infirmity. The narrator of the frame is suffering from an unspecified disease and has been sent to Edinburgh to combine her education with Dr Dawson's treatments. She lives a depressingly spartan existence with her governess, Miss Duncan, punctuated by the convivial gatherings around the invalid Mrs Dawson's sofa, where the assembled company entertain one another with "something, either of information, tradition, history, or legend" (Gaskell 1972: 390).

Gaskell drew this frame from her own experience. After her father's death, Elizabeth was sent to a family friend, Mr Turner, in Newcastle to spend the winter of 1829–30. During the following winter, Mr Turner packed Elizabeth and his daughter Anne off to Edinburgh to escape the cholera epidemic, and here she was welcomed into the modest salon of Mrs Eliza Fletcher, née Dawson, the model for Gaskell's character in *My Lady Ludlow*. Meta Gaskell's description of her mother's visits to the Turner household was intended to dispel the impression that, Jane-Eyre-like, she had been sent to serve as a governess. In a 1909 letter to Clement Shorter, Miss Gaskell corrected the notion "that after her Father's death my Mother was sent out into the world to earn her own living, and that she went to Mr. Turner of Newcastle in order to do so" (Gérin 1980: 40). Rather, these were the quite ordinary visits of a girl to her "connections." Nevertheless, the mysterious illness suffered by the young visitor to the fictional Mrs Dawson's salon suggests that in retrospect Gaskell may have interpreted her own status as an orphan – a young woman sent out into the world alone – as tantamount to having been diseased. More importantly, just as Gaskell identified with the fallen women in some of her other works as symbolizing her own outcast status as a woman writer, here she appears to reflect on her society's perception of female authorship as deforming and disabling women from their proper duties. The infirmity of female authorship would be further exaggerated in a de-formed narrative, like *My Lady Ludlow*.

Infirmity and loss, however, are what enable both Dr Dawson's patient and Margaret Dawson to become storytellers. After the death of Margaret's father, Lady Ludlow, herself a widow, invites the girl to join the small group of orphaned or distressed young gentlewomen she has adopted at her family's estate, Hanbury House. When Margaret is crippled by a fall, Lady Ludlow installs the invalid in her own private sitting-room as her companion and assistant. From this privileged position, Margaret observes the details of Lady Ludlow's life, from which she later constructs her narrative. Now an elderly woman herself, Mrs Dawson holds court from a sofa in her brother's home, gathering an audience around her. Likewise, the narrator of the frame enjoys the company of Mrs Dawson's salon, free from paternal control and daughterly obligations, due to her disease. She, in turn, persuades the elderly invalid to recount her own history, and that of Lady Ludlow. Infirmity, then, figures forth the simultaneously abnormal and privileged position of the female author and her intimate relationships with her audience of sororal sufferers.

Indeed, these diseased or crooked women will tell crooked tales, filled with digressions, *non sequiturs*, irrelevant details, and producing no comforting resolution. Both narrators apologize for the formal inadequacies of their tales. The frame narrator offers the self-deprecating explanation that she has recorded the stories told "round the sofa at the suggestion of Miss Duncan, who imagined it to be a 'good exercise for me, both in memory and composition' " (Gaskell 1972: 216). Mrs Dawson at first demurs from telling her story,

"Nay," said she, smiling, "that would be too long a story. Here are
Signore Sperano and Miss Duncan, and Mr. and Mrs. Preston are
coming to-night, Mr. Preston told me; how would they like to hear
an old-world story which, after all, would be no story at all, neither
beginning, nor middle, nor end, only a bundle of recollections."

(ibid.: 7–8)

At last she agrees, "I will try and tell you about [Lady Ludlow],"
repeating her apology that "It is no story: it has, as I said, neither
beginning, middle, nor end" (ibid.: 9). Gaskell's characters suffer from
a peculiarly feminine discursive complaint: the desire to tell the history
of their own experience, which refuses to conform to the norms of
patriarchal narrative.[8]

Mrs Dawson begins her story with a reflection on space, time, and
narrative, akin to the historical retrospections common in George Eliot's
novels.[9] "I am an old woman now and things are very different to what
they were in my youth," she remarks.

Then we, who travelled, travelled in coaches, carrying six inside, and
making a two days' journey out of what people now go over in a
couple of hours with a whizz and a flash, and a screaming whistle,
enough to deafen one. Then letters came in but three times a week;
indeed, in some places in Scotland where I have stayed when I was a
girl, the post came in but once a month; but letters were letters then;
and we made great prizes of them, and read them and studied them
like books. Now the post comes rattling in twice a day, bringing short,
jerky notes, some without beginning or end, but just a little sharp
sentence, which well-bred folks would think too abrupt to be spoken.
Well, well! they may all be improvements – I dare say they are; but
you will never meet with a Lady Ludlow in these days.

(ibid.)

Margaret Dawson expresses a nostalgia for a particular sort of text, and
relationship to texts. Here, at the outset, she treats this narrative form
as if it were a moral principle: this is the way she has learned that stories
should be told. Yet, just as her auditors "will never meet with a Lady
Ludlow in these days," neither will they be able to produce or consume
the sort of Fieldingesque narrative eschewed in *Middlemarch* in this age
of "short, jerky notes, some without beginning or end." They will not
"travel" with other readers, but construct meanings in private. What is
more, they will not study the "jerky notes" which make up the narratives
of the present day as if they were books – or indeed, the Book – seeking
out a "well-bred," privileged meaning. However, as a result of the
dialectical relationship between Margaret Dawson's disjointed narrative

and the conventionalized romance told by Lady Ludlow, Dawson will come to appreciate the value of her own "ill"-bred narrative method.

Lady Ludlow, it would seem, is an eminently healthy narrator. Within her parish, Lady Ludlow's authority is without rival; her word is law. In the space left by the deaths of her husband and nine children, she is able to construct herself as the patriarch, just as if George Eliot's narrator had been able to erase Fielding and his sons from literary history. Gaskell shows Lady Ludlow using her power to correct the mistakes of a misguided patriarchy, as when she takes up the cause of a ne'er-do-well tenant accused of poaching. When the young Evangelical clergyman, Mr Gray, brings her the plight of Job Gregson, confined to jail by a neighbouring magistrate while his children languish, Lady Ludlow reacts like a stock aristocratic villain, siding unquestioningly with the judgment of her peer. But after visiting the Gregsons' hovel, she demands of the Justice, Mr Lathom, that he release Job on bail, which she proposes to pay. "It is against the law, my lady," he objects.

> "Bah! Bah! Bah! Who makes the laws? [asks Lady Ludlow.] Such as I, in the House of Lords – such as you, in the House of Commons. We, who make the laws in St. Stephen's, may break the mere forms of them, when we have right on our sides, on our own land, and amongst our own people. . . . A pretty set you and your brother magistrates are to administer justice through the land! I always said a good despotism was the best form of government; and I am twice as much in favour of it now I see what a quorum is!"
>
> (ibid.: 38–9)

In this instance at least, Lady Ludlow's brand of despotism improves considerably on that granted by Fielding to his Squire Allworthy, for it benefits from the ability to draw back the curtain of appearances and see into the nature of things – a power Fielding reserves to himself, as author. In her creation of the female paternalist, Gaskell offers us the fantasy of despot as fairy godmother, and temporarily brackets the restrictions on her power as a woman.

Gaskell scrutinizes that fantasy, however, in her presentation of the female paternalist as historian. Although Lady Ludlow's tragic tale of Clément and Virginie, victims of the Terror, starts sixty pages into Margaret Dawson's reminiscences (and takes up fully a third of the novel), it is important to treat this story first. With Lady Ludlow's story, Gaskell insists on preserving a role for conventional narrative in constructing women's histories; further, the novel's other narratives provide feminist interpretive strategies for reading the female paternalist's romance.[10] Not only the content of this story, but the narrative conventions by which it is structured, suggest how the female paternalist represents her past as the rationale for her present actions.

Lady Ludlow narrates the sort of continuous history for which Margaret Dawson expresses nostalgia at the outset of her reminiscences, one with a cathartic and reassuring – if illusory – beginning, middle, and end. It locates the origins of the French Revolution in a discrete phenomenon: the newly acquired ability of the lower orders to read their masters' texts. The plot progresses through the coherent stages of a star-crossed romance between an aristocratic hero and heroine and their betrayal by an unprincipled upstart, and it culminates in the tragic union of the lovers in death. Lady Ludlow is reminded of the story when she discovers that her agent has taught Job Gregson's son to read. Briefly, Lady Ludlow's tale involves a family of French aristocrats, whom she befriends in England where they have fled to escape the terror. Clément De Créquy, the son, whose instinctive noble bearing and undisguisable beauty place him in the tradition of the romance hero, returns to France to rescue his cousin, Virginie. Their plan for escape is discovered when the young son of the concierge who has been hiding Virginie reads a note from Clément that has been concealed in a nosegay she has sent him to buy. The boy betrays them to his uncle, Morin, a jealous rival for Virginie's affections whose suit is rendered hopeless by virtue of his class. Clément and Virginie are imprisoned and guillotined. In England, Clément's mother dies of grief, and the family becomes extinct.

Gaskell historicizes Lady Ludlow's authority to narrate this tale by attributing it to both class and generation. As Lady Ludlow comments at the end of her story,

> People seldom arrive at my age without having watched the beginning, middle, and end of many lives and many fortunes. We do not talk about them, perhaps; for they are often so sacred to us, from having touched us into the very quick of our own hearts, as it were, or into those of others who are dead and gone, and veiled over from human sight, that we cannot tell the tale as if it was a mere story. But young people should remember that we have had this solemn experience of life, on which to base our opinions and form our judgements, so that they are not mere untried theories.
>
> (ibid.: 126)

Whether or not the elderly Lady Ludlow's experience produces a reliable historical hindsight, the fact remains that she believes in the tragic coherence of her past and its sacred significance, and strives to author her life, and those of her dependants, accordingly. "Young people," and those "who, both by position and age, must have had [their] experience confined to a very narrow circle" (ibid.), as Lady Ludlow puts it, must remember the narratives of the female paternalist because of her present authority. The romance genre, melodramatic plot, heroic characters, and tragic closure of her tale – the discourse by which the aristocracy represents itself – all reveal the ideology which informs the discursive politics of a still potent ruling class.

What is more, the contradictions in Lady Ludlow's status as a *female* paternalist reveal the fissures in the ruling class's privileged discourse. Margaret Dawson commented at the time that Mr Gray should hear the story of Clément and Virginie in order that he might understand Lady Ludlow's reasons for opposing his paupers' school. But Lady Ludlow maintains that her power transcends textuality. Other people might have to justify the authority of their stories, but her speech is simply legitimized by virtue of her class: "he ought not to require reasons from me," she replies, "nor to need such explanation of my arguments (if I condescend to argue), as going into relation of the circumstances on which my arguments are based in my own mind would be" (ibid.). What he might discover from Lady Ludlow's narrative is not only the sense of a tragic past on which her class, in her opinion, predicates its current paternalism, but also the peculiar perspective of the *female* paternalist on the fate of her class, and, to some extent, women in general. For example, Lady Ludlow presents Virginie as the victim of a failed patriarchy. Her father indoctrinates her in the philosophy of Rousseau, to which Lady Ludlow attributes the girl's earlier rejection of Clément's marriage proposal, and what presumably would have been a happy ending. More importantly, her father's conviction that his radical politics places his family above the wrath of the revolutionaries leads them all like lambs to the slaughter. Furthermore, Virginie naïvely puts herself at the mercy of the concierge, Mme Babette, failing to consider how sorely that woman's extreme want will try her loyalty. Squeezed between the needs of her son, and the demands of her greedy brother, Morin, Mme Babette is herself a victim of the patriarchy, who will collude in Virginie's betrayal in order to survive. Finally, in true Gothic fashion, Lady Ludlow constructs Virginie's persecution in sexual as well as economic terms. Morin's pathological desire for Virginie leads him to kill that which he cannot possess.

Above all, Mr Gray, as a poor clergyman and a social reformer, might well wonder of what use such a fiction would be to a woman like Lady Ludlow. Why, after all, would a woman, whose privilege is apparently secure, react to her discovery that a pauper child has been taught to read by telling such a fearful tale of threatened virtue? As American male writers of the nineteenth century thematized their anxieties in "melodramas of beset manhood," Lady Ludlow authors a past that enables her to make emotional sense of a present in which she is under attack. However, although her reaction may be exaggerated, Lady Ludlow, as a woman dependent on the patriarchy, is hardly guilty of a paranoid fantasy. During Margaret Dawson's residence at Hanbury House, Lady Ludlow's last surviving child, a son, dies, rendering the family's extinction inevitable. The estate she inherited from her family, the Hanburys, has been deeply mortgaged by her husband to improve his lands in Scotland, forcing her, like so many of Gaskell's female characters, into hopelessly inadequate "elegant economies." Without the providential assistance of her inferiors, Lady Ludlow would surely have lost her home. She is as likely, therefore, to identify with her character Mme Babette as she is with Mme De Créquy.

Certainly, Lady Ludlow's narrative is compensatory, substituting narrative authority for threatened economic and social power. Yet it is also evident that while Lady Ludlow mourns the demise of an aristocratic patriarchy, she also recognizes that it cannot be recovered, that it may even be understood to be the disease from which she suffers as a female paternalist. Patricia Meyer Spacks's assessment of storytelling in *Cranford* might be applied to the female paternalist's history as well: "Gaskell invites awareness of the fragility and the courage of female structures of self-protection, but also of their exclusionary force" (Spacks 1985: 189). In the case of Lady Ludlow, the power of the female paternalist, not only to defend herself but to do good for others, stems from a system that excludes not only those upon whom she must depend, but ultimately excludes even her.

With her other narrators, Gaskell offers alternative discursive structures which revise the purpose of historical narrative and the nature of narrative desire. The web of Margaret Dawson's narrative is made of lace, specifically the lace worn by her mother to distinguish herself from "rich democratic manufacturers, all for liberty and the French Revolution" (Gaskell 1972: 9). From the description of that lace, itself the product of a lost art, Mrs Dawson embroiders her own past. With affectionate condescension she remembers her mother, who "was so innocently happy when she put [the lace collar and cuffs] on – often, poor dear creature, to a very worn and threadbare gown – that I think, even after all my experiences of life, they were a blessing to the family" (ibid.: 10). This apparently irrelevant detail in fact provides both a clue to the experiences that have shaped Mrs Dawson's politics and her connection to the subject of her story, Lady Ludlow. The lace, once owned by a common ancestress, is the symbol of a matriarchy that links these women across generations and social circumstances.

This use of detail situates Mrs Dawson's narrative within the project of realism, which, as Naomi Schor has observed is, "at least at the outset . . . intimately bound up with the *sublimation of details*, and this sublimation constitutes the very condition of the passage of the detail into the field of artistic representation" (Schor 1987: 146). Schor argues further that,

To the extent . . . that the exclusion of the detail from the field of representation in classical and neo-classical aesthetics is based on the sure discrimination of the great and the small, the rise of realism cannot but involve an interrogation of that hierarchy.

(ibid.: 145)

Margaret Dawson's story celebrates the feminine detail, from Lady Ludlow's "delicate Italian writing – writing which contained far more in the same space of paper than all the sloping, or masculine handwritings of the present day," (Gaskell 1972: 10) to the lady's bureau, the myriad drawers of which are filled with miniatures that "had even to be looked at through a microscope before you could see the individual expression of the faces" (ibid.: 44) to the appearance of the lady herself: "very small of stature, and very upright" (ibid.: 15).[11]

If not within the whole of *My Lady Ludlow*, where each narrative is called into question by the others, then at least on its own terms, Margaret Dawson's story challenges patriarchal histories of great men with an epistemological model predicated on the potentially infinite regression of magnification. Like the microscope with which George Eliot's narrator inspects the match-making activities of Mrs Cadwallader in *Middlemarch*, Mrs Dawson's attention to detail encourages the reader to abandon the great scheme of things – the plot constructed by the exclusion of recalcitrant detail – to dwell rather indiscriminately on apparent triviality. As Schor notes of realism generally, the regressive potential of Mrs Dawson's narrative is held in check by sublimating detail to the presence of its subject, Lady Ludlow. Ultimately, no detail is trivial, but, as Margaret Dawson sees it, each contributes to an understanding of Lady Ludlow, and Margaret herself. Nevertheless, not only does the challenge to conventional discursive hierarchies stand, but in the conflicts among Margaret Dawson's story and the other narratives of *My Lady Ludlow* the import of this sublimation is put in doubt. The production of history seems aimed less at self-definition and self-protection than at circulating communal texts of shared female society.

One last narrator in *My Lady Ludlow*, Miss Galindo, makes obvious the unacknowledged desire which narrative, including history, fulfils, not for meaning, but for a dialogic intimacy – to hear and tell stories in order to be part of a narrative community. Miss Galindo is introduced as the practical answer to the crisis precipitated by Henry Gregson's literacy – the same crisis which elicits the story of Clément and Virginie. But she will also provide the discursive solution lacking from that tale. Lady Ludlow, faced with her agent's demand for a clerk to assist in the administration of her increasingly troubled finances, prefers to appoint a distressed gentlewoman, Miss Galindo, to the post rather than trust her affairs to the poacher's son, Henry. Miss Galindo appears to share her mistress's class prejudices, yet she begins to challenge the social order by executing her duties as well as a man, while producing a running critique on life at Hanbury House and the village. Wildly opinionated, an eccentric spinster who takes in a series of misfit servants who must be looked after by their mistress, the benefactress of her dead lover's illegitimate daughter, Miss Galindo is an exaggerated version of Lady Ludlow. The difference between them is that Miss Galindo's inferior social status forces conversation on her, while Lady Ludlow can exist in the silent isolation of her authority.

Miss Galindo chides Lady Ludlow for disparaging her new clerk's role as the village scold. Lady Ludlow need not scold, Miss Galindo reminds her, "because your ladyship has people to do it for you" (Gaskell 1972: 135).

> Begging your pardon, my lady, it seems to me the generality of people may be divided into saints, scolds, and sinners. Now, your ladyship is a saint, because you have a sweet and holy nature, in the first place; and have people to do your anger and vexation for you, in the second place. And Jonathan Walker is a sinner, because he is sent to prison. But here am I, half way, having but a poor kind of disposition at best, and yet hating sin, and all that leads to it, such as wasting, and extravagance, and gossiping – and yet all this lies right under my nose in the village, and I am not saint enough to be vexed at it; and so I scold. And though I had rather be a saint, yet I think I do good in my way.
>
> (ibid.)

The good of Miss Galindo's "scolding" is to circulate the stories that bring disparate individuals into contact with one another. For example, her comically hyperbolic denunciations of Mr Gray generally serve to introduce some unknown aspect of his character which will recommend him to Lady Ludlow. She no more has declared that "Rousseau and Mr Gray are birds of a feather," than she endears him to her mistress by relating some act of charity he has performed. As scold, she is the recording angel, the historian of everyday life.

Indeed, it is with a letter from Miss Galindo, chock-full of Hanbury gossip, that Margaret Dawson's narrative ends. "You ask for news of us all," Miss Galindo opens. "Don't you know there is no news in Hanbury? Did you ever hear of an event here?" Whereupon she launches into a breathless series of anecdotes, each one tailored to the interests and desires of her correspondent, Margaret Dawson. The pleasure of this intimacy is underscored when we are abruptly thrust out of the narrative. Miss Galindo's letter closes with a description of a tea party at Hanbury House to which Lady Ludlow has invited guests she had previously excluded on the basis of strict moral, religious, or political principles. Miss Galindo's declaration, "I would not change places with any in

England," is followed by three terse sentences by Margaret Dawson reporting the deaths of Lady Ludlow and Mr Gray. The narrator of the frame, with the manuscript of "My Lady Ludlow" lying before her, recalls imploringly, "Oh, dear! I wish some one would tell us another story!" The charmed circle has been broken, drawing attention to the fragility of our discursive relationship. "In reading other people's published letters," Patricia Meyer Spacks has argued, "we seek reassurance not only about the stability of a continuous self but about the possibility of intimacy, of fruitful human exchange" (Spacks 1985: 77–8). Cast out of Miss Galindo's letter, of Margaret Dawson's story, of the frame narrator's manuscript – of a diverse community of female storytellers – the reader is left orphaned, infirm, dis-eased. That is, however, poised to write history, and to create yet another frame.

Ultimately, the politics of this novel may be unstable, riddled with conflicts. But *My Lady Ludlow* provides for women's histories a full range of "conceptual weapons with which they can understand and begin to overcome their universal subordination" (Balbus 1987: 120). Narrative authority is dispersed among a range of speakers, whose relative power is left unresolved. The result resembles a post-modernist sort of perspectivism that at once insists on detail as the ground of history, and problematizes adjudicating between the conflicting points of view. Likewise, the ideological demands of the various literary conventions employed by the novel's narrators – autobiography, romance, moral exemplum, letters, and history itself – prevent the reader from privileging one discourse over another and thereby excluding any story, even that of the female paternalist. Gaskell makes good on the claim of one of her narrators that this tale has "no beginning, middle or end," by disrupting any inevitable sense of causal or moral progress, suggesting the diversity of female desire and practice in the production of historical narrative.[12]

NOTES

I am grateful to Claudia L. Johnson for her insightful and patient assistance in revising this chapter.

1 For a discussion of the scandal caused by *The Life of Charlotte Brontë*, see Gérin (1980: 189–201).
2 Gaskell's aim in accommodating Lady Ludlow's recuperative romance of Clément and Virginie might be seen as compatible with Teresa de Lauretis's proposition that "feminist work in film should be not anti-narrative or anti-oedipal but quite the opposite. It should be narrative and oedipal with a vengeance, working, as it were, with and against narrative in order to represent not just a female desire which Hollywood, in the best tradition of Western literature and iconography, has classically represented as the doomed power of the fetish (a fetish empowered for the benefit of men and doomed to disempower women); but working, instead, to represent the duplicity of

the oedipal scenario itself and the specific contradiction of the female subject in it" (de Lauretis 1987: 108).

3 In "Disciplining Women: Michael Foucault and the Power of Feminist Discourse" Isaac D. Balbus describes continuous history in this way: "Since the eighteenth century the prevailing true discourse of the West has been what Foucault calls 'anthropology' of the discourse of 'continuous history.' Practitioners of continuous history – traditional historians – seek to disclose the truth of the present by uncovering its origins in the past; they are committed to a concept of historical continuity, the necessary presupposition of which is the assumption that history is the unfolding of the essential attributes of man" (1988: 139).

4 In "Feminism and the Power of Foucaldian Discourse" Jana Sawicki argues that the dilemma Balbus sees Foucault as posing for feminist theory can be avoided if we recognize first that "the isolation of discontinuities is the starting point of genealogy, not its aim" (168). Having done so, we can use Foucaldian methodology "to bring to light the heterogeneous forms that gender embodiment . . . and power relations producing gendered individuals take" (1988: 171).

5 *My Lady Ludlow* is treated in a few sentences in Lansbury (1975), Basch (1975), and Stoneman (1987). In fact, *My Lady Ludlow* has attracted little critical attention since its publication in Dickens's *Household Words* in 1858. Judging from her letters alone, it would seem that Gaskell's own interest in the novel consisted primarily in its potential as a money-maker. In 1859 she republished it, along with others of her *Household Words* stories, under the title *Round the Sofa*, in order to raise money for a trip to the continent (Gaskell 1967: no. 418). In 1861 she pressured Chapman to settle her account on "The Moorland Cottage" so that it could be included in *My Lady Ludlow and Other Tales*, published by Sampson Low (Gaskell 1967: no. 486).

6 Feminist and Marxist critics have transformed Gaskell's image as Mrs Gaskell, the author of *Cranford* – Lord David Cecil's quaint observer of village life who suffered briefly from the delusion that she had something of social relevance to say (Cecil 1958: 10). Thanks to Aina Rubenius, Raymond Williams, Coral Lansbury, Elaine Showalter, Catherine Gallagher, Patsy Stoneman, and others, the social novels, *Mary Barton* (1848), *Ruth* (1853), and *North and South* (1855), stand at the center of the Gaskell canon. By attending to questions of gender, feminist critics have extended the historical significance of these novels to include a recognition of Gaskell's critiques of women's economic and sexual exploitation. Yet, as Patsy Stoneman points out, "Of all the enormous output of feminist literary criticism during the last fifteen years, none has been concerned to any major extent with Elizabeth Gaskell" (Stoneman 1987: 7).

7 A. W. Ward, author of the generally enthusiastic introductions to the 1906 Knutsford edition of Gaskell's works, concluded of *My Lady Ludlow* "that in this story Mrs. Gaskell either attempted too much, or allowed herself insufficient space and time for harmonizing all that she attempted." The several engaging tales comprising the novel "fail to make up in sum for its chief defect – a want of balance in its construction, discernible in the midst of its many characteristic beauties" (Gaskell 1972: xvi-xvii). This absence of "harmony" and "balance" rendered the work an aesthetic and thematic failure. It was, as one of the novel's narrators describes her own tale, "no story at all, neither beginning, nor middle, nor end, only a bundle of recollections" (ibid.: 8). For several generations of critics following Ward, *My Lady Ludlow*

could be dismissed on the grounds that it lacked organic unity. Edgar Wright (1989: n. 3), editor of the 1989 World Classics edition of *My Lady Ludlow*, summarizes the brief discussions of the story by the current principal Gaskell critics: Angus Easson, Arthur Pollard, Margaret Ganz, Coral Lansbury, and John G. Sharps. Whether finally recuperating or dismissing *My Lady Ludlow*, they share the conviction that the story breaks into two parts, only superficially connected to each other. In *Mrs Gaskell: The Basis for Reassessment* (1965: 10), Wright gives the novel rather more extensive treatment as part of his general contention that Gaskell's "work can be seen to have a unity and a development." By taking change itself to be the theme of *My Lady Ludlow*, he is able to bestow approval on its episodic structure, despite the "catastrophic lapse of judgment [which] makes the essential unity of theme and tone difficult to realize" (Wright 1965: 156).

8 These dis-eased narratives provide a clue to the etiology of the ailment suffered by George Eliot's narrator in *Middlemarch*, who complained of being a "belated historian" whose attempt at an authoritative, universalizing narrative would sound as if it were "delivered from a campstool in a parrot house" (Eliot 1965: 170).

9 In addition to the famous passage on historical narrative in *Middlemarch*, quoted above, George Eliot constructs retrospection specifically along the parallel between travel and recollection in *Scenes from Clerical Life*, *Adam Bede*, *Romola*, and the prelude to *Middlemarch*. Andrew Saunders, in his introduction to *Sylvia's Lovers* (Gaskell 1982), notes the influence of George Eliot's early retrospective novels on Gaskell's first historical novel. Cross-fertilization seems more than likely.

10 I am paraphrasing Rosemarie Bodenheimer's chapter title, "The Romance of the Female Paternalist" in Bodenheimer (1988).

11 David Cecil paid Gaskell the back-handed compliment that her works display an unfailing "feminine command of detail" (1958: 189). Schor would, I believe, concur that "this feminine eye for detail is closely associated with a feminine subtlety" (ibid.: 191).

12 Teresa de Lauretis (1987: 137) sets a similar goal for women's cinema. She cites Helen Fehervary's claim that "the relationship between history and so-called subjective processes is not a matter of grasping the truth in history as some objective entity, but in finding the truth of the experience. Evidently, this kind of experiential immediacy has to do with women's own history and self-consciousness." De Lauretis continues, "that, how, and why our histories and our consciousness are different, divided, even conflicting, is what women's cinema can analyze, articulate, reformulate. And, in so doing, it can help us create something."

WORKS CITED

Balbus, Isaac D. (1987) "Disciplining Women: Michel Foucault and the Power of Feminist Discourse", in Seyla Benhabib and Drucilla Cornell (eds) *Feminism as Critique*, Minneapolis: University of Minnesota Press

—— (1988) "Disciplining Women: Michel Foucault and the Power of Feminist Discourse" (revised), in Jonathan Arac (ed.) *After Foucault: Humanistic Knowledge, Postmodern Challenges*, New Brunswick: Rutgers University Press, pp. 138–60.

Basch, Françoise (1975) *Relative Creatures: Victorian Women in Society and the Novel, 1837–67*, trans. Anthony Rudolf, London: Allen Lane.

Bodenheimer, Rosemarie (1988) *The Politics of Story in Victorian Social Fiction*, Ithaca, NY: Cornell University Press.

Cecil, David (1958) *Victorian Novelists: Essays in Revaluation*, Chicago: University of Chicago Press. First published 1935.

David, Deirdre (1987) *Intellectual Women and Victorian Patriarchy: Harriet Martineau, Elizabeth Barrett Browning, George Eliot*, Ithaca, NY: Cornell University Press.

de Lauretis, Teresa (1987) *Technologies of Gender: Essays on Theory, Film and Fiction*, Bloomington: Indiana University Press.

Doody, Margaret A. (1980) "George Eliot and the Eighteenth-Century Novel," *Nineteenth-Century Fiction*, 35: 260–91.

Eliot, George (1965) *Middlemarch*, Intro. W. J. Harvey, Harmondsworth: Penguin. First published 1871–2.

Gaskell, Elizabeth (1967) *The Letters of Elizabeth Gaskell*, ed. J. A. V. Chapple and Arthur Pollard, Cambridge, MA: Harvard University Press.

—— (1972) "Round the Sofa," in *The Works of Mrs. Gaskell*, vol. 5, Introduction by A. W. Ward, New York: AMS Press. First published 1859.

—— (1982) *Sylvia's Lovers*, Introduction by Andrew Saunders, Oxford: Oxford University Press.

Gérin, Winifred (1980) *The Life of Charlotte Brontë: a Biography*, Oxford: Oxford University Press.

Lansbury, Coral (1975) *Elizabeth Gaskell: the Novel of Social Crisis*, New York: Harper & Row.

Poovey, Mary (1988) *Uneven Developments: The Ideological Work of Gender in Mid-Victorian England*, Chicago: University of Chicago Press.

Rubenius, Aina (1950) *The Woman Question in Mrs Gaskell's Life and Works*, Cambridge, MA: Harvard University Press.

Sawicki, Jana (1988) "Feminism and the Power of Foucauldian Discourse," in Jonathan Arac (ed.) *After Foucault: Humanistic Knowledge, Postmodern Challenges*, New Brunswick: Rutgers University Press, pp. 161–78.

Schor, Naomi (1987) *Reading in Detail: Aesthetics and the Feminine*, New York: Methuen.

Spacks, Patricia Meyer (1985) *Gossip*, New York: Alfred A. Knopf.

Stoneman, Patsy (1987) *Elizabeth Gaskell*, Bloomington: Indiana University Press.

Valenze, Deborah M. (1985) *Prophetic Sons and Daughters: Female Preaching and Popular Religion in Industrial England*, Princeton, NJ: Princeton University Press.

Wright, Edgar (1965) *Mrs Gaskell: the Basis for Reassessment*, Oxford: Oxford University Press.

—— (1989) "*My Lady Ludlow*: Forms of Social Change and Forms of Fiction," *The Gaskell Society Journal*, 3: 29–41.

Afterword
Ideology and the subject as agent

Linda M. Shires

Looking back at the beginnings of this project, I am able to see my intentions for the volume and the unforeseen and exciting ways in which the essays developed their own shaping power. The book directly addresses various ways in which history writes gender relations and how gender relations write history. At the same time, it concentrates on how men and women of the middle class consolidated power and sometimes subverted that power. Finally, it demonstrates, I believe, that "dominant" kinds of representations such as the novel, popular poetry, genre painting, and the public press all admit ideological contradictions while continuing to endorse assumptions about the middle class. In those very contradictions, however, it is possible to see not only Victorian nostalgia for older forms of life, such as previous class systems, and an agrarian order, but also the seeds of an internal dissent which served radical ends, such as increased women's rights.

Yet I am also left with the need to highlight two related issues which continue to vex Victorian studies today: the problem in reading Victorian representations without attending enough to their ideological instability and the difficulty faced by post-structuralist critics in theorizing the subject as agent.

Most contemporary readings of Victorian texts take for granted the capability of dominant groups (groups of people dominating others by sex, class, race, or nation for example) to make their own interests appear to others as natural. Few such readings, however, show how this capability is secured. This is the process – universalizing the sectional – which Judith Newton carefully analyzes in her chapter on the middle class and the *Edinburgh Review*. She demonstrates convincingly how private interests become naturalized public ones by force of rhetoric. Her analysis also demonstrates the complex, multiple intersections and divergences of attitudes, beliefs, desires, and interests which comprise the social field. Yet in my judgment, many of us who study the nineteenth century still overemphasize the fixity of the ideological. Sally Shuttleworth points to this problem in her chapter as she demonstrates the instability of ideologies of the maternal. Many of us, however, remain unwilling or unable to analyze ideologies which seem totally entrenched in the period, such as "separate spheres" or "the white man's burden." We are too easily seduced by what appears as the homogenization of culture and middle-class hegemony.

As a result, we all too frequently tend to ignore what is most Victorian about Victorianism. The instability of any ideology in the period and the even more radical instability of Victorian representations must count as defining characteristics of the age. In fact, Victorian representations are noted for simultaneously venting various ideological positions, airing multiple points of view, letting them comment on each other, and closing off, with affairs left largely as they stood in the beginning. They are also known for their formal accommodation of various points of view and for the invention or hybridization of generic forms (such as the dramatic monologue or double-plot "baggy monster" novels) which promote multiple perspectives.

Though ideological representations often present themselves as coherent, while internally unstable, I am arguing that Victorian representations foreground instability. I would argue this point even of that most "coherent" of forms, the realist novel. The airing of multiple points of view fosters intervention into the status quo, and thus challenges hegemony. If it is true that particular philosophies hold sway among the bourgeoisie during the Victorian era, such as utilitarianism, it is also true that Victorian representations, particularly verbal ones, are rife with dissent. Furthermore, as would be true in any era, a representation could be used to support practically any politics: progressive, conservative, or radical, given the social context and social actors involved. But I think it is especially true of the Victorian period that representations can be used simultaneously to support opposing political frameworks.

We may turn to many writers of the Victorian period whose works demonstrate a typically magnificent display of ideologies at odds with each other – Barrett-Browning, Christina Rossetti, Thackeray, Browning, Carlyle and others – but the Poet Laureate in 1850, Alfred Lord Tennyson, because of his central cultural position, perhaps can best teach us an important lesson about the Victorians and their representations. We do not have to turn to marginal figures to demonstrate the force of resistance to prevailing ideology. The Victorian example illustrates that even those in the dominant group are not wholeheartedly committed to dominant ideologies.

Tennyson's writing appeals ideologically, because he responds waveringly to a Victorian middle-class program which is itself characteristically unclear. His poems admit contradictions, espouse various points of view, and remain beautifully noncommittal. They reach the broadest of audiences and, although poetry itself as a genre is becoming more culturally marginal, they largely succeed because they endorse the assumptions and confusions of the class for which they are written. For example, on one hand, "Locksley Hall" espouses bourgeois progressivism, but, on the other hand, it speaks a nostalgia for an older aristocratic social order. *In Memoriam* supports heterosexual love and religious faith; alternatively, it supports homoerotic love and scientific skepticism.

Taking for granted the instability of Victorian ideologies in representations produced during the period, we must also turn the question around. To what degree in any era, we must ask, is social, political, and cultural engagement ideologically circumscribed and to what degree is it negotiable? Contemporary feminist theory, studies of Third World cultures, African-American studies, and culture studies still require a theory of the subject as agent. One of the major tensions in contemporary criticism remains that which pits constitutive against voluntarist emphases on cultural, political, and social engagement. In spite of the gains of structuralism and post-structuralism – such as an emphasis on spacing through difference, the decentering of the subject, the syntagmatic and paradigmatic axes, a critique of the metaphysics of presence, etc – these theoretical movements fail to provide a theory of agency; they view culture as constitutive of the subject. Such a position is not new. Indeed, it has long been one half of a struggle in the field of the sociology of culture: voluntarism vs. constitutivism. Yet while it is very fashionable to declare that the Cartesian self is dead and that the individual is a mere effect of social forces which intersect at a sign once called the self, the search for a way to give some power to the agent in culture has become more and more insistent. As a close look at Donna Haraway's (1987) work on situated knowledges will demonstrate, the search to empower a subject also includes the need to preserve the best insights of structuralism and post-structuralism. How can we account for the fact that the subject is contradictory, in process, fragmented, produced by ideological hailings, but also able to constitute herself politically?

Mary Poovey's analysis of how gender shapes ideology in her book *Uneven Developments* (Poovey 1988) is just one example of recent feminist work on Victorian culture which confronts such a dilemma. In spite of the admirable analysis put forward by Poovey, the book appears to stress a deterministic culture in spite of itself, as Poovey locates and analyzes fissures in master ideologies and hegemonic institutions. However, the problem of agency is one which Poovey faces head on in her introduction. She writes:

> I have found myself torn between focusing on individuals as if they were agents of change and dispensing altogether with individual life

stories in order to create the impression that individuals are merely points at which competing cultural forces intersect.

(Poovey 1988: 20)

She proceeds to explain the middle course that she adopts, a compromise which she expects will displease readers at either theoretical extreme. When discussing figures important to her, such as Caroline Norton or Florence Nightingale, she employs a narrative life paradigm, but de-authorizes their individual stories by weaving together several at a time and by showing how they are all conditioned by culture. Drawing on a cultural narrative about gender, power, and institutions, she de-emphasizes causation and teleology and stresses the randomness of history.

It is apparent that what Poovey lacks here is a theory of agency that can also reap the benefits of poststructuralism, with the unhappy result that she is led to a compromise that pleases everyone, and yet no one. The problem we face as theorists can be summarized, I think, by a sentence in Michèle Barrett's socialist-feminist analysis *Women's Oppression Today*, a sentence which has struck my eye repeatedly during various readings. Without explaining herself in these terms precisely, Barrett confronts the difference between the discursive production of selves and events and the belief in a self and an event as actual. She maintains that there is a difference between discursive struggle and actual social struggle: "Are we really to see," demands Barrett, "the Peterloo massacre, the storming of the Winter Palace in Petrograd, the Long March, the Grunwick picket – as the struggle of discourses?" (Barrett 1988: 95). In other words, are these battles, marches, and demonstrations by the oppressed only the struggle of ideological representations of the subject and the subjected? Do they not involve actual people who thought they were in an actual place at a specific time doing something, whether they might name it dissent, resistance, rebellion, or revolution?

While knowing what "truly" happened is, finally, impossible except through partial perspectives and shifting values – an ever-moving intersection of "horizons of expectation" in Hans Robert Jauss's terms – the desire for some fixity and for something firm that we can improbably know remains vital. That desire for the actual marks us as subjects in history and in cultural history. Paradoxically, perhaps, it is a product of the Romantic ideology of selfhood, a legacy which continues to inform nearly all of our intellectual endeavours, no matter how much we attempt to dismantle it. The persistent return of this defense of the actual, in response to attacks on the actual from different quarters, is itself a symptom of the need for a theory of agency and for a post-post-structuralist theory of subjectivity which can account for motivation and political will. The defense argues not merely for the actual, then, but also for the human. In Paulo Freire's (1990) terms, our activity consists of the dialogism of action and reflection, praxis and theory, and cannot be reduced to one or the other. The return of the actual is the return of humanism (if, in fact, it ever left), but with a difference. For the fact of the subject as fragile, of the agent as contingent, of our self-consciousness as fraught and ever-changing, which, it can be argued, is actually embedded in classical humanism, has been rearticulated by post-modernist theory.

Cultural change always comes about by at least a three-pronged process of readjustment: a reorganization of the material conditions of production, a reorganization of cultural symbols, and a rearticulation of current vocabulary in new ways (Kroll 1990: 7; 1991: chs 1 and 2). Such alterations are not imposed from without, but occur from within the cultural formation by agents and collectives of agents. For any theory of agency to account for such cultural change, we need to start with definitions of action and event, and an articulation of the relationship between consciousness and action. We also need to take account of an actor's performance of an act and his or her understanding of that performance. Finally, and most importantly, a theory of time and space is crucial to a theory of agency.

If action may be defined as conduct, in the sense of a performance of bodily movements devised with a goal in advance, event may be defined as that which occurred and that which an individual or a group of people have *recursively* endowed with meaning. To return to Barrett's example, it is clear that the march and the demonstration took place, but the actual is that which men and women construct for themselves from intersubjective experiences and discursive negotiation. Consciousness and reflection go hand in hand with action and event. For the translation of action into event and the meanings of the actual are negotiated by agents. Although ideologies may be constitutive, they are also dialectically constructed so as to allow for dissent and critique from within. *Pace* Foucault, agents use discourses. All discourse is political in nature; agents take up specific discourses at specific moments and in specific contexts with results.

Yet how can one theorize subjectivity as at once fragmented and as capable of social action? First, I agree that, as Anthony Giddens advises, we need to take account of the self-awareness of the social actor – all too commonly caricatured these days, partly because of the Althusserian influence, as a social idiot. Human beings reflexively monitor their actions via the knowledge they have of the parameters of their activity (Giddens 1986: 72). This monitoring, as Anthony Giddens persuasively argues, both draws on and reconstitutes the institutional organization of society. Giddens points out that the knowledge can be varied: it can be unconscious; it can be conscious in a way that can stimulate action but that still can't be articulated; it can be discursively conscious. Behavior, attitudes, and self-understanding, dynamically intervene in and transform the social. As John Thompson warns, however, even though the social structure is reproduced and can be transformed by action, the range of options available to individuals and groups of individuals are "differentially distributed and structurally circumscribed" (Held and Thompson 1989: 75). In terms of discourse, the critique from within will have to be framed in the codes of hegemony or it will not be understood, but possibilities for success with such discourse are not equal. Success occurs, one may argue, when an individual or group exploits the options provided by the dominant discourse and makes it their own, while simultaneously compromising their own point of view by adopting the dominant discourse. So critique and transformation will involve both gain (over the dominant) and loss of separatist perspective (by the individual or group).

In an essay entitled "What is Cultural Studies Anyway?" Richard Johnson claims that there is no existing theory of the subjective aspects of struggle. There is no theory, he says, which accounts for a "moment in subjective flux when social subjects (individual and collective) produce accounts of who they are, as conscious political agents" (Johnson 1986–7: 69). I do not introduce Johnson to add to the call for a theory of agency, but to emphasize his conceptualization of the problem in terms of temporality. Johnson is sensitive to the dialectical nature of subjectivity – the flux and the fixing moments of self-definition. It is in our nature to provide narratives of and for ourselves, since this narrativizing remains the predominant way we make meaning. Yet there is always a temporal break between action and meaning. This time lag occurs in at least three different relationships: the self's relationship to itself (personal history), the self's relationship to another (intersubjectivity), and the relationship between act and event (the creation of History or Culture out of the continually flowing stream of acts). The temporal break occurs in between moments of reconstitution (of the self, of interaction, of applying meaning). This In-between Time is indeterminate but also retroactively determining and forward-looking. Drawing on the insights of Saussure concerning the construction of meaning through syntagmatic and paradigmatic operations, we may hypothesize that both the social formation and the constitution of the agent operate through relations of presence and absence recursively awarded meaning. Taking such a hypothesis further and using it to analyze specific historical and textual instances will enable Victorian Studies and feminisms to consolidate the gains of various theoretical traditions in the 1990s.

WORKS CITED

Barrett, Michèle (1988) *Women's Oppression Today*, revised edn, New York: Verso.

Freire, Paulo (1990) *Pedagogy of the Oppressed*, New York: Continuum.

Giddens, Anthony (1986) *Central Problems in Social Theory*, Berkeley: University of California Press.

Haraway, Donna J. (1987) "Situated Knowledges: The Science Question in Feminism and the Privilege of Partial Perspective," in *Simians, Cyborgs, and Women: The Reinvention of Nature*, New York: Routledge.

Held, David and Thompson, John B. (1989) *Social Theory of Modern Societies: Anthony Giddens and his Critics*, Cambridge: Cambridge University Press.

Johnson, Richard (1986–7) "What is Cultural Studies Anyway?" *Social Text* Winter: 38–80.

Kroll, Richard (1990) "The Emergence of Theory, Dissent from Within, and Rochester's 'A Ramble in St James's Park,' " unpublished manuscript.

—— (1991) *The Material Word: Literate Culture in the Restoration and Early Eighteenth Century*, Baltimore, MD: Johns Hopkins University Press.

Poovey, Mary (1988) *Uneven Developments: The Ideological Work of Gender in Mid-Victorian England*, Chicago: University of Chicago Press.

Index